1968

TWELVE POETS
ALTERNATE EDITION

12 POETS
ALTERNATE EDITION,

1561

GEOFFREY CHAUCER

BEN JONSON

JOHN MILTON

ANDREW MARVELL

JOHN DRYDEN

WILLIAM BLAKE

GEORGE GORDON, LORD BYRON

ALFRED, LORD TENNYSON

THOMAS HARDY

JOHN CROWE RANSOM

ARCHIBALD MACLEISH

THEODORE ROETHKE

Edited by Glenn Leggett and Henry-York Steiner
Grinnell College

HOLT, RINEHART AND WINSTON, NEW YORK
CHICAGO   SAN FRANCISCO   TORONTO

ACKNOWLEDGMENTS

GEOFFREY CHAUCER

All Chaucer's poems are from *Chaucer,* edited by F. N. Robinson.
Boston, Mass.: Houghton Mifflin, Riverside Edition, 1957. Reprinted
by permission of Houghton Mifflin Company.

THOMAS HARDY

All poems are reprinted from *Collected Poems of Thomas Hardy*
by permission of The Estate of Thomas Hardy, Macmillan & Co.,
Ltd., London and The Macmillan Company of Canada Limited.

"A Cathedral Facade at Midnight," "Circus Rider to Ringmaster,"
"Last Week in October," "The Graveyard of Dead Creeds," "A
Beauty's Soliloquy During Her Honeymoon," "Cynic's Epitaph,"
"Epitaph on a Pessimist," "The Six Boards" are reprinted by per-
mission of The Macmillan Company from *Collected Poems of*

821.08
P514

ACKNOWLEDGMENTS

Thomas Hardy copyright 1925 by The Macmillan Company. Renewed 1953 by Lloyd's Bank Ltd.

JOHN CROWE RANSOM

"Winter Remembered," "Miriam Tazewell," "Spectral Lovers," "Necrological," "Bells for John Whiteside's Daughter," "Here Lies a Lady," "Judith of Bethulia," "Captain Carpenter," copyright 1924 by Alfred A. Knopf, Inc., and renewed 1952 by John Crowe Ransom. Reprinted from *Selected Poems by John Crowe Ransom* by permission of the publisher.

"Dead Boy," "Blue Girls," "Piazza Piece," "Parting Without a Sequel," "Janet Waking," "Little Boy Blue," "Two in August," "Survey of Literature," "The Equilibrists" copyright 1927 by Alfred A. Knopf, Inc., and renewed 1955 by John Crowe Ransom. Reprinted from *Selected Poems by John Crowe Ransom* by permission of the publisher.

ARCHIBALD MACLEISH

"Tricked by Eternity the Heart," copyright 1948 by Archibald MacLeish. Reprinted from *Act Five and Other Poems*, by permission of Random House, Inc.

"Pole Star," "Speech to the Detractors," "Dover Beach—a note to that poem," "The Sunset Piece," and the following four poems from "The Woman on the Stair": "The Quarrel," "The Reconciliation," "The Room by the River," "The Remembrance" from *Public Speech* by Archibald MacLeish. Copyright 1936, © 1964 by Archibald MacLeish. Reprinted by permission of Holt, Rinehart and Winston, Inc.

"The Silent Slain," "Mother Goose's Garland," "The End of the World," "Memorial Rain," "Ars Poetica," "Not Marble Nor the Gilded Monuments," "You, Andrew Marvell," "Immortal Au-

v

tumn," "Men," "Lines for an Interment," "Calypso's Island," "Crossing" are reprinted by permission of Houghton Mifflin Company.

THEODORE ROETHKE

"Death Piece" and "No Bird," copyright 1934 by Theodore Roethke; "Prayer," copyright 1935 by Theodore Roethke; "Interlude" and "The Bat," copyright 1938 by Theodore Roethke; "Open House," "To My Sister," "Mid-country Blow," "On the Road to Woodlawn," and "Academic," copyright 1941 by Theodore Roethke; "The Cycle," copyright 1941 by *The University of Virginia Quarterly Review,* The University of Virginia; "My Papa's Waltz," copyright 1942 by Hearst Magazines, Inc.; "Pickle Belt," copyright 1943 by The American Mercury, Inc.; "Weed-Puller," and "Child on Top of a Greenhouse," copyright 1946 by Editorial Publications, Inc.; "The Return" and "Night Crow," copyright 1947 by Theodore Roethke; "Elegy for Jane," copyright 1950 by Theodore Roethke; "The Dance" from "Four for Sir John Davies," copyright 1952 by The Atlantic Monthly Company; "The Vigil" from "Four for Sir John Davies" and "The Waking," copyright 1953 by Theodore Roethke; "The Dream," "All the Earth, All the Air," "Words for the Wind," and "Snake," copyright © 1955 by Theodore Roethke; "The Shimmer of Evil," copyright © 1955 by New Republic, Inc.; "She," copyright © 1956 by Theodore Roethke; and "The Surly One" and "Plaint," copyright © 1957 by Theodore Roethke; all from *The Collected Poems of Theodore Roethke.* Reprinted by permission of Doubleday & Company, Inc.

PREFACE

Twelve Poets in its original edition consists of fairly numerous selections from Shakespeare, Donne, Pope, Wordsworth, Keats, Browning, Dickinson, Housman, Yeats, Robinson, Frost, and T. S. Eliot. This edition, the alternate one, consists of selections from Chaucer, Ben Jonson, Milton, Marvell, Dryden, Blake, Byron, Tennyson, Hardy, Ransom, MacLeish, and Roethke. In this edition, as in the other, I have responded to my feeling that the careful reading of a number of poems by the same poet allows the students to hear enough of the poet's speaking voice to feel some security in their response, and though this response is not the same thing as understanding, it is a necessary preparation for understanding. Surely this is what we mean when we say that we have read Dryden or Blake or Hardy and so on. The language of the individual poems keeps adding up, and redefining itself, so that Poem 1 really does not come into its own with us until we hear it sounding through Poem 20, where it works simultaneously to effect our response to that poem and to others by the same poet, those read and those still to be read.

As in the original edition, I wanted in the total combination of "twelve poets" a good historical representation and a general although not exclusive lyrical emphasis. But I wished none of these premises of selection to interfere radically with my personal preference for certain poets. Accordingly, some choices were easy. Jonson, Marvell, Dryden, Blake, Byron, Tennyson, Hardy, and Ransom had all been considered and reluctantly passed over in the original edition. Having used Donne then, I thought it proper to choose Ben Jonson for this edition. Similarly, Dryden for Pope, Blake for Wordsworth, Byron for Keats, Tennyson for Browning, Hardy for Housman, though Coleridge, Shelley, and Arnold were also possibilities. As for Chaucer—the original edition began with Shakespeare, and I wanted the alternate edition to begin with a titan, too. The middle seventeenth century is not represented in the original edition; its poetry is especially to my liking and I make up for the omission in the original by including both Milton and Marvell in this edition. Milton is difficult to anthologize (if one wants several complete poems and a minimum of apparatus), and I omitted him in the original edition for that reason. I have represented him here with the shorter, earlier poems, as I did with some anxiety with T. S. Eliot's poetry in the original edition. Marvell is a personal favorite, what I call a perfect minor poet.

Six of the poets in the original edition can be said to be "major" moderns—Dickinson, Housman, Yeats, Robinson, Frost, Eliot. Indeed, this is almost an exhaustive list, if one adds Auden, who presents copyright difficulties that are insurmountable. But a number of modern poets present an excellence that I thought well worth collecting in a volume of this kind. Hart Crane, Lowell, MacLeish, Pound, Ransom, Roethke, Stevens, Tate, Warren, Wilbur, Williams all came to mind. I picked MacLeish, mostly for the poetry he wrote between 1920 and 1940. In listening to the post World War I "lost generation" tone of him, that sound of innocence just lost, overtly pessimistic but unconsciously responsible about the world, I wonder why contemporary young people have not "rediscovered" him. I chose Ransom, because, like Marvell, he strikes me as special and perfect. And I included Roethke because I think he is the greatest American poet of my generation.

But the premises of selection are endlessly arguable, and the important thing in this edition as in the original one is the poetry itself. As I said then, critical helps for the reader are limited to a brief biographical sketch of each poet and rather full notes to the "hard" words in the poems. I thought it neither wise nor necessary to supply any elaborate critical apparatus. I think it best that the student rely as much as possible on his own intelligence, his instructor, and his fellow students and not be encumbered with the help of too much tailor-made criticism. I still believe that in the beginning, at any rate, the poem and the reader ought to be kept in a pure relationship with each other. If this purity results in ambiguity (and it often does), it is best to take up the problem then, not before the poem has been allowed to do its initial work with the reader.

For help in preparing this volume I am especially indebted to Mrs. David K. Leonard of the University of Chicago.

Glenn Leggett
Grinnell, Iowa
May 1967

CONTENTS

JOHN MILTON: [1608–1674]

ANDREW MARVELL: [1621–1678]

JOHN DRYDEN: [1631–1700]

WILLIAM BLAKE: [*1757–1827*]

GEORGE GORDON, LORD BYRON: [*1788–1824*]

ALFRED, LORD TENNYSON: [1809–1892]

THOMAS HARDY: [1840–1928]

CONTENTS

JOHN CROWE RANSOM: [1888–   ]

CONTENTS

ARCHIBALD MACLEISH: [1892–   ]

THEODORE ROETHKE: [1908–1963]

CONTENTS

TWELVE POETS
ALTERNATE EDITION

GEOFFREY CHAUCER

[*1340–1400*]

Although many of the details of Geoffrey Chaucer's career are obscure, the general pattern of his life can be pieced together with some accuracy. He was born about 1340, probably in London. His father and grandfather were wealthy vintners, who occasionally held offices in the king's court. Nothing is known of Chaucer's education, though his knowledge of Latin and French literature and his father's position suggest that he received some formal training. The first definite record of the young man is dated 1357, when he was in the service of Elizabeth, Countess of Ulster. In 1359 he went on a military expedition in France, was captured and later was ransomed. By September 12, 1366, he had married Philippa, who was probably the daughter of Sir Payne Roet.

In 1367 Chaucer was made a "yeoman of the court," and from 1368 to 1378 he was one of the king's esquires. Among his varied duties was that of entertaining the court with songs and stories. In 1369 he composed THE BOOK OF THE DUCHESS *in honor of John of Gaunt's first wife, Blanche. During this period he also performed diplomatic services in France and Italy. On these missions he had the opportunity, unique among Englishmen, to study the works of Boccaccio and Dante. Chaucer's later writings show how strongly he was influenced by the two poets.*

From 1374 to 1386 he was comptroller of the customs and of the subsidy of wools. During these years he wrote THE HOUSE OF FAME, THE PARLIAMENT OF FOWLS, TROILUS AND CRISEYDE, *and* THE LEGEND OF GOOD WOMEN. *In 1386, probably due to a shift in political power, Chaucer lost his comptrollership and became a justice of the peace in Kent. Three years later Richard II reasserted his power, and Chaucer became clerk of the king's works, responsible for maintaining the Tower, the West Palace, the king's highways and waterworks and other royal possessions. In 1891 he relinquished his clerkship, thereafter living primarily on pensions granted by* the King and the Gaunt family. THE CANTERBURY TALES *was probably written during this later period in Chaucer's life. Upon his death in 1400, Chaucer was paid the tribute of a burial in Westminster Abbey, an almost unprecedented honor (at that time) for a commoner. His grave is now the center of the famous "Poet's Corner."*

The definitive biography of Chaucer is J. M. Manly's SOME NEW LIGHT ON CHAUCER *(1926). The foremost edition of Chaucer's works is that of F. N. Robinson (1933; rev. ed., 1957).* THE CANTERBURY TALES *was edited by J. M. Manly and E. Rickert in eight volumes (1940);* TROILUS AND CRISEYDE *by R. K. Root (1926). Recent criticism on Chaucer includes H. S. Bennett,* CHAUCER AND THE FIFTEENTH CENTURY *(1947), W. W. Laurence,* CHAUCER AND THE CANTERBURY TALES *(1950), C. Muscatine,* CHAUCER AND THE FRENCH TRADITION *(1957), and W. C. Curry,* CHAUCER AND THE MEDIEVAL SCIENCES *(rev. ed., 1960).*

FROM THE GENERAL PROLOGUE
TO THE CANTERBURY TALES

Whan that Aprill with his° shoures soote°	its/sweet
The droghte° of March hath perced to the roote,	drought
And bathed every veyne in swich° licour°	such/moisture
Of° which vertu° engendred is the flour;°	from/strength/ flower
5 Whan Zephirus eek° with his sweete breeth	also
Inspired hath in every holt° and heeth°	grove/meadow
The tendre croppes, and the yonge sonne	
Hath in the Ram his halve cours yronne,°	run
And smale foweles maken melodye,	
10 That slepen al the nyght with open ye°	eye
(So priketh hem° nature in hir corages);°	them/desires, hearts
Thanne longen folk to goon° on pilgrimages,	go
And palmeres for to seken straunge strondes,°	strands, shores
To ferne halwes,° kowthe° in sondry londes;	foreign altars/ known

5 *Zephirus:* the West wind.   7 *yonge sonne:* the sun is halfway through Aries, the sign of the Ram, the first sign of the zodiacal year.   13 *palmeres:* pilgrims, especially those who had been to Palestine where palms are found and were used to identify Christian pilgrims.

¹⁵ And specially from every shires ende
Of Engelond to Caunterbury they wende,
The hooly blisful martir for to seke,
That hem hath holpen° whan that they were seeke.°   helped/sick
   Bifil that in that seson on a day,
²⁰ In Southwerk at the Tabard as I lay
Redy to wenden on my pilgrymage
To Caunterbury with ful° devout corage,   very
At nyght was come into that hostelrye
Wel nyne and twenty in a compaignye,
²⁵ Of sondry folk, by aventure° yfalle   chance
In felaweshipe, and pilgrimes were they alle,
That toward Caunterbury wolden° ryde.   would
The chambres and the stables weren wyde,
And wel we weren esed° atte beste.   eased, accommo-
   dated

³⁰ And shortly, whan the sonne was to reste,
So hadde I spoken with hem everichon°   every one
That I was of hir felaweshipe anon,
And made forward erly for to ryse,
To take oure wey ther as I yow devyse.°   tell
³⁵   But nathelees,° whil I have tyme and space,   nonetheless
Er° that I ferther in this tale pace,°   before/pass by
Me thynketh it acordaunt to resoun°   reason
To telle yow al the condicioun
Of ech of hem, so as it semed me,
⁴⁰ And whiche they weren, and of what degree,
And eek in what array that they were inne;
And at a knyght that wol I first bigynne.
   A KNYGHT ther was, and that a worthy man,
That fro the tyme that he first bigan
⁴⁵ To riden out, he loved chivalrie,
Trouthe° and honour, fredom° and curtesie.   integrity/openness
   of spirit

Ful worthy was he in his lordes werre,°   war
And therto hadde he riden, no man ferre,°   further
As wel in cristendom as in hethenesse,°   heathen **dominions**
⁵⁰ And evere honoured for his worthynesse.
At Alisaundre he was whan it was wonne.

---

17 *martir:* St. Thomas à Becket, assassinated in Canterbury Cathedral in 1170.   20
Southwerk: on the south bank of the Thames, at that time outside London, the site of the
Tabard Inn.   33 *made forward:* made plans.   51 *Alisaundre:* Alexandria. The knight
had fought against the Moslems in the Near East; against the northern heathen in Prussia,
Lithuania, and Russia; and against the Moors in North Africa and Spain.

Ful ofte tyme he hadde the bord bigonne
Aboven alle nacions in Pruce;
In Lettow hadde he reysed° and in Ruce,   raided
55 No Cristen man so ofte of his degree.
In Gernade at the seege eek hadde he be
Of Algezir, and riden in Belmarye.
At Lyeys was he and at Satalye,
Whan they were wonne; and in the Grete See
60 At many a noble armee hadde he be.
At mortal batailles hadde he been fiftene,
And foughten for oure feith at Tramyssene
In lystes thries,° and ay° slayn his foo.   thrice/always
This ilke° worthy knyght hadde been also   same
65 Somtyme with the lord of Palatye
Agayn° another hethen in Turkye.   against
And everemoore he hadde a sovereyn prys;°   reputation
And though that he were worthy, he was wys,° wise
And of his port° as meeke as is a mayde.   deportment,
                                      manners
70 He nevere yet no vileynye° ne sayde   rudeness
In al his lyf unto no maner wight
He was a verray,° parfit° gentil knyght.   true/perfect
But, for to tellen yow of his array,
His hors° were goode, but he was nat gay.° horses/ostentatious
75 Of fustian° he wered° a gypon°   coarse fabric/wore/
                                        tunic
Al bismotered° with his habergeon,°   rust-spattered/
                                      hauberk, chain mail
For he was late ycome from his viage,°   voyage
And wente for to doon° his pilgrymage.   perform
  With hym ther was his sone, a yong SQUIER,
80 A lovyere and a lusty bacheler,
With lokkes crulle° as they were leyd° in presse. curled/laid
Of twenty yeer of age he was, I gesse.
Of his stature he was of evene° lengthe,   moderate, average
And wonderly delyvere,° and of greet strengthe. quick, agile
85 And he hadde been somtyme in chyvachie° horse raids, cavalry
                                        skirmishes

52 . . . *bigonne:* i.e., had sat at the head of table at many a victory feast.   59 *Grete See:* the Mediterranean.   65 *Palatye:* a Moslem ruler. During the Crusades it was sometimes convenient for Christians and pagan rulers to make brief alliances.   68 . . . *worthy:* i.e., in spite of the fact that he was a knight.   71 . . . *wight:* any sort of person. The four negatives in these two lines are a Middle English intensive device.

In Flaundres, in Artoys, and Pycardie,
And born hym weel, as of so litel space,
In hope to stonden in his lady° grace.   *lady's*
Embrouded° was he, as it were a meede°   *embroidered/ meadow*

90 Al ful of fresshe floures, whyte and reede.°   *red*
Syngynge he was, or floytynge,° al the day;   *fluting? whistling?*
He was as fressh as is the month of May.
Short was his gowne, with sleves longe and wyde.
Wel koude he sitte on hors and faire ryde.
95 He koude songes make and well endite,°   *compose*
Juste° and eek daunce, and weel purtreye° and write.   *joust/sketch*
So hoote° he lovede that by nyghertale°   *hotly/nighttime*
He sleep namoore than dooth a nyghtyngale.
Curteis he was, lowely,° and servysable,   *humble*
100 And carf° biforn° his fader° at the table. . . .   *carved/before/ father*

There was also a Nonne, a PRIORESSE,
That of hir smylyng was ful symple and coy;°   *modest*
Hire gretteste ooth° was but Seinte Loy;   *oath*
And she was cleped° madame Eglentyne.   *named*
105 Ful weel she soong° the service dyvyne,   *sang*
Entuned° in hir nose ful semely,°   *intoned/pleasingly*
And Frensh, she spak ful faire and fetisly,°   *elegantly*
After the scole of Stratford atte Bowe,
For Frenssh of Parys was to hire unknowe.
110 At mete° wel ytaught was she with alle: *meat, meals*
She leet° no morsel from hir lippes falle,   *let*
Ne wette hir fyngres in hir sauce depe;
Wel koude she carie a morsel and wel kepe°   *guard*
That no drope ne fille upon hire brest.
115 In curteisie was set ful muchel hir lest.
Hir over-lippe wyped she so clene
That in hir coppe° ther was no ferthyng° sene   *cup/bit*
Of grece, whan she dronken hadde hir draughte.
Ful semely after hir mete she raughte.°   *reached*
120 And sikerly° she was of greet desport°   *certainly/cheeriness*
And ful plesaunt, and amyable of port°   *manner*

---

86 . . . *Pycardie:* sites of conflict between English and French.   87 . . . *litel space:* i.e.,
in such a little time.   103 *Seinte Loy:* Eloi, Eligius.   108 *Stratford atte Bowe*: a con-
vent school in which the standard of French was disparaged. Parisian French had long been
standard.   115 . . . *hir lest:* i.e., good manners were most important to her.

And peyned° hire to countrefete cheere°

pains took/
behavior

Of court, and to been estatlich° of manere,

stately

And to ben° holden digne° of reverence.

be/worthy

125 But, for to speken of hire conscience,

She was so charitable and so pitous°

pitying

She wolde wepe, if that she saugh a mous

Kaught in a trappe, if it were deed° or bledde.

dead

Of° smale houndes hadde she that she fedde

some

130 With rosted flesh, or milk an dwastel-breed.°

bread

But soore wepte she if oon° of hem were deed,

one

Or if men smoot it with a yerde° smerte;°

stick/smartly

And al was conscience and tendre herte.

Ful semyly hir wympul pynched° was,

pleated

135 Hir nose tretys,° hir eyen° greye as glas,

well-shaped/eyes

Hir mouth ful smal, and thereto softe and reed;

But sikerly she hadde a fair forheed;

It was almoost a spanne° brood, I trowe;°

hand-breadth/
think

For, hardily,° she was nat undergrowe.°

truly/petite

140 Ful fetys° was hir cloke, as I was war.°

becoming/aware

Of smal coral aboute hire arm she bar

A peire° of bedes, gauded° al with grene,

string/decorated

And thereon heng a brooch of gold ful sheene,°

shining, bright

On which ther was first write a crowned A,

145 And after *Amor vincit omnia.* . . .

A CLERK ther was of Oxenford also,

That unto logyk hadde longe ygo.

As leene was his hors as is a rake,

And he nas nat right fat, I undertake,

150 But looked holwe°, and therto sobrely.

hollow

Ful thredbare was his overeste° courtepy;°

outer/jacket

For he hadde geten hym yet no benefice,°

ecclesiastical living

Ne was so worldly for to have office.°

secular position

For hym was levere have at his beddes heed°

head

155 Twenty bookes, clad in blak or reed,

Of Aristotle and his philosophie,

Than robes riche, or fithele,° or gay sautrie.°

fiddle/psaltery,
harp

---

145 . . . *omnia:* "Love conquers all."   146 *clerk:* the term "clerk" derives from "cleric" and applied to all students since they had to assert ecclesiastical intentions to enter medieval universities.   147 . . . *ygo:* i.e., he had long since advanced to the study of logic. 154 . . . *levere:* i.e., he would rather.

But al be that he was a philosophre,
Yet hadde he but litel gold in cofre;°   *coffer, strongbox*
160 But al that he myghte of his freendes hente,°   *take*
On bookes and on lernynge he it spente,
And bisily gan for the soules preye°   *pray*
Of hem that yaf° hym wherwith to scoleye.°   *gave/study*
Of studie took he moost cure° and moost heede.   *care*
165 Noght o word spak he moore than was neede,
And that was seyd in° forme° and reverence,   *with/formality*
And short and quyk and ful of hy sentence;°   *meaning, signifi-*
    cance

Sownynge° in moral vertu was his speche,   *resounding*
And gladly wolde he lerne and gladly teche. . . .
170   A good WIF was ther OF biside BATHE,
But she was somdel° deef, and that was scathe.   *somewhat/a pity*
Of clooth-makyng she hadde swich an haunt,'   *skill*
She passed hem of Ypres and of Gaunt.
In al the parisshe wif ne was ther noon
175 That to the offrynge bifore hire sholde goon;
And if ther dide, certeyn so wrooth° was she,   *angry*
That she was out of all charitee.
Hir coverchiefs ful fyne weren of ground;°   *texture*
I dorste° swere they weyden ten pound   *dare*
180 That on a Sonday weren upon hir heed.
Hir hosen weren of fyn scarlet reed,
Ful streite° yteyd, and shoes ful moyste° and newe.   *tightly/unworn*
Boolde was hir face, and fair,° and reed of hewe.   *attractive*
She was a worthy womman al hir lyve:
185 Housbondes at chirche dore she hadde fyve,
Withouten° oother compaignye in youthe,—   *besides*
But therof nedeth nat to speke as nowthe.°   *now*
And thries hadde she been at Jerusalem;
She hadde passed many a straunge° strem;   *foreign*
190 At Rome she hadde been, and at Coloigne.
In Galice at Seint-Jame, and at Coloigne.
She koude° muchel° of wandrynge by the weye.   *knew/much*
Gat°-tothed was she, soothly° for to seye.   *gap/truly*
Upon an amblere° esily she sat,   *riding horse*
195 Ywympled° wel, and on hir heed an hat   *veiled*
As brood° as is a bokeler° or a targe;°   *broad/shield/target*

---

158 *philosophre:* word play with its definition of alchemist.   173 *Ypres . . . Gaunt:*
textile centers in Flanders. "Gaunt" = Ghent.   185 . . . *dore:* medieval weddings
were held at the church door.   191 . . . *Coloigne:* sites of shrines in France, Spain,
and Germany.

A foot-mantel° aboute hir hipes large,   *riding skirt*
And on hir feet a paire of spores° sharpe.   *spurs*
In felaweshipe wel koude she laughe and carpe.°   *chat*
200 Of remedies of love she knew per chaunce,
For she koude of that art the olde daunce. . . .
   The MILLERIE was a stout carl° for the nones;   *fellow*
Ful byg he was of brawn,° and eek° of bones.   *muscle/also*
That proved wel, for over al ther he cam,
205 At wrastlynge he wolde have alwey the ram.
He was short-sholdred, brood,° a thikke knarre;°   *broad/stout fellow*
Ther was no dore that he nolde° heve of° harre,°   *would not/from/hinges*

Or breke it at a rennyng° with his heed.   *running*
His berd as any sowe or fox was reed,
210 And therto brood, as though it were a spade.
Upon the cop° right of his nose he hade   *ridge*
A werte,° and theron stood a toft of herys,°   *wart/hairs*
Reed as the brustles° of a sowes erys;°   *bristles/ears*
His nosethirles° blake° were and wyde.   *nostrils/black*
215 A swerd and bokeler bar° he by his syde.   *bore*
His mouth as greet was as a greet forneys.°   *furnace*
He was a janglere° and a goliardeys,°   *chatterer/liar*
And that was moost of synne and harlotries.°   *obscenities*
Wel koude he stelen corn and tollen thries;
220 And yet he hadde a thombe of gold, pardee.
A whit cote and a blew hood wered he.
A baggepipe wel koude he blowe and sowne,°   *sound*
And therwithal he broghte us out of towne. . . .
   With hym ther rood a gentil PARDONER
225 Of Rouncivale, his freend and his compeer,°   *comrade*
That streight was comen fro the court of Rome.
Ful loude he soong, "Com hider, love, to me!"
This Somonour bar to hym a stif burdoun;
Was nevere trompe° of half so greet a soun.   *trumpet*
230 This Pardoner hadde heer° as yelow as wex,   *hair*
But smothe it heeng as dooth a strike° of flex;   *bunch*

---

201 . . . *the olde daunce:* i.e., as it happened, she knew all the tricks of that game.
205 *ram:* a conventional prize for wrestling matches.   219 *tollen thries:* take toll thrice, i.e., he deducted more than the legal percentage.   220 . . . *thumb of gold:* i.e., still, he was honest, as millers go.   224 *hym:* the Summoner, another pilgrim. A pardoner had the power to sell Papal indulgences and often sold other means of divine forgiveness. 225 *Rouncivale:* the hospital of Roncesvalle in Spain, which had a branch near Charing Cross in London.   228 *burdoun:* carried him along with a loud vocal accompaniment, ground melody.

By ounces° henge his lokkes that he hadde,   stringy strands
And therwith he his shuldres overspradde;
But thynne it lay, by colpons° oon and oon.   shreds
35   But hood, for olitee,° wered he noon,   sport
For it was trussed up in his walet.°   pack
Hym thoughte he rood al of the newe jet;°   style
Dischevelee,° save his cappe, he rood al bare.   hair disheveled
Swiche glarynge° eyen hadde he as an hare.   bright
40   A vernycle hadde he sowed upon his cappe.
His walet lay biforn hym in his lappe,
Bretful° of pardoun, comen from Rom all hoot.°   brimful/hot
A voys he hadde as smal° as hath a goot.°   fine/goat
No berd hadde he, ne nevere sholde have;
45   As smothe it was as it were late shave.
I trowe he were a geldyng or a mare.
But of his craft, from Berwyk into Ware,
Ne was ther swich another pardoner.
For in his male° he hadde a pilwe-beer.°   bag/pillow cover
50   Which that he seyde was Oure Lady° veyl: Lady's
He seyde he hadde a gobet° of the seyl   bit
That Seint Peter hadde, whan that he wente
Upon the see, til Jhesu Crist hym hente.°   seized
He hadde a croys° of latoun ful of stones,   cross
255   And in a glas he hadde pigges bones.
But with thise relikes,° whan that he fond°   relics/found
A povre° person° dwellynge upon lond,°   poor/parson/in the country

Upon° a day he gat hym moore moneye   in
Than that the person gat in monthes tweye;°   two
260   And thus, with feyned° flaterye and japes,°   feigned, pretended/tricks

He made the person and the peple his apes.°   fools
But trewely to tellen atte laste,
He was in chirch a noble ecclesiaste.
Wel koude he rede a lessoun or a storie,°   biblical narrative
265   But alderbest° he song an offertorie;   best of all
For wel he wiste,° whan that song was songe,   knew
He moste° preche and well affile° his tonge   must/file
To wynne silver, as he ful wel koude;
Therefore he song the murierly° and loude. . . .   merrily

240 *vernycle:* a small replica of the handkerchief of St. Veronica, lent to Jesus at a Station of the Cross and reputed to have retained the imprint of his face.   254 *latoun:* a metal alloy of copper and zinc. The stones give it a false weight.   255 *pigges bones:* the pardoner represents them as bones of saints.

THE PRIORESS'S TALE

    There was in Asye, in a greet° citee,   great
Amonges Cristene folk, a Jewerye,°   ghetto
Sustened by a lord of that contree
For foule usure° and lucre of vileynye,°   usury, interest/
                                        shame
5 Hateful to Crist and to his compaignye;
And thurgh° the strete men myghte ride or wende,° through/pass
For it was free and open at eyther ende.

    A litel scole° of Cristen folk ther stood   school
Doun at the ferther ende, in which ther were
10 Children an heep,° ycomen of Cristen blood,   crowd
That lerned in that scole yeer by yere
Swich° manere° doctrine as men used there,   such/manner of
This is to seyn,° to syngen and to rede,   say, recite
As smale children doon° in hire° childhede.°   do/their/childhood

15 Among thise children was a wydwes° sone,   widow's
A litel clergeon,° seven yeer of age,   pupil
That day by day to scole was his wone,°   custom, habit
And eek° also, where as he saugh th'y mage   moreover
Of Cristes mooder,° hadde he in usage,   mother
20 As hym was taught, to knele adoun and seye
His *Ave Marie,* as he goth by the weye.

    Thus hath this wydwe hir litel sone ytaught
Oure blisful Lady, Cristes mooder deere,
To worshipe ay,° and he forgat it naught,   always
25 For sely child wol alday soone leere.
But ay, whan I remembre on this mateere,
Seint Nicholas stant evere in my presence,
For he so yong to Crist dide reverence.

    This litel child, his litel book lerynge,
30 As he sat in the scole at his prymer,

19 . . . *usage:* i.e., he was accustomed.   25 . . . *leere:* for the blessed child wished to
do nothing but learn.   28 *reverence:* a reference to the legend that St. Nicholas was so
devout that as a nursing baby he took only one swallow on Wednesdays and Fridays

He *Alma redemptoris* herde synge,
As children lerned hire antiphoner;°   anthem book
And as he dorste,° he drough° hym ner and ner,   dared/drew
And herkned ay° the wordes and the noote,°   always to/tune
35 Til he the firste vers koude° al by rote.   knew

Noght wiste° he what this Latyn was to seye,°   knew/mean
For he so yong and tendre was of age.
But on a day his felawe° gan he preye   companion
T'expounden hym this song in his langage,
40 Or telle hym why this song was in usage;
This preyde° he hym to construe° and declare   begged/explain
Ful often tyme upon his knowes° bare.   knees

His felawe, which that elder was than he,
Answerde hym thus: "This song, I have herd geye,
45 Was maked of° our blisful Lady free,°   concerning/
                                                  gracious

Hire to salue,° and eek° hire for to preye   hail/also
To been oure help and socour° whan we deye.°   help/die
I kan° namoore expounde in this mateere;   know
I lerne song, I kan but smal grammeere."°   literary criticism,
                                                  explication

50 "And is this song maked in reverence
Of Cristes mooder?" seyde this innocent.
"Now, certes, I wol do my diligence
To konne° it al er Cristemasse be went.   learn
Though that I for my prymer shal be shent,°   scolded
55 And shal be beten thries° in an houre,
I wol it konne Oure Lady for to honoure!"

His felawe taughte hym homward prively,°   privately
Fro° day to day, til he koude° it by rote,   from/knew
And thanne he song it wel and boldely,
60 Fro word to word, acordynge with the note.
Twies a day it passed thurgh his throte,
To scoleward and homward whan he wente;
On Cristes mooder set was his entente.°   attention

As I have seyd, thurghout the Juerie,
65 This litel child, as he cam to and fro,
Ful murily° than wolde he synge and crie   merrily

31 *Alma redemptoris:* an anthem in the Roman breviary. "Our redemptive (Mother)."

O Alma redemptoris everemo.
The swetnesse hath his herte perced so
Of Cristes mooder that, to hire to preye,
70 He kan nat stynte of syngyng by the weye.

    Oure firste foo,° the serpent Sathanas,°   foe/Satan
That hath in Jues herte his waspes nest,
Up swal,° and seide, "O Hebrayk peple, allas!   swelled
Is this to yow a thyng that is honest,
75 That swich a boy shal walken as hym lest°   pleases
In youre despit, and synge of swich sentence,° a theme
Which is agayn youre lawes reverence?"

    Fro thennes forth the Jues han° conspired   had
This innocent out of this world to chace.
80 An homycide° therto han they hyred,   murderer
That in an aleye° hadde a privee° place;   alley/hidden
And as the child gan forby for to pace,
This cursed Jew hym hente,° and heeld° hym faste, seized/held
And kitte° his throte, and in a pit hym caste. cut

85 I seye that in a wardrobe° they hym threwe   privy
Where as thise Jewes purgen° hire entraille.° cleaned/bowels
O cursed folk of Herodes al newe,°   renewed
What may youre yvel entente yow availe?
Mordre wol out, certeyn, it wol nat faille,
90 And namely ther th'onour of God shal sprede;
The blood out crieth on youre cursed dede.

    O martir, sowded° to virginitee,   confirmed
Now maystow° syngen, folwynge evere in oon may'st thou
The white Lamb celestial—quod she—
95 Of which the grete evaungelist, Seint John,
In Pathmos wroot,° which seith that they that goon wrote
Biforn this Lamb, and synge a song al newe,
That nevere, flesshly, wommen they ne knewe.

    This poure wydwe awaiteth al that nyght
100 After hir litel child, but he cam noght;

---

70 *He ... syngyng:* He could not refrain from singing.   76 *... despit:* to your scorn
shame.   82 *... pace:* walked by.   87 *Herodes:* king of the Jews 4–39 A.D.
93 *... oon:* i.e., following continually.   96 *Pathmos:* an island where St. John was thoug
to have written his gospel.

For which, as soone as it was dayes lyght,
With face pale of drede° and bisy thoght,   dread
She hath at scole and elleswhere hym soght,
Til finally she gan so fer espie°   found out
That he last seyn was in the Juerie.

With moodres° pitee in hir brest enclosed,   mother's
She gooth, as she were half out of hir mynde,
To every place where she hath supposed
By liklihede hir litel child to fynde;
And evere on Cristes mooder meeke and kynde
She cride, and atte laste thus she wroghte:°   brought to pass
Among the cursed Jues she hym soghte.

She frayneth° and she preyeth pitously   asked
To every Jew that dwelte in thilke° place,   that
To telle hire if hir child wente oght forby.
They seyde "nay"; but Jhesu, of his grace,
Yaf° in hir thoght, inwith a litel space,   gave
That in that place after hir sone she cryde,
Where he was casten in a pit bisyde.

O grete God, that parfournest° thy laude°   performs/praise
By mouth of innocentz, lo, heere thy myght!
This gemme of chastite, this emeraude,°   emerald
And eek of martirdom the ruby bright,
Ther he with throte ykorven lay upright,
He *Alma redemptoris* gan to synge
So loude that al the place gan to rynge.

The Cristene folk that thurgh the strete wente
In coomen for to wondre upon this thyng,
And hastily they for the provost° sente;   magistrate
He cam anon withouten tariyng,
And herieth° Crist that is of hevene kyng,   worshiped
And eek his mooder, honour of mankynde,
And after that the Jewes leet° he bynde.   let

This child with pitous lamentacioun
Up taken was, syngynge his song alway,
And with honour of greet processioun
They carien hym unto the nexte° abbay.°   nearby/abbey

115 . . . *forby:* sometimes past.   117 . . . *space:* so that in a short time.

13

His mooder swownynge° by the beere° lay;   swooning/bier
Unnethe° myghte the peple that was theere   hardly
140 This newe Rachel brynge fro his beere.

    With torment and with shameful deeth echon°   each one
This provost dooth° thise Jewes for to sterve°   committed/star
That of this mordre wiste,° and that anon.   knew
He nolde° no swich cursednesse observe.   did not wish/
                                                 favor

145 "Yvele shal have that yvele wol deserve";
Therfore with wilde hors he dide hem drawe,°   tear apart
And after that he heng hem by the lawe.

    Upon this beere ay° lith° this innocent   all that time/
                                                    lay
Biforn the chief auter,° whil masse laste;   altar
150 And after that, the abbot with his covent°   order, monks
Han sped hem for to burien hym ful faste;
And whan they hooly water on hym caste,
Yet° spak this child, whan spreynd was hooly water,   again, still
And song O Alma redemptoris mater!

155   This abbot, which that was an hooly man,
As monkes been—or elles oghte be—
This yonge child to conjure he bigan,
And seyde, "O deere child, I halse° thee,   implore
In° vertu° of the hooly Trinitee,   by/the power
160 Tel me what is thy cause for to synge,
Sith that thy throte is kut to my semynge?"°   judgment

    "My throte is kut unto my nekke boon,"
Seyde this child, "and, as by wey of kynde,°   nature
I sholde have dyed, ye, longe tyme agon.
165 But Jesu Crist, as ye in bookes fynde,
Wil° that his glorie laste and be in mynde,   desires
And for the worship of his Mooder deere
Yet may I synge O Alma loude and cleere.

    "This welle of mercy, Cristes mooder sweete,
170 I loved alwey, as after my konnynge;°   understanding
And whan that I my lyf sholde forlete,°   abandon
To me she cam, and bad me for to synge

140 *Rachel:* a reference to Rachel weeping for her children. Matthew 2:18.

This anthem verraily in my deyynge,°   dying
As ye han herd, and whan that I hadde songe,
75 Me thoughte she leyde a greyn upon my tonge.

"Wherfore I synge, and synge moot° certeyn,   most
In honour of that blisful Mayden free,
Til fro my tonge of° taken is the greyn;   off
And after that thus seyde she to me:
180 'My litel child, now wol I fecche thee,
Whan that the greyn is fro thy tonge ytake.
Be nat agast, I wol thee nat forsake.'"

This hooly monk, this abbot, hym meene I,
His tonge out caughte, and took awey the greyn,
85 And he yaf up the goost ful softely.
And whan this abbot hadde this wonder seyn,
His salte teeris trikled doun as reyn,
And gruf° he fil° al plat° upon the grounde,   face down/fell/flat
And stille he lay as he had ben ybounde.

190 The covent eek lay on the pavement
Wepynge, and herying Cristes mooder deere,
And after that they ryse, and forth been went,
And tooken awey this martir from his beere;
And in a tombe of marbul stones cleere°   splendid
195 Enclosen they his litel body sweete.
Ther he is now, God leve° us for to meete!   grant

O yonge Hugh of Lyncoln, slayn also
With° cursed Jewes, as it is notable,   by
For it is but a litel while ago,
200 Preye eek for us, we synful folk unstable,
That, of his mercy, God so merciable
On us his grete mercy multiplie,
For reverence of his mooder Marie.
        Amen

175 *greyn:* probably a pearl.   197 *Hugh of Lyncoln:* murdered by Jews in 1255, according to the Annals of Waverly.

THE NUN'S PRIEST'S TALE

A povre wydwe, somdeel° stape° in age somewhat/
advanced

Was whilom° dwellyng in a narwe cotage, once
Biside a grove, stondynge in a dale.
This wydwe, of which I telle yow my tale,
5 Syn thilke° day that she was last a wyf, that
In pacience ladde a ful symple lyf;
For litel was hir catel° and her rente.° property/income
By housbondrie° of swich as God hire sente thrift
She foond° hirself and eek hir doghtren two. provided for
10 Thre large sowes hadde she, and namo,
Three keen°, and eek a sheep that highte° Malle. kine, cows/was called

Ful sooty was hire bour° and eek hir halle, bedroom
In which she eet ful many a sklendre° meel. skimpy
Of poynaunt° sauce hir neded never a deel. spicy
15 No deyntee morsel passed thurgh hir throte;
Hir diete was accordant to hir cote.° cottage
Repleccioun° ne made hire nevere sik; repletion, over-eating

Attempree° diete was al hir phisik,° a temperate/medicine

And exercise, and hertes suffisaunce.° contentment
20 The goute lette° hire nothyng for to daunce, hindered
N'apoplexie shente° nat hir heed. harmed
No wyn ne drank she, neither whit ne reed;
Hir bord was served moost with whit and blak,—
Milk and broun breed, in which she foond no lak,° fault
25 Seynd° bacoun, and somtyme an ey° or tweye;° singed, broiled/egg/two

For she was, as it were, a maner° deye.° kind of/dairymaid

A yeerd° she hadde, enclosed al aboute yard
With stikkes, and a drye dych withoute,° outside, around
In which she hadde a cok, hight Chauntecleer.
30 In al the land, of crowyng nas° his peer. was not

---

20 . . . *daunce:* i.e., the gout did not stop her from dancing.

His voys was murier than the murie orgon
On messe° days that in the chirche gon. *mass*
Wel° sikerer° was his crowyng in the logge° *more/certain/
lodging*

Than is a clokke or an abbey orlogge.° *hour log, clock*
35 By nature he knew ech ascencioun
Of the equynoxial in thilke toun;
For whan degrees fiftene weren ascended,
Thanne crew he, that it myghte nat been amended.° *bettered*
His coombe was redder than the fyn coral,
40 And batailled° as it were a castel wal; *notched*
His byle° was blak, and as the jeet° it shoon; *bill/jet*
Lyk asure° were his legges and his toon;° *azure/toes*
His nayles whitter than the lylye flour,
And lyk the burned gold was his colour.
45 This gentil cok hadde in his governaunce
Sevene hennes for to doon al his plesaunce,° *pleasure*
Which were his sustres° and his paramours,° *sisters/mistresses*
And wonder lyk to hym, as of colours;
Of whiche the faireste hewed on hir throte
50 Was cleped° faire damoysele° Pertelote. *called/Miss*
Curteys she was, discreet, and debonaire,° *mild*
And compaignable, and bar hyrself so faire,
Syn thilke day that she was seven nyght oold,
That trewely she hath the herte in hoold
55 Of Chauntecleer, loken° in every lith;° *locked/limb*
He loved hire so that wel° was hym therwith. *content*
But swich a joye was it to here hem synge,
Whan that the brighte sonne gan to sprynge,
In sweete accord, "My lief is faren in londe!"
60 For thilke° tyme, as I have understonde, *at that*
Beestes and briddes° koude speke and synge. *birds*
    And so bifel that in a dawenynge,
As Chauntecleer among his wyves alle
Sat on his perche, that was in the halle,
65 And next hym sat this faire Pertelote,
This Chauntecleer gan gronen in his throte,
As man that in his dreem is drecched° soore. *wretched*
And whan that Pertelote thus herde hym roore,
She was agast, and seyde, "Herte deere,

35 . . . *ascencioun:* i.e., he instinctively knew the celestial equator's progression, which was
believed to be 360 degrees in twenty-four hours or 15 degrees in one hour (37).
59 . . . *londe:* the refrain of a medieval song. "My love has gone to the country."

70 What eyleth yow, to grone in this manere?
   Ye been a verray° sleper; fy, for shame!"   sound
      And he answerde, and seyde thus: "Madame,
   I pray yow that ye take it nat agrief.°   amiss
   By God, me mette° I was in swich meschief   dreamed
75 Right now, that yet° myn herte is soore afright.   still
   Now God," quod he, "my swevene° recche° aright,   dream/interpret
   And kepe my body out of foul prisoun!
   Me mette how that I romed up and doun
   Withinne our yeerd, wheer as I saugh a beest
80 Was lyk an hound, and wolde han maad areest
   Upon my body, and wolde han had me deed.
   His colour was bitwixe yelow and reed,
   And tipped was his tayl and bothe his eeris°   ears
   With blak, unlyk the remenant of his heeris;   hairs
85 His snowte smal, with glowynge eyen° tweye.   eyes
   Yet of his look for feere almoost I deye;
   This caused me my gronyng, doutelees."
      "Avoy!"° quod she, "fy on yow, hertelees!   fie
   Allas!" quod she, "for, by that God above,
90 Now han ye lost myn herte and al my love.
   I kan nat love a coward, by my feith!
   For certes, what so any womman seith,
   We all desiren, if it myghte bee,
   To han housebondes hardy, wise, and free,°   generous
95 And secree,° and no nygard,° ne no fool,   discreet/miser
   Ne hym that is agast of every tool,
   Ne noon avauntour,° by that God above!   braggart
   How dorste° ye seyn, for shame, unto youre love   dare
   That any thyng myghte make yow aferd?
100 Have ye no mannes herte, and han a berd?
   Allas! and konne° ye been agast of swevenys?   can
   Nothyng, God woot,° but vanitee° in sweven is.   knows/illusion
   Swevenes engendren° of replecciouns,   come
   And ofte of fume° and of complecciouns,°   gas/humors
105 Whan humours been to habundent in a wight.
   Certes this dreem, which ye han met to-nyght,
   Cometh of the greete superfluytee
   Of youre rede° colera,° pardee,   red/bile
   Which causeth folk to dreden° in hir dremes   dread, fear
110 Of arwes,° and of fyr with rede lemes,°   arrows/flames

74 . . . *meschief:* i.e., I dreamed that I was in such trouble.   105 . . . *wight:* assum
that an excess of one of the bodily humors affects the temperament of a person.

Of rede beestes, that they wol hem byte,
Of contek,° and of whelpes,° grete and lyte;°   conflict/dogs/little
Right° as the humour of malencolie   just
Causeth ful many a man in sleep to crie
15 For feere of blake° beres, or boles° blake,   black/balls
Or elles blake develes wole hem take.
Of othere humours koude I telle also
That werken many a man sleep° ful wo;   asleep
But I wol passe as lightly° as I kan.   quickly
20   Lo Catoun, which that was so wys a man,
Seyde he nat thus, 'Ne do no fors of dremes?'
    Now sire," quod she, "whan we flee fro the bemes,°   beams
For Goddes love, as taak som laxatyf.
Up° peril of my soule and of my lyf,   upon
25 I conseille yow the beste, I wol nat lye,
That bothe of colere and of malencolye
Ye purge yow; and for° ye shal nat tarie,   so
Though in this toun is noon apothecarie,
I shal myself to herbes techen yow
30 That shul been for youre hele° and for youre prow;° health/betterment
And in oure yeerd tho herbes shal I fynde
The whiche han of hire propretee by kynde°   nature
To purge yow bynethe and eek above.
Foryet° nat this, for Goddes owene love!   forget
35 Ye been ful coleryk of compleccioun;
Ware° the sonne in his ascencioun   beware that
Ne fynde yow nat repleet° of humours hoote.°   filled/hot
And if it do, I dar wel leye a grote,°   coin
That ye shul have a fevere terciane,
40 Or an agu, that may be youre bane.°   death
A day or two ye shul have digestyves
Of wormes, er ye take youre laxatyves
Of lawriol, centaure, and fumetere,
Or elles of ellebor, that groweth there,
45 Of katapuce, or of gaitrys beryis,
Of herbe yve, growyng in oure yeerd, ther mery° is;   pleasant
Pekke hem up right as they growe and ete hem yn.
Be myrie, housbonde, for youre fader kyn!
Dredeth no dreem, I kan sey yow namoore."

120 *Catoun:* Dionysius Cato, to whom were attributed a book of proverbial sayings used in
lementary medieval education.   121 . . . *dremes:* i.e., make nothing of the force of
reams.   139 . . . *terciane:* tertian fever, so called because it was thought to involve a
ertiary, or three-day, cycle of rise and fall.   143 *lawriol:* an herb, like those mentioned
elow, used in medieval cathartics.   148 . . . *kyn:* i.e., you are your father's son.

150   "Madame," quod he, "graunt mercy° of youre loore.°   thanks/lore
But, nathelees, as touchying daun° Catoun   don, master
That hath of wysdom swich a greet renoun,
Though that he bad no dremes for to drede,
By God, men may in olde bookes rede
155 Of many a man moore of auctorite°   authority
Than evere Caton was, so moot I thee,°   prosper
That al the revers seyn of this sentence,°   sentence
And han wel founden by experience
That dremes been significaciouns
160 As wel of joye as of tribulaciouns
That folk enduren in this lif present.
Ther nedeth make of this noon argument;
The verray preeve° showeth it in dede.   experience
    Oon of the gretteste auctour° that men rede   authors
165 Seith thus: that whilom two felawes wente
On pilgrimage, in a ful good entente;
And happed so, they coomen in a toun
Wher as ther was swich congregacioun
Of peple, and eek so streit° of herbergage,°   scarce/lodging
170 That they ne founde as muche as o° cotage   one
In which they bothe myghte ylogged° bee.   lodged
Wherfore they mosten° of necessitee,   must
As for that nyght, departen compaignye;
And ech of hem gooth to his hostelrye,
175 And took his loggyng as it wolde falle.
That oon of hem was logged in a stalle,
Fer in a yeerd, with oxen of the plough;
That oother man was logged wel ynough,
As was his aventure° or his fortune,   chance
180 That us governeth alle as in commune.
    And so bifel that, longe er it were day,
This man mette in his bed, ther as he lay,
How that his felawe gan upon hym calle,
And seyde, "Allas! for in an oxes stalle
185 This nyght I shal be mordred ther I lye.
Now help me, deere brother, or I dye.
In alle haste com to me!' he sayde.
This man out of his sleep for feere abrayde;°   got up
But whan that he was wakened of his sleep,
190 He turned hym, and took of this no keep.°   heed
Hym thoughte his dreem nas but a vanitee.

164 *auctour:* both Cicero and Valerius Maximus tell this story.

Thus twies in his slepyng dremed hee;
And atte thridde tyme yet his felawe
Cam, as hym thoughte, and seide, 'I am now slawe.°   slain
Bihoold my bloody woundes depe and wyde!
Arys up erly in the morwe tyde,
And at the west gate of the toun,' quod he,
'A carte ful of dong° ther shaltow° se,   dung/shalt thou
In which my body is hid ful prively;
Do thilke carte arresten° boldely.   stop
My gold caused my mordre, sooth to sayn.'
And tolde hym every point how he was slayn,
With a ful pitous face, pale of hewe.
And truste wel, his dreem he foond° ful trewe,   found
For on the morwe, as soone as it was day,
To his felawes in° he took the way;   inn
And whan that he cam to this oxes stalle,
After his felawe he bigan to calle.

The hostiler° answerde hym anon.   innkeeper
And seyde, 'Sire, your felawe is agon.
As soone as day he wente out of the toun.'

This man gan fallen in suspecioun,
Remembrynge on his dremes that he mette,
And forth he gooth—no lenger wolde he lette—°   delay
Unto the west gate of the toun, and fond
A dong-carte, wente as it were to donge° lond,   dump manure on
That was arrayed in that same wise
As ye han herd the dede man devyse.°   describe
And with an hardy herte he gan to crye
Vengeance and justice of this felonye.'
'My felawe mordred is this same nyght,
And in this carte he lith gapyng upright.
I crye out on the ministres,'° quod he,   officers
'That sholden kepe and reulen this citee.
Harrow!° allas! heere lith my felawe slayn!'   alarm
What sholde I moore unto this tale sayn?
The peple out sterte° and caste the cart to grounde,   started
And in the myddel of the dong they founde
The dede man, that mordred was al newe.

O blisful God, that art so just and trewe,
Lo, how that thou biwreyest° mordre alway!   reveal
Mordre wol out, that se we day by day.
Mordre is so wlatsom° and abhomynable   loathsome

196 . . . *tyde:* i.e., in the morning.

To God, that is so just and resonable,
235 That he ne wol nat suffre it heled° be   concealed
Though it abyde a yeer, or two, or thre.
Mordre wol out, this my conclusioun.
And right anon, ministres of that toun
Han hent° the carter and so soore hym pyned,°   seized/tortured
240 And eek the hostiler so soore engyned,°   racked
That they biknewe° hire wikkednesse anon,   confessed
And were anhanged by the nekke-bon.
    Heere may men seen that dremes been to drede.
And certes in the same book I rede,
245 Right in the nexte chapitre after this—
I gabbe° nat, so have I joye or blis—   lie
Two men that wolde han passed over see,
For certeyn cause, into a fer contrarie,
If that the wynd ne hadde been contrarie,
250 That made hem in a citee for to tarie
That stood ful myrie upon an haven°-syde;   harbor
But on a day, agayn° the even-tyde,   toward
The wynd gan chaunge, and blew right° as hem   just/
   leste.°   wished
Jolif° and glad they wente unto hir reste,   jolly
255 And casten° hem ful erly for to saille.   decided
But to that o° man fil° a greet mervaille: one/befell
That oon of hem, in slepyng as he lay,
Hmn mette a wonder dreem agayn the day.
Hym thoughte a man stood by his beddes syde,
260 And hym comanded that he sholde abyde,
And seyde hym thus: 'If thou tomorwe wende,°   travel
Thow shalt be dreynt;° my tale is at an ende.'   drowned
He wook, and tolde his felawe what he mette,
And preyde hym his viage for to lette;
265 As for that day, he preyde hym to byde.
His felawe, that lay by his beddes syde,
Gan for to laughe, and scorned him ful faste.°   hard, harshly
'No dreem,' quod he, 'may so myn herte agaste
That I wol lette for to do my thynges.
270 I sette° nat a straw by thy dremynges,   care
For swevenes been but vanytees and japes.°   frauds
Men dreme alday of owles and of apes,
And eek of many a maze° therwithal;   delusion
Men dreme of thyng that nevere was ne shal.

243 . . . *drede:* are worth being feared.

22

275	But sith I see that thou wolt heere abyde,	
	And thus he took his leve, and wente his way.	waste/time
	God woot, it reweth° me; and have good day!'	sorrows
	And thus he took his leve, and wente his way.	
	But er that he hadde half his cours yseyled,	
280	Noot° I nat why, ne what myschaunce it eyled,°	know/ailed
	But casuelly° the shippes botme rente,°	accidentally/tore, split

	And ship and man under the water wente	
	In sighte of othere shippes it bisyde,	
	That with hem seyled at the same tyde.	
285	And therfore, faire Pertelote so deere,	
	By swich ensamples olde maistow° leere°	may'st thou/learn
	That no man sholde been to recchelees°	reckless
	Of dremes; for I seye thee, douteleees,	
	That many a dreem ful soore is for to drede.	
290	Lo, in the lyf of Seint Kenelm I rede,	
	That was Kenulphus sone, the noble kyng	
	Of Mercenrike, how Kenelm mette a thyng;	
	A lite° er he was mordred, on a day,	little
	His mordre in his avysioun° he say.°	dream/saw
295	His norice° hym expowned° every deel°	nurse/explained/ entirely

	His sweven, and bad hym for to kepe° hym weel	guard
	For traisoun; but he nas but seven yeer oold,	
	And therfore litel tale hath he toold	
	Of any dreem, so hooly was his herte.	
300	By God! I hadde levere than my sherte	
	That ye hadde rad° his legende, as have I.	read
	Dame Pertelote, I sey yow trewely,	
	Macrobeus, that writ the avisioun	
	In Affrike of the worthy Cipioun,	
305	Affermeth° dremes, and seith that they been	affirms
	Warnynge of thynges that men after seen.	
	And forthermoore, I pray yow, looketh wel	
	In the olde testament, of Daniel,	
	If he heeld° dremes any vanitee.	believed
310	Reed eek of Joseph, and ther shul ye see	

290 *Kenelm:* became king of Mercia in 821 at the age of seven (297) and was assassinated by his aunt and guardian. 300 . . . *sherte:* i.e., I would rather give up my shirt. 303 *Macrobeus:* ca. 400 A.D. he wrote an elaborate commentary on Book VI of Cicero's *De Republica,* in which is told the dream of Scipio. 308 *Daniel:* Daniel's dreams are in Daniel 2, 4, 7, 8, and 10. 310 *Joseph:* Genesis 37, 40, 41.

Wher dremes be somtyme— I sey nat alle—
Warnynge of thynges that shul after falle.
Looke of Egipte the kyng, daun Pharao,
His bakere and his butiller also,
315 Wher they ne felte noon effect in dremes.
Whoso wol seken actes of sondry remes°   realms
May rede of dremes many a wonder thyng.
Lo Cresus, which that was of Lyde° kyng,   Lydia
Mette he nat that he sat upon a tree,
320 Which signified he sholde anhanged bee?
Lo heere Andromacha, Ectores° wyf,   Hector's
That day that Ector sholde lese° his lyf,   lose
She dremed on the same nyght biforn
How that the lyf of Ector sholde be lorn,°   lost
325 If thilke day he wente into bataille.
She warned hym, but it myghte nat availle;
He wente for to fighte natheles,
But he was slayn anon of Achilles.
But thilke tale is al to longe to telle,
330 And eek it is ny° day, I may nat dwelle.   nigh, near
Shortly I seye, as for conclusioun,
That I shal han of this avisioun
Adversitee; and I seye forthermoor,
That I ne telle of laxatyves no stoor,°   store
335 For they been venymous, I woot it weel;
I hem diffye, I love hem never a deel!
    Now let us speke of myrthe, and stynte° al this.   stop
Madame Pertelote, so have I blis,
Of o thyng God hath sent me large grace;
340 For whan I se the beautee of youre face,
Ye been so scarlet reed° aboute youre yen,°   red/eyes
It maketh al my drede for to dyen;
For al so siker° as *In principio,*   certain
Mulier est hominis confusio,—
345 Madame, the sentence° of this Latyn is,   meaning
'Womman is mannes joye and al his blis.'
For whan I feele a-nyght your softe syde,
Al be it that I may nat on yow ryde,
For that oure perche is maad so narwe, allas!

334 *ne telle of:* i.e., set by.   343 *In principio:* i.e., as sure as gospel. These are the first
words of the Gospel of St. John, which are essential to much Christian doctrine: "In the
beginning was the Word."   344 . . . *confusio:* woman is man's ruin.

350 I am so ful of joye and of solas,°   contentment,
                                       pleasure

That I diffye bothe sweven and dreem."
And with that word he fley doun fro the beem,
For it was day, and eke his hennes alle,
And with a chuk he gan hem for to calle,
355 For he hadde founde a corn, lay in the yerd.
Real° he was, he was namoore aferd.   royal
He fethered° Pertelote twenty tyme,   embraced
And trad° hire eke as ofte, er it was pryme.°   trod, copulated
                                      with/9 A.M.

He looketh as it were a grym leoun,°   lion
360 And on his toos he rometh up and doun;
Hym deigned nat to sette his foot to grounde.
He chukketh whan he hath a corn yfounde,
And to hym rennen thanne his wyves alle.
Thus roial, as a prince is in his halle,
365 Leve I this Chauntecleer in his pasture,
And after wol I telle his aventure.
   Whan that the month in which the world bigan,
That highte March, whan God first maked man,
Was compleet, and passed were also,
370 Syn March began, thritty dayes and two,
Bifel that Chauntecleer in al his pryde,
His sevene wyves walkynge by his syde,
Caste up his eyen to the brighte sonne,
That in the signe of Taurus hadde yronne
375 Twenty degrees and oon, and somwhat moore,
And knew by kynde,° and by noon oother loore,   nature
That it was pryme, and crew with blisful stevene.°   voice
"The sonne," he seyde, "is clomben up on hevene
Fourty degrees and oon, and moore ywis.
380 Madame Pertelote, my worldes blis,
Herkneth thise blisful briddes° how they synge,   birds
And se the fresshe floures how they sprynge;
Ful is myn herte of revel and solas!"
But sodeynly hym fil° a sorweful cas,°   befell/accident
385 For evere the latter ende of joye is wo.
God woot that worldly joye is soone ago;°   to go

---

368 . . . *man:* the creation was thought to have taken place at the vernal equinox.
370 . . . *and two:* i.e., April 3, although 374-375 yield May 3 when the sun would have passed 20 degrees through Taurus the Bull, the second zodiacal sign.

And if a rethor° koude faire° endite,°   rhetorician/well/
    write

He in a cronycle saufly° myghte it write   safely
As for a sovereyn° notabilitee.°   certain/observa-
    tion, fact

390 Now every wys man, lat him herkne me;
This storie is also° trewe, I undertake,   as
As is the book of Launcelot de Lake,
That wommen holde in ful greet reverence.
Now wol I torne agayn to my sentence.°   theme
395   A col°-fox, ful of sly iniquitee,   black
That in the grove hadde woned° yeres three,   lived
By heigh° ymaginacioun° forncast,°   divine/will/fore-
    cast

The same nyght thurghout the hegges° brast°   hedges/burst
Into the yerd ther Chauntecleer the faire
400 Was wont, and eek his wyves, to repaire;
And in a bed of wortes° stille he lay,   cabbages
Til it was passed undren° of the day,   midmorning
Waitynge his tyme on Chauntecleer to falle,
As gladly doon thise homycides alle
405 That in await° liggen° to morde men.   ambush/lie
O false mordrour, lurkynge in thy den!
A newe Scariot,° newe Genylon,   Iscariot, Judas
False dissymulour, o Greek Synon,
That broghtest Troye al outrely° to sorwe!   utterly
410 O Chauntecleer, acursed be that morwe°   morning
That thou into that yerd flaugh fro the bemes!
Thou were ful wel ywarned by thy dremes
That thilke day was perilous to thee;
·But what that God forwoot° moot nedes bee,   foreknows
415 After the opinioun of certein clerkis.
Witnesse on hym that any parfit clerk is,
That in scole is greet altercacioun
In this mateere, and greet disputisoun,°   disputation
And hath been of an hundred thousand men.
420 But I ne kan nat bulte° it to the bren°   sift/bran, husks
As kan the hooly doctour Augustyn,

---

392 . . . *de Lake:* a popular medieval romance; i.e., it is not true.   407 *Genylon:* Ganelon betrayed Roland to the Saracens in the medieval French epic, *The Song of Roland.* 408 *Synon:* persuaded the Trojans to take the wooden horse into their city.   421–422 *Augustyn, Boece, Bradwardyn:* St. Augustine (d. 430), the orthodox authority on predestination and "necessity," and whether they restricted free will; Boethius (d. 524), a Roman

Or Boece, or the Bisshop Bradwardyn,
Wheither that Goddes worthy forwityng
Streyneth° me nedely° for to doon a thyng,—   constrains/neces-
    sarily

425   "Nedely" clepe I symple necessitee;
Or elles, if free choys be graunted me
To do that same thyng, or do it noght,
Though God forwoot it er that was wroght;
Or if his wityng° streyneth never a deel°   knowledge/not at
    all

430   But by necessitee condicioneel.
I wol nat han to do of swich mateere;
My tale is of a cok, as ye may heere,
That tok his conseil° of his wyf, with sorwe,   advice
To walken in the yerd upon that morwe
435   That he hadde met that dreem that I yow tolde.
Wommennes conseils been full ofte colde;°   fatal
Wommannes conseil broghte us first to wo,
And made Adam fro Paradys to go,
Ther as he was ful myrie and wel at ese.
440   But for I noot° to whom it myght displese,   know not
If I conseil of wommen wolde blame,
Passe over, for I seyde it in my game.°   jest
Rede auctours, where they trete of swich mateere,
And what they seyn of wommen ye may heere.
445   Thise been the cokkes wordes, and nat myne;
I kan noon harm of no womman divyne.°   guess
    Faire in the soond,° to bathe hire myrily,   sand
Lith° Pertelote, and alle hire sustres by,   lies
Agayn° the sonne, and Chauntecleer so free°   in/noble
450   Soong murier than the mermayde in the see;
For Phisiologus seith sikerly
How that they syngen wel and myrily.
And so bifel that, as he caste his ye
Among the wortes on a boterflye,
455   He was war° of this fox, that lay ful lowe.   aware
Nothyng ne liste hym thanne for to crowe,
But cride anon, "Cok! cok!" and up he sterte

---

philosopher whose *Consolation of Philosophy* Chaucer translated, distinguished between "simple necessity" and "conditional necessity" (425–430), the latter term involving a large measure of free will; Thomas Bradwardine (Archbishop of Canterbury, d. 1349) lectured at Oxford on predestination.   451 *Phisiologus:* to whom was attributed the Latin bestiary, a series of moral and theological descriptions of animals real and imaginary.

As man that was affrayed in his herte.
For natureelly a beest desireth flee
460   Fro his contrarie, if he may it see,
Though he never erst° hadde seyn it with his ye.   *before*
  This Chauntecleer, whan he gan hym espye,
He wolde han fled, but that the fox anon
Seyde, "Gentil sire, allas! wher wol ye gon?
465   Be ye affrayed of me that am youre freend?
Now, certes, I were worse than a feend,
If I to yow wolde harm or vileynye!
I am nat come youre conseil for t'espye,   *secrets*
But trewely, the cause of my comynge
470   Was oonly for to herkne how that ye synge.
For trewely, ye have as myrie a stevene
As any aungel hath that is in hevene.
Therwith ye han in musyk moore feelynge
Than hadde Boece, or any that kan synge.
475   My lord youre fader—God his soule blesse!—
And eek youre mooder, of hire gentillesse,°   *gentility*
Han in myn hous ybeen to my greet ese;
And certes, sire, ful fayn° wolde I yow plese.   *gladly*
But, for men speke of syngyng, I wol seye,—
480   So moote I brouke° wel myne eyen tweye,—   *use*
Save yow, I herde nevere man so synge
As dide youre fader in the morwenynge.
Certes, it was of° herte, al that he song.   *from the*
And for to make his voys the moore strong,
485   He wolde so peyne hym that with bothe his yen
He moste wynke,° so loude he wolde cryen,   *shut*
And stonden on his tiptoon therwithal,
And strecche forth his nekke long and smal.
And eek he was of swich discrecioun
490   That ther nas no man in no regioun
That hym in song or wisedom myghte passe.
I have wel rad in 'Daun Burnel the Asse,'
Among his vers, how that ther was a cok,
For that a preestes sone yaf hym a knok
495   Upon his leg whil he was yong and nyce,°   *foolish*
He made hym for to lese° his benefice.   *lose*

---

492 . . . *the Asse':* Master Bounellus, a donkey unhappy about the shortness of his tail, is the satirical hero of a twelfth century poem by Nigel Wireker.   496 . . . *benefice:* i.e., he lost his living because the cock, when the boy was grown, let him oversleep and he missed his ordination.

But certeyn, ther nys no comparisoun
Bitwixe the wisedom and discrecioun
Of youre fader and of his subtiltee.°   skill
500 Now syngeth, sire, for seinte° charitee;   holy
Lat se, konne ye youre fader countrefete?"
    This Chauntecleer his wynges gan to bete,
As man that koude his traysoun nat espie,
So was he ravysshed with his flaterie.
505   Allas! ye lordes, many a fals flatour°   flatterer
Is in youre courtes, and many a losengeour,°   deceiver
That plesen yow wel moore, by my feith,
Than he that soothfastnesse° unto yow seith.   truth
Redeth Ecclesiaste of flaterye;
510 Beth war, ye lordes, of hir trecherye.
    This Chauntecleer stood hye upon his toos,
Strecchynge his nekke, and heeld his eyen cloos,
And gan to crowe loude for the nones.°   occasion
And daun Russell the fox stirte up atones,°   at once
515 And by the gargat° hente° Chauntecleer,   throat/seized
And on his bak toward the wode hym beer,
For yet ne was ther no man that hym sewed.°   followed
    O destinee, that mayest nat been eschewed!°   evaded
Allas, that Chauntecleer fleigh fro the bemes!
520 Allas, his wyf ne roghte° nat of dremes!   interpreted
And on a Friday fil al this meschaunce.
    O Venus, that art goddesse of plesaunce,
Syn that thy servant was this Chauntecleer,
And in thy servyce dide al his poweer,
525 Moore for delit than world to multiplye,
Why woldestow suffre hym on thy day to dye?
    O Gaufred, deere maister soverayn,
That whan thy worthy kyng Richard was slayn
With shot,° compleynedest his deeth so soore,   a missile
530 Why ne hadde I now thy sentence° and thy loore,°   wisdom/
                                         lore, learning
The Friday for to chide, as diden ye?
For on a Friday, soothly,° slayn was he.   truly
Thanne wolde I shewe yow how that I koude pleyne°   complain, lament
For Chauntecleres drede° and for his peyne.   doubt
535   Certes, swich cry ne lamentacion,

---

509 *Ecclesiaste:* The Book of Ecclesiasticus in the Apocrypha (Chapter 12).   527
Gaufred: Geoffrey of Vinsanf, medieval rhetorician, who wrote a lamentation of the death of Richard I as a specimen of the lament. Richard received his wound and died on a Friday.

Was nevere of ladyes maad whan Ylion°   Ilion, Troy
Was wonne, and Pirrus with his streite swerd,°   sword
Whan he hadde hent kyng Priam by the berd,
And slayn hym, as seith us *Eneydos,*°   the *Aeneid*
540 As maden alle the hennes in the clos,°   yard
Whan they had seyn of Chauntecleer the sighte.
But sovereynly° dame Pertelote shrighte°   royally/shrieked
Ful louder than dide Hasdrubales wyf,
Whan that hir housbonde hadde lost his lyf,
545 And that the Romayns hadde brend° Cartage.   burned
She was so ful of torment and of rage°   madness
That wilfully into the fyr she sterte,°   leaped
And brende hirselven with a stedefast herte.
    O woful hennes, right so criden ye,
550 As, whan that Nero brende the citee
Of Rome, cryden senatoures wyves
For that hir husbondes losten alle hir lyves,—
Withouten gilt this Nero hath hem slayn.
Now wole I turne to my tale agayn.
555   This sely° wydwe and eek hir doghtres two   innocent
Herden thise hennes crie and maken wo,
And out at dores stirten they anon,
And syen° the fox toward the grove gon,   saw
And bar upon his bak the cok away,
560 And cryden, "Out! harrow! and weylaway!
Ha! ha! the fox!" and after hym they ran,
And eek with staves many another man.
Ran Colle oure dogge, and Talbot and Gerland,
And Malkyn, with a dystaf in hir hand;
565 Ran cow and calf, and eek the verray hogges,
So fered° for the berkyng of the dogges   panicked
And shoutyng of the men and wommen eeke,
They roone so hem thoughte hir herte breeke.
They yolleden as feendes doon in helle;
570 The dokes° cryden as men wolde hem quelle;°   ducks/kill
The gees for feere flowen° over the trees;   flew
Out of the hyve cam the swarm of bees.
So hydous was th noyse, a, *benedicitee!*°   bless me
Certes, he Jakke Straw and his meynee

537 *Pirrus:* the Greek who killed Priam.   543 *Hasdrubales wyf:* Hasdrubal was king of Carthage when the Romans burned it in 146 B.C.   550 *Nero:* burned a portion of Rome in 64 A.D. and, according to legend, killed many senators at the same time.   574 *Jakke Straw:* a leader of the Peasant's Revolt in 1381. Resident Flemings were attacked (line 576) because they encouraged wool production to supply Flemish weavers and the peasants did not want farm land turned into sheep pasturage.

575 Ne made nevere shoutes half so shrille
Whan that they wolden any Flemyng kille,
As thilke day was maad upon the fox.
Of bras they broghten bemes,° and of box,°   trumpets/box-
                                                 wood
Of horn, of boon,° in whiche they blewe and powped,°   bone/puffed
580 And therwithal they skriked° and they howped.°   shrieked/whooped
It semed as that hevene sholde falle.
    Now, goode men, I prey yow herkneth alle:
Lo, how Fortune turneth° sodeynly   reverses
The hope and pryde eek of hir enemy!
585 This cok, that lay upon the foxes bak,
In al his drede° unto the fox he spak,   dread, fear
And seyde, "Sire, if that I were as ye,
Yet sholde I seyn, as wys° God helpe me,   surely
'Turneth agayn, ye proude cherles° alle!   peasants
590 A verray pestilence upon yow falle!
Now am I come unto the wodes syde;
Maugree youre heed, the cok shal heere abyde.
I wol hym ete, in feith, and that anon!'"
    The fox answerde, "In feith, it shal be don."
595 And as he spak that word, al sodeynly
This cok brak from his mouth delyverly,°   nimbly
And heighe upon a tree he fleigh anon.
And whan the fox saugh that the cok was gon,
    "Allas!" quod he, "O Chauntecleer, allas!
600 I have to yow," quod he, "ydoon trespas,°   wrong
In as muche as I maked yow aferd
Whan I yow hente and broghte out of the yerd.
But, sire, I dide it in no wikke° entente.   wicked
Com doun, and I shal telle yow what I mente;
605 I shall seye sooth to yow, God help me so!"
    "Nay thanne," quod he, "I shrewe° us bothe two.   curse
And first I shrewe myself, bothe blood and bones,
If thou bigyle° me ofter° than ones.   beguile/oftener
Thou shalt namoore, thurgh thy flaterye,
610 Do° me to synge and wynke with myn ye;   make
For he that wynketh, whan he sholde see,
Al wilfully, God lat him nevere thee!"°   thrive
    "Nay," quod the fox, "but God yeve hym
        meschaunce,
That is so undiscreet of governaunce°   self-control
615 That jangleth° whan he sholde holde his pees."   talks

592 *Maugree youre heed:* i.e., in spite of what you wish; literally: despite your head.

Lo, swich it is for to be recchelees° reckless
And necligent, and truste on flaterye.
But ye that holden this tale a folye,
As of a fox, or of a cok and hen,
620 Taketh the moralite, goode men.
For seint Paul seith that al that writen is,
To oure doctrine° it is ywrite, ywis; instruction
Taketh the fruyt, and lat the chaf be stille.
Now, goode God, if that it be thy wille,
625 As seith my lord, so make us alle goode men,
And brynge us to his heighe blisse! Amen.

621 *seint Paul:* Romans 15:4.

FROM THE PARDONER'S TALE

In Flaundres whilom° was a campaignye once
Of yonge folk that haunteden° folye, engaged in
As riot,° hasard,° stywes,° and tavernes wildness/gambling/brothels

Where as with harpes, lutes, and gyternes,° guitars
5 They daunce and pleyen at dees° both day and nyght, dice
And eten also and drynken over hir myght,
Thurgh which they doon° the devel sacrifise performed to
Withinne that develes temple, in cursed wise,
By superfluytee° abhomynable. excesses
10 Hir othes been so grete and so dampnable° damnable
That it is grisly for to heere hem swere.
Oure blissed Lordes body they totere,—
Hem thoughte that Jewes rente° hym noght ynough; tore
And ech of hem at otheres synne lough° laughed
15 And right anon° thanne comen tombesteres° soon/dancing girls
Fetys° and smale,° and yonge frutesteres,° shapely/slender/fruit-selling girls

Syngeres with harpes, baudes,° waferes,° pimps/cake-selling girls

Whiche been the verray develes officeres
To kyndle and blowe the fyr of lecherye,
20 That is annexed° unto glotonye. akin

6 . . . *myght:* more than they could handle.   12 *totere:* i.e., by swearing by God's blood, bones, teeth, etc., they tear his body.

The hooly writ take I to my witnesse
That luxurie° is in wyn° and dronkenesse.   excess/wine
    Lo, how that dronken Looth, unkyndely,°   unnaturally
Lay by his doghtres two, unwityngly;
25   So dronke he was, he nyste° what he wroghte.   knew not
    Herodes, whoso wel the stories soghte,°   looked up
Whan he of wyn was repleet at his feeste,
Right at his owene table he yaf° his heeste°   gave/command
To sleen° the Baptist John, ful giltelees.   slay
30   Senec seith a good word doutelees;
He seith he kan no difference fynde
Bitwix a man that is out of his mynde
And a man which that is dronkelewe,°   drunk
But that woodnesse, yfallen in a shrewe,
35   Persevereth lenger than doth dronkenesse.
O glotonye, ful of cursednesse!
O cause first of oure confusioun!°   fall
O original of oure dampnacioun,°   damnation
Til Crist hadde boght us with his blood agayn!
40   Lo, how deere, shortly for to sayn,
Aboght° was thilke° cursed vileynye!   bought, paid for/
                                                              that

Corrupt was al this world for glotonye.
    Adam oure fader, and his wyf also,
Fro° Paradys to labour and to wo°   from
45   Were dryven for that vice, it is no drede.°   doubt
For whil that Adam fasted, as I rede,
He was in Paradys; and whan that he
Eet° of the fruyt deffended° on the tree,   ate/forbidden
Anon he was out cast to wo and peyne.°   pain
50   O glotonye, on thee wel oghte us pleyne!   complain
O, wiste° a man how manye maladyes   knew
Folwen° of excesse and of glotonyes,   follow
He wolde been the moore mesurable°   moderate
Of his diete, sittynge at his table.
55   Allas! the shorte throte, the tendre mouth,
Makest that est and west and north and south,
In erthe, in eir, in water, men to swynke°   labor
To gete a glotoun deyntee mete and drynke!
Of this matiere, o Paul, wel kanstow trete:

23 *Looth:* Lot, see Genesis 19:30–36.   26 *Herodes:* see Mark 6:17–29.   30 *Senec:*
Seneca, the Roman Stoic philosopher.   34 *woodnesse . . . shrewe:* i.e., madness, happening
to an evil man.   59 *Paul:* St. Paul. See I Corinthians 6:13.

60   "Mete unto wombe,° and wombe eek° unto mete,   belly/also
     Shal God destroyen bothe," as Paulus seith.
     Allas! a foul thyng is it, by my feith,
     To seye this word, and fouler is the dede,
     Whan man so drynketh of the white and rede
65   That of his throte he maketh his pryvee,°   privy
     Thurgh thilke cursed superfluitee.
       The apostel wepyng ·seith ful pitously,
     "Ther walken manye of whiche yow toold have I—
     I seye it now wepyng, with pitous voys—
70   That they been enemys of Cristes croys,°   cross
     Of which the ende is deeth, wombe is hir god!"
     O wombe! O bely! O stynkyng cod,
     Fulfilled° of dong° and of corrupcioun!   filled full/dung
     At either ende of thee foul is the soun.°   sound
75   How greet labour and cost is thee to fynde!°   provide for
     Thise cookes, how they stampe,° and streyne, and   pound
        grynde,
     And turnen substaunce into accident,
     To fulfille al thy likerous° talent!°   greedy/appetite
     Out of the harde bones knokke they
80   The mary,° for they caste noght awey   marrow
     That may go thurgh the golet° softe and swoote   gullet/sweetly
     Of spicerie° of leef, and bark, and roote   spices
     Shal been° his sauce ymaked by delit,   be
     To make hym yet a newer appetit.
85   But, certes,° he that haunteth swiche° delices°   truly/such/delight
     Is deed,° whil that he lyveth in tho° vices.   dead/those
       A lecherous thyng is wyn, and dronkenesse
     Is full of stryvyng° and of wrecchednesse.   fighting
     O dronke man, disfigured is thy face,
90   Sour is thy breeth, foul artow° to embrace,   art thou
     And thurgh thy dronke nose semeth the soun
     As though thou seydest ay° "Sampsoun, Sampsoun!" always
     And yet, God woot,° Sampsoun drank nevere no wyn. knows
     Thou fallest as it were a styked° swyn;   stuck
95   Thy tonge is lost, and al thyn honeste cure;
     For dronkenesse is verray sepulture°   burial
     Of mannes wit° and his discrecioun.   intellect
     In whom that drynke hath dominacioun

---

71 . . . *god!":* see Phillippians 3:18.   77 . . . *accident:* substance has inner reality whil[e]
outward appearance is accident, according to medieval philosophy.   95 . . . *cure:* i.e., car[e]
for honesty, self-respect.

He kan no conseil° kepe, it is no drede.   *confidence*
100 Now kepe yow fro the white and fro the rede,
And namely° fro the white wyn of Lepe,   *particularly*
That is to selle in Fysshstrete or in Chepe.
The wyn of Spaigne crepeth subtilly
In othere wynes, growynge faste° by,   *near*
105 Of which ther ryseth swich fumositee°   *fumes*
That whan a man hath dronken draughtes thre,
And weneth° that he be at hoom in Chepe,   *believes*
He is in Spaigne, right at the toune of Lepe,—
Nat at the Rochele, ne at Burdeux toun;
110 And thanne wol he seye "Sampsoun, Sampsoun!"
 But herkneth, lordynges, o° word, I yow preye,   *one*
That alle the sovereyn° actes, dar I seye,   *mighty*
Of victories in the Olde Testament,
Thurgh verray God, that is omnipotent,
115 Were doon in abstinence and in preyere.
Looketh° the Bible, and there ye may it leere.°   *look at/learn*
 Looke, Attilla, the grete conquerour,
Deyde in his sleep, with shame and dishonour,
Bledynge ay° at his nose in dronkenesse.   *continually*
120 A capitayn sholde lyve in sobrenesse.
And over al this, avyseth° yow right wel   *think*
What was comaunded unto Lamuel—
Nat Samuel, but Lamuel, seye I;
Redeth the Bible, and fynde it expresly
125 Of wyn-yevyng° to hem that han° justise.   *giving/give*
Namoore of this, for it may wel suffise.
 And now that I have spoken of glotonye,
Now wol I yow deffenden° hasardrye.°   *resist/gambling*
Hasard is verray mooder° of lesynges,°   *mother/lies*
130 And of deceite, and cursed forswerynges,
Blaspheme of Crist, manslaughtre, and wast° also   *waste*
Of catel° and of tyme; and forthermo,   *possessions*
It is repreeve° and contrarie of honour   *shame*
For to ben° holde° a commune hasardour.   *be/held*
135 And ever the hyer he is of estaat,
The moore is he yholden desolaat.°   *dissolute*
If that a prynce useth hasardrye,
In alle governaunce and policye

---

101 *Lepe:* Spanish town. 102 . . . *Chepe:* market streets in London. 117 *Attilla:* war leader of the Huns who overran Rome in the fifth century. 122 *Lamuel:* Lemuel was taught by his mother that rulers must not drink. See Proverbs 31:4-5.

He is, as by commune opinioun,
140 Yholde the lasse° in reputacioun.   less
    Stilboun, that was a wys embassadour,
Was sent to Cornynthe, in ful greet honour,
Fro Lacidomye,° to make hire alliaunce.   Sparta
And whan he cam, hym happede,° par chaunce,   it happened
145 That alle the gretteste that were of that lond,
Pleyynge atte hasard he hem fond.°   found
For which, as soone as it myghte be,
He stal° hym hoom agayn to his contree,   stole away
And seyde, "There wol I nat lese° my name,°   lose/reputation
150 Ne I wol nat take on me so greet defame,°   dishonor
Yow for to allie unto none° hasardours.   any
Sendeth othere wise embassadours;
For, by my trouthe, me were levere dye
Than I yow shold to hasardours allye.
155 For ye, that been so glorious in honours,
Shul nat allyen yow with hasardours
As by my wyl, ne as by my tretee."°   treaty
This wise philosophre, thus seyde hee.
    Looke eek that to the kyng Demetrius,
160 The kyng of Parthes,° as the book seith us,   Parthia
Sente him a paire of dees of gold in scorn,
For he hadde used hasard ther-biforn;
For which he heeld his glorie or his renoun
At no value or reputacioun.
165 Lordes may fynden oother maner pley
Honest ynough to dryve the day awey.
    Now wol I speke of othes false and grete
A word or two, as olde bookes trete.
Gret sweryng is a thyng abhominable,
170 And fals sweryng is yet moore reprevable.°   reprovable
The heighe God forbad sweryng at al,
Witnesse on Mathew; but in special
Of sweryng seith the hooly Jeremye,
"Thou shalt swere sooth° thyne othes,° and   true/oaths
    nat lye,
175 And swere in doom, and eek in rightwisnesse";
But ydel sweryng is a cursednesse.

141 *Stilboun:* Chilon, taken from a medieval history of politics, as is the story in lines 159 f
153 . . . *dye:* i.e., I would rather die.   172 . . . *Mathew:* "But I say unto you, Swea
not at all." Matthew 5:34   173 *Jeremye:* Jeremiah 4:2.   175 . . . *rightwisnesse:* i.e
in justice and also in righteousness.

Bihoold and se that in the firste table°   tablet
Of heighe Goddes heestes° honurable,   commandments
Hou that the seconde heeste of hym is this:
180 "Take nat my name in ydel or amys."
Lo, rather he forbedeth swich sweryng
Than° homycide or many a cursed thyng;   before
I seye that, as by ordre, thus it stondeth;
This knoweth, that his heestes understondeth,
185 How that the seconde heeste of God is that.
And forther over, I wol thee telle al plat,°   flat
That vengeance shal nat parten° from his hous   depart
That of his othes is to outrageous.
"By Goddes precious herte," and "By his nayles,"° fingernails, nails
                                                   of the cross

190 And "By the blood of Crist that is in Hayles,
Sevene is my chaunce, and thyn is cynk° and   five
   treye!"°   three
"By Goddes armes, if thou falsly pleye,
This daggere shal thurghout thyn herte go!"—
This fruyt cometh of the bicched° bones° two,   cursed/dice
195 Forsweryng, ire, falsnesse, homycide.
Now, for the love of Crist, that for us dyde,
Lete° youre othes, bothe grete and smale.   abandon
But, sires, now wol I telle forth my tale.
   Thise riotoures° thre of whiche I telle,   merrymakers
200 Longe erste° er prime° rong of any belle   before/9 A.M.
Were set hem in a taverne for to drynke,
And as they sat, they herde a belle clynke
Biforn a cors,° was caried to his grave.   corpse
That oon of hem gan callen to his knave:°   servant
205 "Go bet,"° quod he, "and axe° redily°   well, quickly/ask/
                                                  immediately

What cors is this that passeth heer forby;
And looke° that thou reporte his name weel."°   see to it/well
   "Sire," quod this boy, "it nedeth never-a-deel;° not at all
It was me toold er ye cam heer two houres.
210 He was, pardee, an old felawe of youres;
And sodeynly he was yslayn to-nyght,°   last night
Fordronke,° as he sat on his bench upright.   very drunk
Ther cam a privee° theef men clepeth° Deeth,   sneak/call

185 *seconde heeste:* the third Protestant commandment. Catholicism treats the first two
commandments as one and divides the Protestant tenth.   190 *Hayles:* Gloucestershire abbey
which possessed a phial containing what was believed to be a portion of Jesus' blood.

That in this contree al the peple sleeth,°   slays
215 And with his spere he smoot his herte atwo,
And wente his wey withouten wordes mo.
He hath a thousand slayn this° pestilence.   during this
And, maister, er ye come in his presence,
Me thynketh that it were necessarie
220 For to be war of swich an adversarie.
Beth redy for to meete hym everemoore;
Thus taughte me my dame;° I sey namoore."   mother
"By seinte Marie!" seyde this taverner,
"The child seith sooth, for he hath slayn this yeer,
225 Henne° over a mile, withinne a greet village,   hence
Bothe man and womman, child, and hyne,° and   laborer
    page;
I trowe° his habitacioun be there.   think
To been avysed° greet wysdom it were,   warned
Er that he dide a man a dishonour."
230   "Ye, Goddes armes!" quod this riotour,
"Is it swich peril with hym for to meete?
I shal hym seke by wey° and eek by strete,   highway
I make avow to Goddes digne° bones!   respected
Herkneth, felawes, we thre been al ones;°   agreed, of one mind
235 Lat ech of us holde up his hand til° oother,   to
And ech of us bicomen otheres brother,
And we wol sleen this false traytour Deeth.
He shal be slayn, he that so manye sleeth,
By Goddes dignitee, er it by nyght!"
240   Togidres han thise thre hir trouthes° plight°   honors/pledged
To lyve and dyen ech of hem for oother,
As though he were his owene ybore° brother.   born
And up they stirte,° al dronken in this rage,   started
And forth they goon towardes that village
245 Of which the taverner hadde spoke biforn.
And many a grisly ooth thanne han they sworn,
And Cristes blessed body al torente°—   tore apart
Deeth shal be deed, if that they may hym hente!°   seize
   Whan they han goon nat fully half a mile,
250 Right as they wolde han troden over a stile,
An oold man and a povre° with hem mette.   poor one
This olde man ful mekely hem grette,°   greeted
And seyde thus, "Now, lordes, God yow see!"
   The proudeste of thise riotoures three
255 Answerde agayn, "What, carl,° with sory grace!   peasant
Why artow al forwrapped save thy face?

Why lyvestow so longe in so greet age?"
   This olde man gan looke in his visage,
And seyde thus: "For° I ne kan nat fynde   because
260 A man, though that I walked into Ynde,°   India
Neither in citee ne in no village,
That wolde chaunge his youthe for myn age;
And therefore moot° I han myn age stille,   must
As longe tyme as it is Goddes wille.
265 Ne Deeth, allas! ne wol nat han my lyf
Thus walke I, lyk a restelees kaityf,°   captive
And on the ground, which is my moodres gate,
I knokke with my staf, bothe erly and late,
And seye 'Leeve° mooder, leet me in!   allow me
270 Lo how I vanysshe, flessh, and blood, and skyn!
Allas! whan shul my bones been at reste?
Mooder, with yow wolde I chaunge° my cheste   exchange
That in my chambre longe tyme hath be,
Ye, for an heyre clowt° to wrappe in me!'   haircloth, shroud
275 But yet to me she wol nat do that grace,
For which ful pale and welked° is my face.   withered
   But, sires, to yow it is no curteisye
To speken to an old man vileynye,°   rudeness
But° he trespasse in word, or elles in dede.   unless
280 In Hooly Writ ye may yourself wel rede:
'Agayns° an oold man, hoor° upon his heed,   near/hoar
Ye sholde arise;' wherfore I yeve yow reed,°   advice
Ne dooth unto an oold man noon harm now,
Namoore than that ye wolde men did to yow
285 In age, if that ye so longe abyde.
And God be with yow, where ye go° or ryde!   walk
I moot go thider as I have to go."
   "Nay, olde cherl, by God, thou shalt nat so,"
Seyde this oother hasardour anon;
290 "Thou partest nat so lightly, by Seint John!
Thou spak right now of thilke traytour Deeth,
That in this contree alle oure freendes sleeth.
Have heer my trouthe, as thou art his espye,
Telle where he is, or thou shalt it abye,°   suffer for
295 By God, and by the hooly sacrement!
For soothly thou art oon of his assent°   party
To sleen us yonge folk, thou false theef!"
   "Now, sires," quod he, "if that yow be so leef°   desirous
To fynde Deeth, turne up this croked wey,
300 For in that grove I lafte hym, by my fey,°   faith

Under a tree, and there he wole abyde;
Noght for youre boost° he wole him no thyng hyde.   boast
Se ye that ook?° Right there ye shal hym fynde.   oak
God save yow, that boghte agayn mankynde,
305 And yow amende!"° Thus seyde this olde man;   redeem
And everich of thise riotoures ran
Til he cam to that tree, and ther they founde
Of floryns° fyne of gold, ycoyned rounde   coins
Wel ny an eighte busshels, as hem thoughte.
310 No lenger thanne after Deeth they soughte,
But ech of hem so glad was of that sighte,
For that the floryns been so faire and brighte,
That doun they sette hem by this precious hoord.
The worste of hem, he spak the firste word.
315 "Bretheren," quod he, "taak kep° what that I seye;   care
My wit is greet, though that I bourde° and pleye.   jest
This tresor hath Fortune unto us yiven,
In myrthe and joliftee oure lyf to lyven,
And lightly° as it comth, so wol we spende.   as easily
320 Ey! Goddes precious dignitee! who wende°   knew
To-day that we sholde han so fair a grace?
But myghte this gold be caried fro this place
Hoom to myn hous, or elles unto youres—
For wel ye woot° that al this gold is oures—   know
325 Thanne were we in heigh felicitee.
But trewely, by daye it may nat bee.
Men wolde seyn that we were theves stronge,
And for oure owene tresor doon us honge.
This tresor moste ycaried be by nyghte
330 As wisely and as slyly as it myghte.
Wherfore I rede° that cut° among us alle   advise/lots
Be drawe, and lat se wher the cut wol falle;
And he that hath the cut with herte blithe
Shal renne° to the town, and that ful swithe,   run/fast
335 And brynge us breed and wyn ful prively.
And two of us shul kepen subtilly
This tresor wel; and if he wol nat tarie,
Whan it is nyght, we wol this tresor carie,
By oon assent, where as us thynketh best."
340 That° oon of hem the cut broghte in his fest,°   then/fist
And bad hem drawe, and looke where it wol falle;
And it fil on the yongeste of hem alle,
And forth toward the toun he wente anon.
And also° soone as that was gon,   as

40

345 That oon of hem spak thus unto that oother:
"Thow knowest wel thou art my sworen brother;
Thy profit wol I telle thee anon.
Thou woost° wel that oure felawe is agon.   know'st
And heere is gold, and that ful greet plentee,
350 That shal departed° been among us thre.   divided
But nathelees, if I kan shape it so
That it departed were among us two,
Hadde I nat doon a freendes torn° to thee?"   turn
That oother answerde, "I noot° hou that may be.   know not
355 He woot wel that the gold is with us tweye;
What shal we doon? What shal we to hym seye?"
"Shal it be conseil?"° seyde the first shrewe,°   secret/evil one
"And I shal tellen in a wordes fewe
What we shal doon, and brynge it wel aboute."
360 "I graunte," quod the oother, "out of doute,
That, by my trouthe, I wol thee nat biwreye."°   betray
"Now," quod the firste, "thou woost wel we be
tweye,
And two of us shul strenger° be than oon.   stronger
Looke whan that he is set,° that right anoon   seated
365 Arys as though thou woldest with hym pleye,
And I shal ryve° hym thurgh the sydes tweye   pierce
Whil that thou strogelest with hym as in game,
And with thy daggere looke thou do the same;
And thanne shal al this gold departed be,
370 My deere freend, bitwixen me and thee.
Thanne may we bothe oure lustes al fulfille,
And pleye at dees right at oure owene wille."
And thus acorded been thise shrewes tweye
To sleen the thridde, as ye han herd me seye.
375 This yongeste, which that wente to the toun,
Ful ofte in herte he rolleth up and doun
The beautee of thise floryns newe and brighte.
"O Lord!" quod he, "if so were that I myghte
Have al this tresor to myself allone,
380 Ther is no man that lyveth under the trone°   throne
Of God that sholde lyve so murye as I!"
And atte laste the feend, oure enemy,
Putte in his thought that he sholde poyson beye,°   buy
With which he myghte sleen his felawes tweye;
385 For-why° the feend foond hym in swich lyvynge°   because/frame
                                                             of mind

41

That he hadde leve him to sorwe brynge.
For this was outrely° his fulle entente,   clearly
To sleen hem bothe, and nevere to repente.
And forth he gooth, no lenger wolde he tarie,
390   Into the toun, unto a pothecarie,°   apothecary, chemi
And preyde hym that he hym wolde selle
Som poyson, that he myghte his rattes quelle;°   quell, kill
And eek ther was a polcat in his hawe,°   hedge
That, as he seyde, his capouns hadde yslawe,°   slain
395   And fayn° he wolde wreke hym, if he myghte,   gladly
On vermyn that destroyed° hym by nyghte.   ruined
     The pothecarie answerde, "And thou shalt have
A thyng that, also God my soule save,
In al this world ther is no creature,
400   That eten or dronken hath of this confiture°   mixture
Noght but the montance° of a corn° of whete,   amount/grain
That he ne shal his lif anon forlete;°   let go
Ye,° sterve° he shal, and that in lasse° while   yes/die/less
Than thou wolt goon a paas° nat but a mile,   stroll
405   This poysoun is so strong and violent."
     This cursed man hath in his hond yhent°   taken
This poysoun in a box, and sith° he ran   then
Into the nexte strete unto a man,
And borwed of hym large botelles thre;
410   And in the two his poyson poured he;
The thridde he kepte clene for his drynke.
For al the nyght he shoop° hym for to swynke°   plotted/work
In cariynge of the gold out of that place.
And whan this riotour, with sory grace,
415   Hadde filled with wyn his grete botels thre,
To his felawes agayn repaireth he.
     What nedeth it to sermone of it moore?
For right as they hadde cast° his deeth bifoore,   devised
Right so they han hym slayn, and that anon.
420   And whan that this was doon, thus spak that oon:
"Now lat us sitte and drynke, and make us merie,
And afterward we wol his body berie."
And with that word it happed hym, par° cas,°   by/chance
To take the botel ther the poyson was,
425   And drank, and yaf his felawe drynke also,
For which anon they storven° bothe two.   died

386 . . . *brynge:* Job 1:12 and 2:6 is the basis for the doctrine that the devil may subver**
man only by God's leave.

42

But certes, I suppose that Avycen
Wroot nevere in no canon, ne in no fen,°   chapter
Mo wonder signes of empoisonyng
430   Than hadde thise wrecches two, er hir endyng.
Thus ended been thise homycides two,
And eek the false empoysonere also.
     O cursed synne of alle cursednesse!
O traytours homycide, O wikkednesse!
435   O glotonye, luxurie, and hasardrye!
Thou blasphemour of Crist with vileynye
And othes grete, of usage° and of pride!   habit
Allas! mankynde, how may it bitide
That to thy creatour, which that the° wroghte,   thee
440   And with his precious herte-blood thee boghte,
Thou art so fals and so unkynde, allas?
     Now, goode men, God foryeve yow youre trespas,
And ware° yow fro the synne of avarice!   beware
Myn hooly pardoun may yow alle warice,°   save
445   So that ye offre nobles or sterlynges,
Or elles silver broches, spoones, rynges.
Boweth youre heed under this hooly bulle!
Cometh up, ye wyves, offreth of youre wolle!°   wool
Youre names I entre heer in my rolle anon;
450   Into the blisse of hevene shul ye gon.
I yow assoille,° by myn heigh power,   absolve
Yow that wol offre, as clene and eek as cleer
As ye were born.—And lo, sires, thus I preche.
And Jhesu Crist, that is oure soules leche,°   healer
455   So graunte yow his pardoun to receyve,
For that is best; I wol yow nat deceyve. . . .

427 *Avycen:* Avicenna, eleventh-century Arabic philosopher, divided his *The Canon of Medicine* into subdivisions called "fens."   445 . . . *sterlynges:* these and "nobles" were valuable coins.

BEN JONSON

[ca. 1573–1637]

Many of the important facts of Ben Jonson's life are still in dispute. Jonson was born in or near London, probably on June 11, 1573. His father died shortly before or after he was born, and the boy was raised by his stepfather, a London bricklayer. He attended a private school in St. Martin's Church and later was sent to Westminster School, where he came under the strong classical influence of William Camden, who became a close friend. It is probable that Jonson received no formal education beyond secondary school, for he seems to have left school in 1588 to work at his stepfather's trade. Sometime before 1592 he fought as a volunteer in the Low Countries.

After his return to England, Jonson worked as a strolling player, and around 1594 he married Anne Lewis. In 1597 he was imprisoned for acting in the "seditious" play, THE ISLE OF DOGS, by Thomas Nashe. Following his release he began to write his own plays, including EVERY MAN IN HIS HUMOUR, in which Shakespeare played a part. In September of 1598, he was again imprisoned; this time for killing an actor in a duel. While in jail he was converted to Roman Catholicism. He was sentenced to hang, but escaped punishment by making the not unusual claim to right of clergy. His reputation as a playwright was beginning to grow among the educated and at court, and he produced many controversial and successful satirical plays as well as elaborate and expensive masques. Among the former were EVERY MAN OUT OF HIS HUMOUR (1599), VOLPONE (1606), EPICOENE (1609), THE ALCHEMIST (1610), and BARTHOLOMEW FAIR (1614).

The most successful period of Jonson's life was from his appointment to the post of poet laureate in 1616 to 1625. During these years he enjoyed the particular favor of the King, and his plays and masques were often produced at court for state occasions. During this time he also wrote poetry, including EPIGRAMS (1615),

THE FOREST (*1616*), *and* UNDERWOODS (*1619, pub. 1640*). *In 1619 the University of Oxford honored him with a Master of Arts degree. Jonson was acquainted and friendly with both the intellectual elite and the fashionable aristocrats of London. He counted among his friends men such as John Donne, William Shakespeare, Sir Francis Bacon, and Sir Walter Raleigh. After 1625, however, his rival and former colleague, Inigo Jones, gained precedence at court, and Jonson's influence and activity waned. After an unsuccessful attempt to win back his audience, Jonson retired on pension in 1634. He died on August 6, 1637, and was buried in Westminster Abbey.*

The definitive edition of Jonson's WORKS, *with an account of his life, an introduction, and critical and textual notes, was compiled by C. H. Herford and P. E. Simpson, in eleven volumes (1925–1952), and a useful general study of the poetry is G. B. Johnston's* BEN JONSON: POET (*1945*). *There are numerous critical studies of Jonson as satirist and playwright.*

HYMN TO DIANA

> Queen and huntress, chaste and fair,
>   Now the sun is laid to sleep,
> Seated in thy silver chair,
>   State in wonted manner keep:
>   Hesperus entreats thy light,   5
>   Goddess excellently bright.
>
> Earth, let not thy envious shade
>   Dare itself to interpose;
> Cynthia's shining orb was made
>   Heaven to clear when day did close: 10
>   Bless us then with wishèd sight,
>   Goddess excellently bright.
>
> Lay thy bow of pearl apart,
>   And thy crystal shining quiver;
> Give unto thy flying hart   15

5 *Hesperus:* evening.

Space to breathe, how short soever:
Thou that makest a day of night,
Goddess excellently bright.

THE GLOVE

Thou more than most sweet glove,
Unto my more sweet love,
Suffer me to store with kisses
This empty lodging that now misses
  The pure rosy hand that wear thee,   5
  Whiter than the kid that bare thee.
    Thou art soft, but that was softer;
    Cupid's self hath kissed it ofter
    Than e'er he did his mother's doves,
    Supposing her the queen of loves   10
    That was thy mistress, best of gloves.

SONG: IF I FREELY MAY DISCOVER

If I freely may discover
What would please me in my lover,
I would have her fair and witty,
Savouring more of court than city;
A little proud, but full of pity;   5
Light and humorous in her toying;
Oft building hopes, and soon destroying;
Long, but sweet in the enjoying;
Neither too easy nor too hard:
All extremes I would have barred.   10

She should be allowed her passions,
So they were but used as fashions;
Sometimes forward, and then frowning,
Sometimes sickish, and then swooning,
Every fit with change still crowning.   15
Purely jealous I would have her,

15 *fit:* period of feeling or emotion, activity or idleness.

Then only constant when I crave her;
'Tis a virtue should not save her.
Thus, nor her delicates would cloy me,
Neither her peevishness annoy me.   20

19 *delicates:* delicacies.

EPITAPH ON S. P.

A child of Queen Elizabeth's Chapel

Weep with me, all you that read
  This little story;
And know, for whom a tear you shed
  Death's self is sorry.
'Twas a child that so did thrive   5
  In grace and feature,
As Heaven and Nature seemed to strive
  Which owned the creature.

Years he numbered scarce thirteen,
  When Fates turned cruel;   10
Yet three filled zodiacs had he been
  The stage's jewel;
And did act, what now we moan,
  Old men so duly,
As sooth the Parcae thought him one,   15
  He played so truly.

So, by error, to his fate
  They all consented;
But, viewing him since—alas, too late!—
  They have repented;   20
And have sought, to give new birth,
  In baths to steep him;
But, being so much too good for earth,
  Heaven vows to keep him.

Epitaph on S. P.: Salomon or Salathiel Pavy, who, after three years as a
child actor with the Children of the Chapel, died in 1603, aged thirteen.
15 *Parcae:* the three Fates.

MAB THE MISTRESS—FAIRY

This is Mab the mistress-fairy
That doth nightly rob the dairy,
And can hurt or help the churning
As she please, without discerning:

She that pinches country wenches   5
If they rub not clean their benches,
And with sharper nails remembers
When they rake not up their embers;
But if so they chance to feast her,
In a shoe she drops a tester.   10

This is she that empties cradles,
Takes out children, puts in ladles;
Trains forth midwives in their slumber
With a sieve the holes to number:
And then leads them from her burrows   15
Home through ponds and water-furrows.

She can start our franklin's daughters
In their sleep with shrieks and laughters,
And on sweet Saint Anne's night
Feed them with a promised sight,   20
Some of husbands, some of lovers,
Which an empty dream discovers.

10 *tester:* sixpence.   17 *franklin:* middle-class landowner.

ON MY FIRST SON

Farewell, thou child of my right hand, and joy!
My sin was too much hope of thee, loved boy;
Seven years thou wert lent to me, and I thee pay,
Exacted by thy fate, on the just day.

Oh, could I lose all father now! For why   5
Will man lament the state he should envy—
To have so soon 'scaped world's and flesh's rage,
And, if no other misery, yet age?
Rest in soft peace, and, asked, say here doth lie
Ben Jonson his best piece of poetry: 10
For whose sake, henceforth, all his vows be such
As what he loves may never like too much.

COME, MY CELIA, LET US PROVE

Come, my Celia, let us prove,
While we can, the sports of love;
Time will not be ours for ever,
He, at length, our good will sever.
Spend not then his gifts in vain: 5
Suns that set may rise again;
But if once we lose this light,
'Tis with us perpetual night.
Why should we defer our joys?
Fame and rumour are but toys.   10
Cannot we delude the eyes
Of a few poor household spies?
Or his easier ears beguile,
Thus removèd by our wile?
'Tis no sin love's fruits to steal,   15
But the sweet thefts to reveal;
To be taken, to be seen.
These have crimes accounted been.

FOOLS

Fools, they are the only nation
Worth men's envy or admiration;
Free from care or sorrow-taking,
Selves and others merry making:

All they speak or do is sterling.   5
Your fool he is your great man's dearling,
And your lady's sport and pleasure;
Tongue and babble are his treasure.
E'en his face begetteth laughter,
And he speaks truth free from slaughter;   10
He 's the grace of every feast,
And sometimes the chiefest guest;
Hath his trencher and his stool,
When wit waits upon the fool.
    Oh, who would not be   15
      He, he, he?

STILL TO BE NEAT

Still to be neat, still to be dressed,
As you were going to a feast;
Still to be powdered, still perfumed:
Lady, it is to be presumed,
Though art's hid causes are not found,   5
All is not sweet, all is not sound.

Give me a book, give me a face,
That makes simplicity a grace;
Robes loosely flowing, hair as free:
Such sweet neglect more taketh me   10
Than all the adulteries of art;
They strike mine eyes, but not my heart.

Still To Be Neat: still: always.

EPITAPH ON ELIZABETH, L. H.

Wouldst thou hear what man can say
In a little? Reader, stay.
Underneath this stone doth lie

Epitaph on Elizabeth, L. H.: the identity of this woman is not known.

As much beauty as could die;
Which in life did harbour give   5
To more virtue than doth live.
If at all she had a fault,
Leave it buried in this vault.
One name was *Elizabeth,*
Th' other, let it sleep with death: 10
Fitter, where it died, to tell
Than that it lived at all. Farewell.

HER TRIUMPH

See the chariot at hand here of Love,
    Wherein my lady rideth!
Each that draws is a swan or a dove,
    And well the car Love guideth.
As she goes, all hearts do duty   5
        Unto her beauty;
And enamoured do wish, so they might
        But enjoy such a sight,
That they still were to run by her side,
Through swords, through seas, whither she would ride.   10

Do but look on her eyes, they do light
    All that Love's world compriseth!
Do but look on her hair, it is bright
    As Love's star when it riseth!
Do but mark, her forehead 's smoother   15
        Than words that soothe her;
And from her arched brows such a grace
        Sheds itself through the face,
As alone there triumphs to the life
All the gain, all the good of the elements' strife.   20

Have you seen but a bright lily grow
    Before rude hands have touched it?
Have you marked but the fall of the snow
    Before the soil hath smutched it?
Have you felt the wool o' the beaver,   25

51

Or swan's down ever?
Or have smelt o' the bud o' the brier,
Or the nard i' the fire?
Or have tasted the bag o' the bee?
Oh so white, oh so soft, oh so sweet is she!   30

28 *nard:* an aromatic plant, spikenard.

THAT WOMEN ARE BUT MEN'S SHADOWS

Follow a shadow, it still flies you;
Seem to fly it, it will pursue:
So court a mistress, she denies you;
Let her alone, she will court you.
Say, are not women truly, then,   5
Styled but the shadows of us men?

At morn and even, shades are longest,
At noon they are or short, or none:
So, men at weakest, they are strongest;
But grant us perfect, they 're not known.   10
Say are not women truly, then,
Styled but the shadows of us men?

TO CELIA: DRINK TO ME ONLY WITH THINE EYES

Drink to me only with thine eyes,
And I will pledge with mine;
Or leave a kiss but in the cup,
And I 'll not look for wine.
The thirst that from the soul doth rise   5
Doth ask a drink divine:
But might I of Jove's nectar sup,
I would not change for thine.

I sent thee late a rosy wreath,
Not so much honouring thee,   10

As giving it a hope that there
    It could not withered be.
But thou thereon didst only breathe,
    And sent'st it back to me:
Since when it grows, and smells, I swear,   15
    Not of itself, but thee.

TO CELIA: KISS ME, SWEET

Kiss me, sweet; the wary lover
Can your favours keep, and cover,
When the common courting jay
All your bounties will betray.
Kiss again; no creature comes.   5
Kiss, and score up wealthy sums
On my lips thus hardly sundered
While you breathe. First give a hundred,
Then a thousand, then another
Hundred, then unto the other   10
Add a thousand, and so more
Till you equal with the store
All the grass that Rumney yields,
Or the sands in Chelsea fields,
Or the drops in silver Thames,   15
Or the stars that gild his streams
In the silent summer nights
When youths ply their stolen delights:
That the curious may not know
How to tell them as they flow;   20
And the envious, when they find
What their number is, be pined.

---

3 *courting jay:* a chattering, foolish fop.   13–14 . . . *in Chelsea fields:*
Rumney is in Wales and Chelsea is on the north bank of the Thames, three
miles from Charing Cross.   22 *pined:* wasted away from grief and
deprivation.

HYMN TO COMUS

Room! room! make room for the bouncing belly,
First father of sauce and deviser of jelly;
Prime master of arts, and the giver of wit,
That found out the excellent engine the spit,
The plough and the flail, the mill and the hopper,   5
The hutch and the bolter, the furnace and copper,
The oven, the bavin, the mawkin, the peel,
The hearth and the range, the dog and the wheel:
He, he first invented the hogshead and tun,
The gimlet and vice too, and taught 'em to run;   10
And since with the funnel and hippocras bag
He has made of himself, that he now cries swag!
Which shows, though the pleasure be but of four inches,
Yet he is a weasel, the gullet that pinches
Of any delight, and not spares from his back   15
Whatever to make of the belly a sack!
Hail, hail, plump paunch! O the founder of taste,
For fresh meats, or powdered, or pickle, or paste;
Devourer of broiled, baked, roasted, or sod,
And emptier of cups be they even or odd: 20
All which have now made thee so wide i' the waist,
As scarce with no pudding thou art to be laced;
But eating and drinking until thou dost nod,
Thou break'st all thy girdles, and break'st forth a god.

Hymn to Comus: Comus: a late Roman mythological figure associated
with revelry.   6 *hutch:* grain box; *bolter:* sieve; *copper:* pan.   7
bavin: stovewood; *mawkin:* ovenmop; *peel:* baker's shovel.   8 *dog and
the wheel:* a mechanical device for spit turning.   9 *hogshead and tun:*
barrels.   10 *gimlet and vice:* devices for keg tapping.   11 *hippocras
bag:* cone-shaped cloth filter.   12 *swag:* a drunken lurch.   13 *but
of four inches:* from teeth to gullet.   19 *sod:* boiled.

GIPSY SONGS

I

The faery beam upon you,
The stars to glister on you;
 A moon of light
 In the noon of night,
Till the fire-drake hath o'ergone you!   5
The wheel of fortune guide you,
The boy with the bow beside you;
 Run aye in the way
 Till the bird of day,   10
And the luckier lot betide you!

II

To the old, long life and treasure,
To the young, all health and pleasure;
 To the fair, their face
 With eternal grace,
And the foul to be loved at leisure!   15
To the witty, all clear mirrors,
To the foolish, their dark errors;
 To the loving sprite,
 A secure delight;
To the jealous, his own false terrors!   20

---

5 ... *the fire-drake* ... : i.e., till the fairies or the will-o'-the-wisp have passed by you.

CHORUS IN A MASQUE

Spring all the Graces of the age,
 And all the Loves of time;
Bring all the pleasures of the stage,
 And relishes of rhyme;
Add all the softnesses of courts,   5

The looks, the laughters, and the sports:
And mingle all their sweets and salts
That none may say, the Triumph halts.

IT WAS A BEAUTY THAT I SAW

It was a beauty that I saw
    So pure, so perfect, as the frame
    Of all the universe was lame,
To that one figure, could I draw,
Or give least line of it a law!   5

A skein of silk without a knot,
    A fair march made without a halt,
    A curious form without a fault,
A printed book without a blot,
All beauty, and without a spot!   10

TO HIMSELF

Where dost thou careless lie
    Buried in ease and sloth?
Knowledge, that sleeps, doth die;
    And this security,
        It is the common moth   5
That eats on wits and arts, and so destroys them both.

Are all the Aonian springs
    Dried up? lies Thespia waste?
Doth Clarius' harp want strings,
    That not a nymph now sings?   10
        Or droop they as disgraced,
To see their seats and bowers by chattering pies defaced?

7 *Aonian springs:* in the region of Mt. Helikon and Kithaeron in Boetia, sacred to the Muses.   8 *Thespia:* literally, "the land of Thespis," the traditional creator of Greek tragedy (*ca.* 600 B.C.).   9 *Clarius:* Apollo, one of whose principal shrines was at Clarius.   12 *pies:* magpies.

If hence thy silence be,
   As 'tis too just a cause,
Let this thought quicken thee: 15
Minds that are great and free,
   Should not on fortune pause;
'Tis crown enough to virtue still, her own applause.

What though the greedy fry
   Be taken with false baits   20
Of worded balladry,
   And think it poesy?
   They die with their conceits,
And only piteous scorn upon their folly waits.

Then take in hand thy lyre,   25
   Strike in thy proper strain,
With Japhet's line, aspire
Sol's chariot for new fire,
   To give the world again:
Who aided him, will thee, the issue of Jove's brain.   30

And since our dainty age
   Cannot endure reproof,
Make not thyself a page
To that strumpet the stage,
   But sing high and aloof,   35
Safe from the wolf's black jaw, and the dull ass's hoof.

---

19 *fry:* young fish, i.e., insignificant persons.   23 *conceits:* affected and fanciful notions.   27 *Japhet's line:* Prometheus, whose father was the titan Iapetus.   30 . . . *of Jove's brain:* Athena.

LOVE AND DEATH

Though I am young and cannot tell
Either what Death or Love is well,
Yet I have heard they both bear darts,
And both do aim at human hearts:
And then again, I have been told,   5
Love wounds with heat, as Death with cold;

So that I fear they do but bring
Extremes to touch, and mean one thing.
As in a ruin we it call
One thing to be blown up, or fall;   10
Or to our end like way may have
By a flash of lightning, or a wave:
So Love's inflamèd shaft or brand,
May kill as soon as Death's cold hand;
Except Love's fires the virtue have   15
To fright the frost out of the grave.

TO HEAVEN

Good and great God! can I not think of thee,
 But it must straight my melancholy be?
Is it interpreted in me disease,
 That, laden with my sins, I seek for ease?
O be thou witness, that the reins dost know   5
 And hearts of all, if I be sad for show;
And judge me after, if I dare pretend
 To aught but grace, or aim at other end.
As thou art all, so be thou all to me,
 First, midst, and last, converted One and Three!   10
My faith, my hope, my love; and, in this state,
 My judge, my witness, and my advocate!
Where have I been this while exiled from thee,
 And whither rapt, now thou but stoop'st to me?
Dwell, dwell here still! O, being everywhere,   15
 How can I doubt to find thee ever here?
I know my state, both full of shame and scorn,
 Conceived in sin, and unto labor born,
Standing with fear, and must with horror fall,
 And destined unto judgment, after all.   20
I feel my griefs too, and there scarce is ground
 Upon my flesh to inflict another wound;
Yet dare I not complain or wish for death
 With holy Paul, lest it be thought the breath
Of discontent; or that these prayers be   25
 For weariness of life, not love of thee.

TO THE MEMORY OF MY BELOVED,
THE AUTHOR, MASTER WILLIAM SHAKESPEARE

To draw no envy, Shakespeare, on thy name,
Am I thus ample to thy book and fame;
While I confess thy writings to be such
As neither man nor Muse can praise too much.
'Tis true, and all men's suffrage. But these ways   5
Were not the paths I meant unto thy praise;
For silliest ignorance on these may light,
Which, when it sounds at best, but echoes right;
Or blind affection, which doth ne'er advance
The truth, but gropes, and urgeth all by chance;   10
Or crafty malice might pretend this praise,
And think to ruin, where it seemed to raise.
These are, as some infamous bawd or whore
Should praise a matron. What could hurt her more?
But thou art proof against them, and indeed,   15
Above the ill fortune of them, or the need.
I therefore will begin. Soul of the age!
The applause, delight, the wonder of our stage!
My Shakespeare, rise! I will not lodge thee by
Chaucer, or Spenser, or bid Beaumont lie   20
A little further, to make thee a room;
Thou art a monument without a tomb,
And art alive still while thy book doth live
And we have wits to read and praise to give.
That I not mix thee so, my brain excuses,   25
I mean with great, but disproportioned Muses;
For if I thought my judgment were of years,
I should commit thee surely with thy peers,
And tell how far thou didst our Lyly outshine,
Or sporting Kyd, or Marlowe's mighty line.   30

5 *suffrage:* agreement, judgment.   7 *silliest:* feeblest.   9 *affection:* feeling, prejudice.   26 *disproportioned:* not capable, inferior.
29 *Lyly:* John Lily (*ca.* 1554–1606), Elizabethan playwright.   30 *Kyd or Marlowe:* Thomas Kyd (1558–1594) and Christopher Marlowe (1564–1593), Elizabethan playwrights.

And though thou hadst small Latin and less Greek,
From thence to honor thee I would not seek
For names; but call forth thundering Aeschylus,
Euripides, and Sophocles to us;
Pacuvius, Accius, him of Cordova dead,   35
To life again, to hear thy buskin tread,
And shake a stage; or, when thy socks were on,
Leave thee alone for the comparison
Of all that insolent Greece or haughty Rome
Sent forth, or since did from their ashes come.   40
Triumph, my Britain, thou hast one to show
To whom all scenes of Europe homage owe.
He was not of an age, but for all time!
And all the Muses still were in their prime,
When, like Apollo, he came forth to warm   45
Our ears, or like a Mercury to charm!
Nature herself was proud of his designs
And joyed to wear the dressing of his lines,
Which were so richly spun, and woven so fit,
As, since, she will vouchsafe no other wit.   50
The merry Greek, tart Aristophanes,
Neat Terence, witty Plautus, now not please,
But antiquated and deserted lie,
As they were not of Nature's family.
Yet must I not give Nature all; thy art,   55
My gentle Shakespeare, must enjoy a part.
For though the poet's matter Nature be,
His art doth give the fashion; and, that he
Who casts to write a living line, must sweat
(Such as thine are) and strike the second heat   60
Upon the Muses' anvil; turn the same
(And himself with it) that he thinks to frame,

33–34 *Aeschylus, Euripides, and Sophocles:* three Greek tragic poets
and playwrights.   35 *Pacuvius, Accius, him of Cordova:* early Roman
tragic poets (second century B.C.). " . . . him of Cordova dead" is Seneca
the Younger (first century A.D.), the chief Roman author of tragedy.
36 *buskin:* the high laced boot emblematic of tragedy.   37 *socks:* emblematic of comedy.   42 *scenes:* stages.   51–52 *Aristophanes, Terence, Plautus:* respectively, a Greek and two Romans, the greatest classical
authors of dramatic comedy.   59 *casts:* tries.

Or, for the laurel, he may gain a scorn;
For a good poet's made, as well as born.
And such wert thou! Look how the father's face   65
Lives in his issue; even so the race
Of Shakespeare's mind and manners brightly shines
In his well-turned, and true-filed lines;
In each of which he seems to shake a lance,
As brandished at the eyes of ignorance.   70
Sweet Swan of Avon! what a sight it were
To see thee in our waters yet appear,
And make those flights upon the banks of Thames,
That so did take Eliza, and our James!
But stay, I see thee in the hemisphere   75
Advanced, and made a constellation there!
Shine forth, thou star of poets, and with rage
Or influence, chide or cheer the drooping stage,
Which, since thy flight from hence, hath mourned like night,
And despairs day, but for thy volume's light.   80

74 *Eliza . . . James:* Queen Elizabeth and King James I.

JOHN MILTON

[1608–1674]

Milton was the eldest son of a well-to-do London scrivener and was raised in an atmosphere of piety, wealth, and cultural refinement. He had a great gift for language and before he left St. Paul's School for Cambridge, at the age of sixteen, he had the command of Latin, Greek, Hebrew, and most modern European tongues. He took his B.A. in 1629, and his M.A. in 1632, and then retired to his father's country house at Horton in Buckinghamshire where he spent five years in constant reading and occasional writing. He wrote COMUS, *a masque, in 1634, and contributed* LYCIDAS *to the volume memorializing his Cambridge classmate, Edward King, in 1637. "On the Morning of Christ's Nativity," "L'Allegro" and "Il Penseroso" were probably written while Milton was still at Cambridge.*

In 1638 Milton's father sent him to Europe to finish his formal education. He traveled on the Continent for two years. He returned home to enter the complex and controversial arena of seventeenth-century English politics and religion by writing tracts against the rule of the English church by bishops. His marriage to Mary Powell, in 1642, lasted only six weeks before she left him to live with her parents, and for the next three years Milton devoted much of his energy to the writing of a series of pamphlets in which he advocated incompatibility and ennui as grounds for divorce. Before the beheading of Charles I in 1649 Milton had also written his defense of the freedom of the press, AREOPAGITICA, *and* OF EDUCATION.

Appointment as Latin Secretary to Cromwell's Council of State gave Milton the opportunity to use his talent for languages and rhetoric but it was exhausting work which damaged his health, especially his eyesight. His wife had returned to him and three daughters had been born, but in 1652 she and an infant son died and in the same year Milton became totally blind. In 1656 he made another marriage to Catherine Woodcock which ended with her death in childbirth in 1658.

The political defeat of the Commonwealth in 1660 brought Milton a short period of imprisonment followed by poverty and isolation. In 1633 he married Elizabeth Minshull and began the composition of PARADISE LOST *(1667).* PARADISE REGAINED *and the verse drama* SAMSON AGONISTES *were published together in 1671.*

The standard text of Milton's writings is the Columbia Milton (eighteen vols., 1931–1938), and the standard biography is David Masson's in seven volumes, published 1859–1894 and revised 1881–1896. Studies of the poetry are innumerable but two good general books are E. M. W. Tillyard's MILTON *(1930, rev. 1949) and J. H. Hanford's* MILTON HANDBOOK *(4th ed., 1946). Other studies of interest include Theodore Banks'* MILTON'S IMAGERY *(1950); Cleanth Brooks' and John Hardy's* POEMS OF JOHN MILTON *(1951); S. E. Sprott's* MILTON'S ART OF PROSODY *(1953); Kester Svendsen's* MILTON AND SCIENCE *(1956); and Arnold Stein's* ANSWERABLE STYLE: ESSAYS ON PARADISE LOST *(1953), and* HEROIC KNOWLEDGE; AN INTERPRETATION OF PARADISE REGAINED AND SAMSON AGONISTES *(1957).*

AT A SOLEMN MUSIC

Blest pair of Sirens, pledges of heaven's joy,
Sphere-born harmonious sisters, Voice, and Verse,
Wed your divine sounds, and mixed power employ
Dead things with inbreathed sense able to pierce,
And to our high-raised fantasy present,   5
That undisturbed song of pure consent,
Aye sung before the saphire-coloured throne
To him that sits thereon
With saintly shout, and solemn jubilee,
Where the bright seraphim in burning row   10
Their loud up-lifted angel trumpets blow,
And the cherubic host in thousand choires
Touch their immortal harps of golden wires,
With those just spirits that wear victorious palms,
Hymns devout and holy psalms   15

1 *Sirens:* seductive female spirits, traditionally evil. Their personification here is of goodness.

Singing everlastingly;
That we on earth with undiscording voice
May rightly answer that melodious noise;
As once we did, till disproportioned sin
Jarred against nature's chime, and with harsh din   20
Broke the fair music that all creatures made
To their great Lord, whose love their motion swayed
In perfect diapason, whilst they stood
In first obedience, and their state of good.
O may we soon again renew that song,   25
And keep in tune with heaven, till God ere long
To his celestial consort us unite,
To live with him, and sing in endless morn of light.

23 *diapason:* harmony.

ON THE NEW FORCERS OF CONSCIENCE
UNDER THE LONG PARLIAMENT

Because you have thrown off your prelate lord,
    And with stiff vows renounced his Liturgy
    To seize the widowed whore Plurality
    From them whose sin ye envied, not abhored,
Dare ye for this adjure the civil sword   5
    To force our consciences that Christ set free,
    And ride us with a classic hierarchy
    Taught ye by mere A. S. and Rutherford?
Men whose life, learning, faith and pure intent
    Would have been held in high esteem with Paul   10
    Must now be named and printed heretics

On the New Forcers of Conscience under the Long Parliament: new
forcers: Presbyterians, with whom Milton had sided against the Church of
England. He found them to be as oppressive, in the Puritan-led Long Parliament, as their predecessors. This is a *sonneto candato* (tailed sonnet), an
Italian form with fourteen lines and two "tails" of three lines each.
1 *prelate lord:* bishop.   3 *Plurality:* the practice of holding more than one
ecclesiastical living by a single priest.   8 *A. S. and Rutherford:* Adam
Stuart and Samuel Rutherford, who were Presbyterian writers.

By shallow Edwards and Scotch what d' ye call:
  But we do hope to find out all your tricks,
  Your plots and packing worse than those of Trent,
                        That so the Parliament 15
May with their wholesome and preventive shears
Clip your phylacteries, though balk your ears,
                        And succor our just fears
When they shall read this clearly in your charge:
New presbyter is but *old priest* writ large.   20

12 . . . *what d'ye call:* Thomas Edwards, author of a three-volume work on Episcopal heresies, *Gangiaena* (1645–1646). "Scotch what d'ye call" is a snide reflection on the unfamiliar sound of Scotch dialect; Presbyterianism was especially strong in Scotland.   14 *Trent:* i.e., the Council of Trent, which was called by the Pope after the Reformation. It had a reputation for political machination.   17 *phylacteries:* symbols of the Law of Moses to orthodox Jews, and here used as symbols of superstition. The amputation of ears was a standard English penalty for sedition by a commoner.

HOW SOON HATH TIME

How soon hath Time, the subtle thief of youth,
  Stolen on his wing my three and twentieth year!
  My hasting days fly on with full career,
  But my late spring no bud or blossom show'th.
Perhaps my semblance might deceive the truth,   5
  That I to manhood am arrived so near,
  And inward ripeness doth much less appear,
  That some more timely-happy spirits endu'th.
Yet be it less or more, or soon or slow,
  It shall be still in strictest measure even   10
  To that same lot, however mean or high,
Toward which Time leads me, and the will of heaven;
  All is, if I have grace to use it so,
  As ever in my great Taskmaster's eye.

8 *endu'th:* endoweth.

ON THE LATE MASSACRE IN PIEDMONT

Avenge, O Lord, thy slaughtered saints, whose bones
  Lie scattered on the Alpine mountains cold,
  Even them who kept thy truth so pure of old
  When all our fathers worshiped stocks and stones,
Forget not: in thy book record their groans   5
  Who were thy sheep and in their ancient fold
  Slain by the bloody Piedmontese that rolled
  Mother with infant down the rocks. Their moans
The vales redoubled to the hills, and they
  To heaven. Their martyred blood and ashes sow   10
  O'er all the Italian fields where still doth sway
The triple tyrant: that from these may grow
  A hundred-fold, who having learnt thy way
  Early may fly the Babylonian woe.

On the Late Massacre in Piedmont: On April 25, 1655, the Waldenses sect
in northern Italy (the Piedmont) was massacred by Catholics at the end of
an agreement which had given them freedom of worship. The Protestant
leaders of Europe brought pressure on the Duke of Savoy to renew that
freedom to the survivors in the summer of 1656, and Milton, as Cromwell's
secretary, was intimately involved in the protest.   12 *triple tyrant:* the
Pope, who wears a triple tiara.   14 ... *woe:* seventeenth-century Protestants identified Roman Catholicism with Babylon as it is depicted in Revelation 16–18.

ON HIS BLINDNESS

When I consider how my light is spent,
  Ere half my days, in this dark world and wide,
  And that one talent which is death to hide,
  Lodged with me useless, though my soul more bent
To serve therewith my Maker, and present   5
  My true account, lest he returning chide,
  "Doth God exact day-labour, light denied?"

I fondly ask; But Patience to prevent
That murmur, soon replies, "God doth not need
  Either man's work or his own gifts, who best   10
  Bear his mild yoke, they serve him best. His state
Is kingly. Thousands at his bidding speed
And post o'er land and ocean without rest:
They also serve who only stand and wait."

8 *fondly:* foolishly.

TO CYRIACK SKINNER

Cyriack, this three years day these eyes, though clear
  To outward view, of blemish or of spot,
  Bereft of light their seeing have forgot.
  Nor to their idle orbs doth sight appear
Of sun or moon or star throughout the year,   5
  Or man or woman. Yet I argue not
  Against heaven's hand or will, nor bate a jot
  Of heart or hope; but still bear up and steer
Right onward. What supports me dost thou ask?
  The conscience, friend, to have lost them overplied   10
  In liberty's defense, my noble task,
Of which all Europe talks from side to side.
  This thought might lead me through the world's vain mask
  Content though blind, had I no better guide.

To Cyriack Skinner: a pupil and close friend of Milton's.   10 *conscience:* consciousness.

ON HIS DECEASED WIFE

Methought I saw my late espoused saint
  Brought to me like Alcestis from the grave,
  Whom Jove's great son to her glad husband gave,

On His Deceased Wife: Milton's second wife, Katherine Woodcock.
2 *Alcestis:* the wife of Admetus, King of Thessaly, whom Hercules (*Jove's
great son,* line 3) rescued from Hades and restored to her husband.

Rescued from death by force though pale and faint.
Mine as whom washed from spot of child-bed taint,   5
   Purification in the old law did save,
   And such, as yet once more I trust to have
   Full sight of her in heaven without restraint,
Came vested all in white, pure as her mind:
   Her face was veiled, yet to my fancied sight,   10
   Love, sweetness, goodness, in her person shined
So clear, as in no face with more delight.
   But O, as to embrace me she enclined,
   I waked, she fled, and day brought back my night.

6 *old law:* see Leviticus 12.   10 . . . *veiled:* Milton was blind when he met and married her.

LYCIDAS

In this Monody the Author bewails a learned friend, unfortunately drowned in his passage from Chester *on the Irish Seas, 1637. And by occasion foretells the ruin of our corrupted Clergy then in their height.*

Yet once more, O ye laurels, and once more
Ye myrtles brown, with ivy never sere,
I come to pluck your berries harsh and crude,
And with forced fingers rude,
Shatter your leaves before the mellowing year.   5
Bitter constraint, and sad occasion dear,
Compels me to disturb your season due:
For Lycidas is dead, dead ere his prime,
Young Lycidas, and hath not left his peer:
Who would not sing for Lycidas? he knew   10
Himself to sing, and build the lofty rhyme.
He must not float upon his watery bier

Monody: a song in Greek drama, sung by one voice; *learned friend:* Edward King (1612–1637).   1 *laurels:* like *Myrtles* and *Ivy* (line 2), symbolic of poetic inspiration.   3 *crude:* unripe.   6 *dear:* moving, with connotation of "dire" and "drear."

Unwept, and welter to the parching wind,
Without the meed of some melodious tear.
   Begin then, sisters of the sacred well, 15
That from beneath the seat of Jove doth spring,
Begin, and somewhat loudly sweep the string.
Hence with denial vain, and coy excuse,
So may some gentle Muse
With lucky words favour my destined urn, 20
And as he passes turn,
And bid fair peace be to my sable shroud.
For we were nursed upon the self-same hill,
Fed the same flock; by fountain, shade, and rill.
   Together both, ere the high lawns appeared 25
Under the opening eye-lids of the morn,
We drove a field, and both together heard
What time the grayfly winds her sultry horn,
Battening our flocks with the fresh dews of night,
Oft till the star that rose, at evening, bright, 30
Toward heaven's descent had sloped his westering wheel.
Meanwhile the rural ditties were not mute,
Tempered to the oaten flute,
Rough satyrs danced, and fauns with cloven heel,
From the glad sound would not be absent long, 35
And old Damaetas loved to hear our song.
   But O the heavy change, now thou art gone,
Now thou art gone, and never must return!
Thee shepherd, thee the woods, and desert caves,
With wild thyme and the gadding vine o'ergrown, 40
And all their echoes mourn.
The willows, and the hazel copses green,
Shall now no more be seen,
Fanning their joyous leaves to thy soft lays.
As killing as the canker to the rose, 45
Or taint-worm to the weanling herds that graze,
Or frost to flowers, that their gay wardrobe wear,

14 *meed:* reward, consolation, tribute.   15 . . . *well:* the Muses.
29 *battening:* feeding.   33 *oaten flute:* the pastoral pipes of Pan.
36 *Damaetas:* a traditional pastoral name, referring perhaps to a Cambridge
tutor.   40 *gadding:* straggling.   45 *canker:* blight, lesion.

When first the white thorn blows;
Such, Lycidas, thy loss to shepherd's ear.
   Where were ye, nymphs, when the remorseless deep   50
Closed o'er the head of your loved Lycidas?
For neither were ye playing on the steep,
Where your old bards, the famous Druids, lie,
Nor on the shaggy top of Mona high,
Nor yet where Deva spreads her wizard stream.   55
Ay me, I fondly dream!
Had ye been there—for what could that have done?
What could the Muse herself that Orpheus bore,
The Muse herself for her inchanting son
Whom universal Nature did lament,   60
When by the rout that made the hideous roar,
His gory visage down the stream was sent,
Down the swift Hebrus to the Lesbian shore.
   Alas! What boots it with uncessant care
To tend the homely slighted shepherd's trade,   65
And strictly meditate the thankless Muse,
Were it not better done as others use,
To sport with Amaryllis in the shade,
Or with the tangles of Neæra's hair?
Fame is the spur that the clear spirit doth raise   70
(That last infirmity of noble mind)
To scorn delights, and live laborious days;
But the fair guerdon when we hope to find,
And think to burst out into sudden blaze,
Comes the blind Fury with the abhorred shears,   75

48 *blows:* blossoms (full-blown).   53 *Druids:* priests of Celtic Gaul and Britain.   54 *Mona:* the isle of Anglesey; *Deva* (line 55) is the river Dee, between Cheshire and North Wales; the Dee was magic (*wizard:* line 55) because the shifts of the fords were interpreted to foretell the future. 58 *Muse:* Calliope, the mother of Orpheus, was the Muse of epic poetry. 59 *inchanting:* connotes both singing and magical incantation.   61 *rout:* mob. Orpheus was torn to bits by the women of Thrace because he refused to join their Bacchic rites. They threw his head into the river *Hebrus* (line 63) and it floated out into the Aegean to Lesbos, still singing.   64 *boots:* profits.   66 . . . *thankless Muse:* i.e., to be a serious poet.   68–69 *Amaryllis, Neaera:* conventional names for pastoral nymphs; i.e., to write love poetry.   73 *guerdon:* prize, reward.   75 *Fury:* Atropos, who cuts the thread of life. She was a Fate, not a Fury, but Milton's change intensifies the bitterness of death.

And slits the thin spun life. But not the praise,
Phoebus replied, and touched my trembling ears;
Fame is no plant that grows on mortal soil,
Nor in the glistering foil
Set off to the world, nor in broad rumour lies,   80
But lives and spreads aloft by those pure eyes,
And perfect witness of all-judging Jove;
As he pronounces lastly on each deed,
Of so much fame in heaven expect thy meed.

   O Fountain Arethuse, and thou honoured flood,   85
Smooth-sliding Mincius, crowned with vocal reeds,
That strain I heard was of a higher mood:
But now my oat proceeds,
And listens to the herald of the sea
That came in Neptune's plea,   90
He asked the waves, and asked the felon winds,
What hard mishap doomed this gentle swain?
And questioned every gust of rugged wings
That blows from off each beaked promontory.
They knew not of his story,   95
And sage Hippotades their answer brings,
That not a blast was from his dungeon strayed,
The air was calm, and on the level brine,
Sleek Panope with all her sisters played.
It was that fatal and perfidious bark   100
Built in the eclipse, and rigged with curses dark,
That sunk so low that sacred head of thine.

   Next Camus, reverend sire, went footing slow,
His mantle hairy, and his bonnet sedge,
Inwrought with figures dim, and on the edge   105

---

77 . . . *ears:* Apollo, god of divine inspiration, touched ears to insure remembrance.   79 *foil:* cheap metal, used as a flashy setting for false jewelry.   80 *rumour:* reputation.   85 *Arethuse:* Arethusa, a Sicilian fountain, was considered the home of Theocritus and pastoral poetry. The *Mincius* (line 86) a river in Lombardy, was associated with Virgil. The reeds are vocal because they were used for Panpipes.   88 *oat:* pipe, i.e., song.   89 *herald:* Triton, who pleads Neptune's innocence in King's death.   96 *Hippotades:* Aeolus, son of Hippotas, and god of wind.   99 *Panope:* a sea nymph.   101 *eclipse:* i.e., at an ill-omened time.   103 *Camus:* the god of the river Cam, slow and shaggy.

Like to that sanguine flower inscribed with woe.
"Ah, who hath reft," quoth he "my dearest pledge?"
Last came, and last did go,
The pilot of the Galilean lake,
Two massy keys he bore of metals twain,   110
(The golden opes, the iron shuts amain)
He shook his mitered locks, and stern bespake,
"How well could I have spared for thee, young swain,
Enow of such as for their bellies sake,
Creep and intrude, and climb into the fold?   115
Of other care they little reckoning make,
Then how to scramble at the shearers' feast,
And shove away the worthy bidden guest;
Blind mouths! that scarce themselves know how to hold
A sheep-hook, or have learned ought else the least   120
That to the faithful herdman's art belongs!
What recks it them? What need they? They are sped;
And when they list, their lean and flashy songs
Grate on their scrannel pipes of wretched straw,
The hungry sheep look up, and are not fed,   125
But swollen with wind, and the rank mist they draw,
Rot inwardly, and foul contagion spread,
Besides what the grim wolf with privy paw
Daily devours apace, and nothing said,
But that two-handed engine at the door,   130
Stands ready to smite once, and smite no more.
    Return Alpheus, the dread voice is past,

---

106 . . . *woe:* the *sanguine flower* is the hyacinth, whose petals carry marks
which the Greeks read as AI, AI, an exclamation of grief at the death of
Hyacinthus, a Greek youth whom Apollo accidentally killed.   107 *pledge:*
child, i.e., of Cambridge.   109 *pilot:* St. Peter, who guards the gate of
heaven.   111 *amain:* firmly.   112 *mitered:* he wears the miter of the
first bishop of Rome.   114 *Enow:* an archaic plural of "enough."
119 *Blind mouths:* those characterized in lines 114–118 as corrupt, non-Puri-
tan clergy. They are poor pastors (shepherds), and their doctrine is false.
122 . . . *them:* i.e., what do they care? . . . *sped:* i.e., they advance rapidly;
they are finished, doomed.   123 *list:* choose; listen.   124 *scrannel:*
scrawny, harsh.   128 *wolf:* Roman Catholicism; *privy:* secret.   130
two-handed engine: an apocalyptic instrument of revenge, perhaps an angelic
sword or the symbolic justice of the English Parliament.   132 *Alpheus:* a
river god who pursued the nymph Arethusa, (line 85) causing her meta-

That shrunk thy streams; return Sicilian Muse,
And call the vales, and bid them hither cast
Their bells, and flowerets of a thousand hues.   135
Ye valleys low where the mild whispers use,
Of shades and wanton winds, and gushing brooks,
On whose fresh lap the swart star sparely looks,
Throw hither all your quaint enameld eyes,
That on the green turf suck the honeyed showers,   140
And purple all the ground with vernal flowers.
Bring the rath primrose that forsaken dies.
The tufted crow-toe, and pale jessamine,
The white pink, and the pansie freaked with jet,
The glowing violet.   145
The musk-rose, and the well attired woodbine,
With cowslips wan that hang the pensive head,
And every flower that sad embroidery wears:
Bid Amaranthus all his beauty shed,
And daffadillies fill their cups with tears,   150
To strew the laureate hearse where Lycid lies.
For so to interpose a little ease,
Let our frail thoughts dally with false surmise.
Ay me! Whilst thee the shores, and sounding seas
Wash far away, where ere thy bones are hurled,   155
Whether beyond the stormy Hebrides
Where thou perhaps under the whelming tide
Visitest the bottom of the monstrous world;
Or whether thou to our moist vows denied,
Sleepest by the fable of Bellerus old,   160
Where the great vision of the guarded mount

---

morphosis. He was associated with the pastoral tradition to which, at this point, Milton returns.

136 *use:* i.e., are heard.   138 *swart star:* Sirius, the Dog Star, which was thought to wither late summer flowers and crops.   142 *rath:* early; . . . *forsaken:* i.e., in the sun's absence.   143 *crow-toe:* wild hyacinth. 144 *freaked:* flecked, freckled.   149 *amaranthus:* an imaginary unfading flower which will fade in mourning for Lycidas.   151 *laureate hearse:* honored coffin, bier.   153 *false surmise:* i.e., that the body can be found and given burial.   159 *moist:* tearful.   160 *Bellerus:* a giant supposed to be buried at Land's End in Cornwall.   161 *guarded mount:* St. Michael's, a rocky island in Mount's Bay, in Cornwall, where the guardian archangel is seen looking out over the Bay of Biscay toward the Spanish coast and the Catholic strongholds of Namancos and Bayona (line 162).

Looks toward Namancos and Bayona's hold;
Look homeward angel now, and melt with ruth.
And, O ye dolphins, waft the hapless youth.
    Weep no more, woeful shepherds, weep no more,   165
For Lycidas, your sorrow, is not dead,
Sunk though he be beneath the watery floor,
So sinks the day-star in the ocean bed,
And yet anon repairs his drooping head,
And tricks his beams, and with new spangled ore,   170
Flames in the forehead of the morning sky:
So Lycidas sunk low, but mounted high,
Through the dear might of him that walked the waves
Where other groves, and other streams along,
With nectar pure his oozy locks he laves,   175
And hears the unexpressive nuptial song,
In the blest kingdoms meek of joy and love.
There entertain him all the saints above,
In solemn troops, and sweet societies
That sing, and singing in their glory move,   180
And wipe the tears for ever from his eyes.
Now, Lycidas, the shepherds weep no more;
Henceforth thou art the genius of the shore,
In thy large recompense, and shalt be good
To all that wander in that perilous flood.   185
    Thus sang the uncouth swain to the oaks and rills,
While the still morn went out with sandals gray;
He touched the tender stops of various quills,
With eager thought warbling his Doric lay:
And now the sun had stretched out all the hills,   190
And now was dropped into the western bay;
At last he rose, and twitched his mantle blue:
Tomorrow to fresh woods, and pastures new.

---

163 *homeward:* toward England; *ruth:* sorrow.   164 *dolphins:* who
carried the legendary Greek poet and musician Arion safely to shore after a
shipwreck.   168 *day-star:* the sun.   170 *tricks:* dresses, renews.
173 . . . *waves:* Matthew 14:25–33.   176 . . . *song:* inexpressible hymn
of joy sung at the "marriage of the Lamb" (Revelation 19).   178 *entertain:* receive.   183 *genius:* spirit.   186 *swain:* unpolished shepherd,
i.e., Milton.   188 *quills:* reed pipes.   189 *Doric:* simple.   192
twitched: pulled close.

L'ALLEGRO

Hence loathed Melancholy
  Of Cerberus, and blackest midnight born,
In Stygian cave forlorn.
  'Mongst horrid shapes, and shrieks, and sights unholy,
Find out some uncouth cell,   5
  Where brooding darkness spreads his jealous wings,
And the night-raven sings;
  There under ebon shades, and low-browed rocks,
As ragged as thy locks,
  In dark Cimmerian desert ever dwell.   10
But come thou goddess fair and free,
In heaven ycleped Euphrosyne,
And by men, heart-easing mirth,
Whom lovely Venus at a birth
With two sister Graces more   15
To ivy-crowned Bacchus bore;
Or whether (as some sager sing)
The frolic wind that breathes the spring,
Zephyr with Aurora playing,
As he met her once a Maying,   20
There on beds of violets blue,
And fresh-blown roses washed in dew,
Filled her with thee a daughter fair,
So buxom, blithe, and debonair.
Haste thee nymph, and bring with thee   25
Jest and youthful Jollity,

L'Allegro: the cheerful, lively man.   2 *Cerberus:* the three-headed dog which guarded the gate of Hades on the river Styx (hence *Stygian* in line 3). The genealogies in this poem are sometimes altered by Milton from their classical form.   10 *Cimmerian:* a fabled land at the edge of the world, shrouded in twilight and mist. The Crimea derives its name from Cimmeria. 12 *ycleped:* named.   15 *Graces:* Aglaia and Tralia, goddesses of beauty and delight.   16 *Bacchus:* god of wine and revelry.   17 *sager:* poets who describe the Graces as daughters of Zephyr, the west wind, and Aurora, the dawn. This version is Milton's invention.   22 *fresh-blown:* newly opened.   24 *buxom:* gay.

Quips and cranks, and wanton wiles,
Nods, and becks, and wreathed smiles,
Such as hang on Hebe's cheek,
And love to live in dimple sleek;   30
Sport that wrinkled Care derides,
And Laughter holding both his sides.
Come, and trip it as you go
On the light fantastic toe,
And in thy right hand lead with thee,   35
The mountain nymph, sweet Liberty;
And if I give thee honor due,
Mirth, admit me of thy crew
To live with her, and live with thee,
In unreproved pleasures free;   40
To hear the lark begin his flight,
And singing startle the dull night,
From his watch-tower in the skies,
Till the dappled dawn doth rise;
Then to come in spite of sorrow,   45
And at my window bid good morrow,
Through the sweet-briar, or the vine,
Or the twisted eglantine.
While the cock with lively din,
Scatters the rear of darkness thin,   50
And to the stack, or the barn door,
Stoutly struts his dames before,
Oft listening how the hounds and horn
Cheerly rouse the slumbering morn,
From the side of some hoar hill,   55
Through the high wood echoing shrill.
Some time walking not unseen
By hedge-row elms, on hillocks green,
Right against the eastern gate,
Where the great sun begins his state,   60
Robed in flames, and amber light,
The clouds in thousand liveries dight,
While the plowman near at hand,

27 . . . *wiles:* jokes and playful tricks.   28 *becks:* curtseys.   29
Hebe: goddess of youth.   55 *hoar:* grey.   60 *state:* procession.
62 *dight:* dressed.

Whistles o're the furrowed land,
And the milkmaid singeth blithe,   65
And the mower whets his scythe,
And every shepherd tells his tale
Under the hawthorn in the dale.
Straight mine eye hath caught new pleasures
Whilst the landscape round it measures,   70
Russet lawns, and fallows gray,
Where the nibbling flocks do stray,
Mountains on whose barren breast
The labouring clouds do often rest;
Meadows trim with daisies pied,   75
Shallow brooks, and rivers wide.
Towers, and battlements it sees
Bosomed high in tufted trees,
Where perhaps some beauty lies,
The cynosure of neighbouring eyes.   80
Hard by, a cottage chimney smokes,
From betwixt two aged oaks,
Where Corydon and Thyrsis met,
Are at their savory dinner set
Of herbs, and other country messes,   85
Which the neat-handed Phyllis dresses;
And then in haste her bower she leaves,
With Thestylis to bind the sheaves;
Or if the earlier season lead
To the tanned haycock in the mead,   90
Some times with secure delight
The up-land hamlets will invite,
When the merry bells ring round,
And the jocond rebecks sound
To many a youth, and many a maid,   95
Dancing in the checkered shade;
And young and old come forth to play
On a sunshine holiday,
Till the live-long day-light fail,
Then to the spicy nut-brown ale,   100

80 *cynosure:* an object much gazed at, literally, the polestar.   83 *Cory-*
don . . . Thyrsis: traditional shepherd's names in pastoral poetry, like Phyllis
and Thestylis in lines 86 and 88.   94 *rebecks:* a three-stringed viol.

With stories told of many a feat,
How Fairy Mab the junkets eat,
She was pinched, and pulled she said,
And by the friar's lantern led
Tells how the drudging goblin sweat,   105
To earn his cream-bowl duly set,
When in one night, ere glimpse of morn,
His shadowy flail hath threshed the corn,
That ten day-labourers could not end,
Then lies him down the lubber fiend.   110
And stretched out all the chimney's length,
Basks at the fire his hairy strength;
And crop-full out of doors he flings,
Ere the first cock his matin rings.
Thus done the tales, to bed they creep,   115
By whispering winds soon lulled asleep.
Towered cities please us then,
And the busy hum of men,
Where throngs of knights and barons bold,
In weeds of peace high triumphs hold,   120
With store of ladies, whose bright eyes
Rain influence, and judge the prize,
Of wit, or arms, while both contend
To win her grace, whom all commend.
There let Hymen oft appear   125
In saffron robe, with taper clear,
And pomp, and feast, and revelry,
With mask, and antique pageantry,
Such sights as youthful poets dream
On summer eves by haunted stream.   130
Then to the well-trod stage anon,
If Jonson's learned sock be on,

---

102 *Mab:* wife to Oberon, king of the fairies.   104 *friar's lantern:* will-o'-the-wisp.   105 *drudging goblin:* Robin Goodfellow, hobgoblin. 110 *lubber fiend:* rude spirit.   111 *chimney's:* fireplace's.   120 *weeds:* dress; *triumphs:* festivals.   122 *influence:* astrologic power, because the ladies' eyes are like stars.   125 *Hymen:* god of marriage.   132 . . . *sock:* the low shoe emblematic of comedy. Ben Jonson (1572–1637) was conventionally considered a *learned,* or classical, poet and playwright as contrasted with Shakespeare's *native,* or natural, gift.

Or sweetest Shakespeare, fancy's child,
Warble his native wood-notes wild,
And ever against eating cares,   135
Lap me in soft Lydian airs,
Married to immortal verse
Such as the meeting soul may pierce
In notes, with many a winding bout
Of linked sweetness long drawn out,   140
With wanton heed, and giddy cunning,
The melting voice through mazes running;
Untwisting all the chains that tie
The hidden soul of harmony.
That Orpheus' self may heave his head   145
From golden slumber on a bed
Of heaped Elysian flowers, and hear
Such strains as would have won the ear
Of Pluto, to have quite set free
His half regained Eurydice.   150
These delights, if thou canst give,
Mirth with thee, I mean to live.

136 *Lydian:* soft, sweet, caressing.   139 *bout:* musical passage, perhaps
referring to counterpoint.   145 *Orpheus:* legendary Greek poet and
musician who went to the underworld to reclaim his wife, Eurydice. His
music so charmed Pluto and the guardians of Hades that she was allowed
to leave, walking behind him, on the condition that he must demonstrate his
faith by not looking back to make sure that she was there. He finally did
look back, however, and Eurydice had to remain behind forever.

IL PENSEROSO

Hence vain deluding joys,
    The brood of folly without father bred,
How little you bestead,
    Or fill the fixed mind with all your toys;
Dwell in some idle brain,   5
    And fancies fond with gaudy shapes possess,

Il Penseroso: the thoughtful, brooding man.   3 *bestead:* help, avail.
4 *toys:* trifles.   6 *fond:* foolish.

As thick and numberless
　　As the gay motes that people the sun beams,
Or likest hovering dreams
　　The fickle pensioners of Morpheus' train.　　　　　10
But hail thou goddess, sage and holy,
Hail divinest Melancholy,
Whose saintly visage is too bright
To hit the sense of human sight;
And therefore to our weaker view,　　　　　　　　15
O'erlaid with black staid Wisdom's hue.
Black, but such as in esteem,
Prince Memnon's sister might beseem,
Or that starred Ethiope queen that strove
To set her beauty's praise above　　　　　　　　20
The sea nymphs, and their powers offended,
Yet thou art higher far descended,
Thee bright-haired Vesta long of yore,
To solitary Saturn bore;
His daughter she (in Saturn's reign,　　　　　　　25
Such mixture was not held a stain)
Oft in glimmering bowers, and glades
He met her, and in secret shades
Of woody Ida's inmost grove,
While yet there was no fear of Jove.　　　　　　　30
Come pensive nun, devout and pure,
Sober, steadfast, and demure,
All in a robe of darkest grain,
Flowing with majestic train,
And sable stole of cypress lawn,　　　　　　　　35
Over thy decent shoulders drawn.
Come, but keep thy wonted state,

10 *pensioners:* followers. Morpheus is the god of sleep and dreams.
18 . . . *sister:* Hemara, sister to an Ethiopian prince who fought for Troy.
Homer characterizes her as a great beauty in *The Odyssey* XI.　　19 . . .
queen: Cassiopeia, who was turned into a constellation for boasting that her
daughter Andromeda was more beautiful than the sea nymphs. (Milton
says she boasted of her own beauty.)　　23 *Vesta:* goddess of the hearth
and purity. Saturn (line 24) was chief of the gods before Zeus-Jove. His
rule from Mt. Ida (line 29) and fatherhood of Melancholy is Milton's
invention.　　33 *grain:* dye, color.　　35 *cypress lawn:* funeral crepe.
37 *wonted state:* usual dignity.

With even step, and musing gait,
And looks commercing with the skies,
Thy rapt soul sitting in thine eyes: 40
There held in holy passion still,
Forget thy self to marble, till
With a sad leaden downward cast,
Thou fix them on the earth as fast.
And join with thee calm Peace, and Quiet,   45
Spare Fast, that oft with gods doth diet,
And hears the Muses in a ring,
Aye round about Jove's altar sing.
And add to these retired Leisure,
That in trim gardens takes his pleasure;   50
But first, and chiefest, with thee bring,
Him that yon soars on golden wing,
Guiding the fiery-wheeled throne,
The cherub Contemplation,
And the mute Silence hist along,   55
'Less Philomel will deign a song,
In her sweetest, saddest plight,
Smoothing the rugged brow of night,
While Cynthia checks her dragon yoke,
Gently o'er th' accustomed oak;   60
Sweet bird that shunn'st the noise of folly,
Most musical, most melancholy!
Thee, chauntress, oft the woods among
I woo to hear thy evensong;
And missing thee, I walk unseen   65
On the dry smooth-shaven green,
To behold the wandering Moon,
Riding near her highest noon,
Like one that had been led astray
Through the heaven's wide pathless way;   70
And oft, as if her head she bowed,
Stooping through a fleecy cloud.
Oft on a plat of rising ground,

55 *hist:* summon quietly.   56 *Philomel:* the nightingale, whose song
is traditionally sad.   59 *Cynthia:* the moon goddess, sometimes described
as driving a team of sleepless dragons.   73 *plat:* plot.

I hear the far-off curfew sound,
Over some wide-watered shore, 75
Swinging slow with sullen roar;
Or if the air will not permit,
Some still removed place will fit,
Where glowing embers through the room
Teach light to counterfeit a gloom, 80
Far from all resort of mirth,
Save the cricket on the hearth,
Or the bellman's drowsy charm,
To bless the doors from nightly harm;
Or let my lamp at midnight hour, 85
Be seen in some high lonely tower,
Where I may oft out-watch the Bear,
With thrice great Hermes, or unsphere
The spirit of Plato to unfold
What worlds, or what vast regions hold 90
The immortal mind that hath forsook
Her mansion in this fleshly nook;
And of those demons that are found
In fire, air, flood, or under ground,
Whose power hath a true consent 95
With planet, or with element.
Some time let gorgeous Tragedy
In sceptered pall come sweeping by,
Presenting Thebes, or Pelops' line,
Or the tale of Troy divine. 100
Or what (though rare) of later age,
Ennobled hath the buskined stage.
But, O sad Virgin, that thy power

---

83 *bellman:* night watchman.   87 *the Bear:* the Big Dipper which, in the northern hemisphere, never sets.   88 *Hermes:* Trismegistus, legendary Egyptian philosopher and mystic whose attributed third- and fourth-century works were an authority to later magicians and alchemists; *unsphere:* i.e., to call back Plato from the heavenly to the earthly sphere.   93 *demons:* spirits which correspond (line 95, *consent*) with the four elements.   98 *sceptered pall:* royal tragic robe.   100 . . . *Troy:* Sophocles wrote of the royal house of Thebes in his Oedipus cycle, Aeschylus of that of Pelops in the Oresteia, and Euripides of Troy in *The Trojan Women.*   102 *buskined:* the high boot emblematic of tragedy.

Might raise Musaeus from his bower,
Or bid the soul of Orpheus sing   105
Such notes as warbled to the string,
Drew iron tears down Pluto's cheek,
And made Hell grant what Love did seek.
Or call up him that left half told
The story of Cambuscan bold,   110
Of Camball, and of Algarsife,
And who had Canacee to wife,
That owned the virtuous ring and glass,
And of the wondrous horse of brass,
On which the Tartar king did ride;   115
And if aught else, great bards beside,
In sage and solemn tunes have sung,
Of tourneys and of trophies hung;
Of forests, and enchantments drear,
Where more is meant than meets the ear,   120
Thus, Night, oft see me in thy pale career,
Till civil-suited Morn appear,
Not tricked and frounced as she was wont,
With the Attic boy to hunt,
But kerchiefed in a comely cloud,   125
While rocking winds are piping loud,
Or ushered with a shower still,
When the gust hath blown his fill,
Ending on the rustling leaves,
With minute drops from off the eaves.   130
And when the sun begins to fling
His flaring beams, me, goddess, bring
To arched walks of twilight groves,
And shadows brown that Sylvan loves
Of pine, or monumental oak,   135
Where the rude ax with heaved stroke,

104 *Musaeus:* Greek poet (ca. 500 B.C.), semilegendary.   105 *Orpheus:*
for his story see 'L'Allegro," line 145 and note.   109 *him:* Chaucer,
whose Squire's Tale (in *The Canterbury Tales*) leaves half told the story
of Cambuscan.   113 *virtuous:* powerful, having (magical) strength.
122 . . . *morn:* Aurora, when hunting with Cephalus of Attica, dressed
plainly and not in bright colors (line 123, *tricked*) or with frizzled hair
(line 123, *frounced*).   134 *Sylvan:* Sylvanus, Roman god of woods.

Was never heard the nymphs to daunt,
Or fright them from their hallowed haunt.
There in close covert by some brook,
Where no profaner eye may look,   140
Hide me from Day's garish eye,
While the bee with honeyed thigh,
That at her flowery work doth sing,
And the waters murmuring
With such consort as they keep,   145
Entice the dewy-feathered Sleep;
And let some strange mysterious dream,
Wave at his wings in airy stream,
Of lively portraiture displayed,
Softly on my eye-lids laid.   150
And as I wake, sweet music breath
Above, about, or underneath,
Sent by some spirit to mortals good,
Or the unseen genius of the wood.
But let my due feet never fail,   155
To walk the studious cloisters pale,
And love the high embowed roof,
With antic pillars massy proof,
And storied windows richly dight,
Casting a dim religious light.   160
There let the pealing organ blow,
To the full voiced choir below,
In service high, and anthems clear,
As may with sweetness, through mine ear,
Dissolve me into ecstasies,   165
And bring all heaven before mine eyes.
And may at last my weary age
Find out the peaceful hermitage,
The hairy gown and mossy cell,
Where I may sit and rightly spell   170
Of every star that heaven doth show,
And every herb that sips the dew;

154 *genius:* spirit.   156 *pale:* enclosure.   158 *antic:* quaintly carved,
antique; *massy proof:* secure because massive.   159 *storied:* storytelling;
dight: dressed.   170 *spell:* study, contemplate.

Till old experience do attain
To something like prophetic strain.
These pleasures Melancholy give,   175
And I with thee will choose to live.

ANDREW MARVELL

[1621–1678]

Andrew Marvell was born in Winestead, Yorkshire, on March 31, 1621. His father, also Andrew Marvell, became master of the Charterhouse (an almshouse) outside Hull in 1624. The younger Marvell attended Hull grammar school and Trinity College, Cambridge, where he received his B.A. in 1639. He would undoubtedly have become a distinguished scholar, but abandoned his education, probably because of the death of his father in 1641. One Latin and one Greek poem survive from these early days. For the next four years Marvell traveled on the continent as a tutor and, upon his return to England, became tutor at Nun Appleton to Lord Fairfax's daughter, Mary. This idyllic setting in Yorkshire inspired many of Marvell's "garden" poems.

In 1653 Marvell was drawn into political life. In that year Milton attempted unsuccessfully to have Marvell appointed his assistant in the Latin Secretaryship. Instead he became tutor to the ward of Cromwell, William Dutton. Marvell was an intensely patriotic man, and demonstrated his reverence for Cromwell in several poems. In 1657 Marvell was appointed Latin Secretary; two years later he was elected to the House of Commons.

Marvell had published his Cromwellian poems anonymously, and his political career did not end with the Restoration; his service as a Member of Parliament continued until the end of his life. His discontent with England's new government was expressed in many anonymous satires. In 1672 he began an open attack against the ecclesiastical policy of the government. His writings were directed against Samuel Parker, Bishop of Oxford, and so skillfully did he draw a line between the policies of the King and those of the clergy that Charles II refused to silence him. Marvell's last great satire, an "Account of the Growth of Popery and Arbitrary Government in England" (1677), was published secretly. Marvell had made many political enemies, and his sudden death on August

18, 1678, aroused suspicions of foul play. These charges have been proved groundless: he died of fever at the hands of an incompetent doctor. In 1681 the volume MISCELLANEOUS POEMS BY ANDREW MARVELL, ESQ. *was published by Mary Palmer, who claimed to have been Marvell's wife, but may have been his housekeeper.*

Marvell's writings were published in four volumes by A. B. Grosart in the COMPLETE WORKS IN PROSE AND VERSE OF ANDREW MARVELL *(1872–1875). His poems and letters were edited by H. M. Margoliouth in two volumes (1927); 2d. ed. 1953), M. C. Bradbrook and M. G. Lloyd have written a biography and critical commentary:* ANDREW MARVELL *(1940). The second half of Ruth Wallerstein's* STUDIES IN SEVENTEENTH-CENTURY POETIC *(1950) is a modern examination of Marvell's poetry.*

ON A DROP OF DEW

See how the orient dew,
  Shed from the bosom of the morn
  Into the blowing roses,
Yet careless of its mansion new;
For the clear region where 'twas born   5
  Round in its self incloses:
  And in its little globes extent,
Frames as it can its native element.
  How it the purple flower does slight,
    Scarce touching where it lies,   10
    But gazing back upon the skies,
    Shines with a mournful light;
      Like its own tear,
  Because so long divided from the sphere.
  Restless it roles and unsecure,   15
    Trembling lest it grow impure:
  Till the warm sun pity its pain,
And to the skies exhale it back again.
    So the Soul, that drop, that ray
Of the clear fountain of eternal day,   20

1 *orient:* the radiant luster peculiar to pearls.

Could it within the human flower be seen,
    Remembering still its former height,
    Shuns the sweet leaves and blossoms green;
    And, recollecting its own light,
Does, in its pure and circling thoughts, express   25
The greater Heaven in a heaven less.
    In how coy a figure wound,
    Every way it turns away:
    So the world excluding round,
    Yet receiving in the day.   30
    Dark beneath, but bright above:
    Here disdaining, there in love.
  How loose and easy hence to go:
  How girt and ready to ascend.
  Moving but on a point below,   35
  It all about does upwards bend.
Such did the manna's sacred dew distil;
White and entire, though congealed and chill.
Congealed on earth: but does, dissolving run
Into the glories of the almighty sun.   40

37 *Manna's:* the divine food that appeared as dew to the host of Moses (Exodus 16:13–36).

BERMUDAS

Where the remote Bermudas ride
In the ocean's bosom unespied,
From a small boat that rowed along
The listening winds received this song.
  "What should we do but sing his praise   5
That led us through the watery maze
Unto an isle so long unknown,
And yet far kinder than our own?
Where he the huge sea-monsters wracks,
That lift the deep upon their backs,   10
He lands us on a grassy stage,
Safe from the storms, and prelates' rage.

He gave us this eternal spring
Which here enamels every thing,
And sends the fowls to us in care   15
On daily visits through the air.
He hangs in shades the orange bright
Like golden lamps in a green night,
And does in the pomegranates close
Jewels more rich than Ormus shows.   20
He makes the figs our mouths to meet,
And throws the melons at our feet;
But apples plants of such a price,
No tree could ever bear them twice.
With cedars chosen by his hand   25
From Lebanon he stores the land;
And makes the hollow seas that roar
Proclaim the ambergris on shore.
He cast (of which we rather boast)
The Gospel's pearl upon our coast;   30
And in these rocks for us did frame
A temple where to sound his name.
O let our voice his praise exalt
Till it arrive at heaven's vault,
Which thence (perhaps) rebounding, may   35
Echo beyond the Mexique bay!"
    Thus sung they, in the English boat,
An holy and a cheerful note:
And all the way, to guide their chime,
With falling oars they kept the time.   40

20 *Ormus:* Hormuz, rich trading port in the Persian Gulf.   23 *apples:*
pineapples.

A DIALOGUE BETWEEN THE SOUL AND BODY

Soul
O who shall, from this dungeon, raise
A soul enslaved so many ways?
With bolts of bones, that fettered stands

In feet; and manacled in hands.
Here blinded with an eye; and there   5
Deaf with the drumming of an ear.
A soul hung up, as 'twere, in chains
Of nerves and arteries, and veins.
Tortured, besides each other part,
In a vain head, and double heart.   10

Body

O who shall me deliver whole,
From bonds of this tyrannic soul?
Which, stretched upright, impales me so,
That mine own precipice I go;
And warms and moves this needless frame: 15
(A fever could but do the same.)
And, wanting where its spite to try,
Has made me live to let me die.
A body that could never rest,
Since this ill spirit it possessed.   20

Soul

What magic could me thus confine
Within another's grief to pine?
Where whatsoever it complain,
I feel, that cannot feel, the pain.
And all my care itself employs,   25
That to preserve, which me destroys:
Constrained not only to endure
Diseases, but what's worse, the cure,
And ready oft the port to gain,
Am shipwrecked into health again.   30

Body

But physic yet could never reach
The maladies thou me dost teach;
Whom first the cramp of hope does tear:
And then the palsy shakes of fear.
The pestilence of love does heat: 35

---

15 *needless frame:* this frame which does not need it.   24 . . . *cannot feel:* the soul can feel emotion though it cannot feel physical sensation.
31 *physic:* medicine.

Or hatred's hidden ulcer eat.
Joy's cheerful madness does perplex:
Or sorrow's other madness vex.
Which knowledge forces me to know;
And memory will not forgo.   40
What but a soul could have the wit
To build me up for sin so fit?
So architects do square and hew,
Green trees that in the forest grew.

TO HIS COY MISTRESS

Had we but world enough, and time,
This coyness, Lady, were no crime.
We would sit down, and think which way
To walk, and pass our long love's day.
Thou by the Indian Ganges' side   5
Shouldst rubies find; I by the tide
Of Humber would complain. I would
Love you ten years before the Flood;
And you should, if you please, refuse
Till the conversion of the Jews.   10
My vegetable love should grow
Vaster than empires, and more slow.
An hundred years should go to praise
Thine eyes, and on thy forehead gaze;
Two hundred to adore each breast;   15
But thirty thousand to the rest:
An age, at least, to every part,
And the last age should show your heart.
For, Lady, you deserve this state;
Nor would I love at lower rate.   20
    But, at my back, I always hear
Time's winged chariot hurrying near:
And yonder, all before us lie

To His Coy Mistress: Coy: obstinate, reserved.   7 *Humber:* English
river which flows through Hull, Marvell's home town.   11 *vegetable:*
lush, verdant, insistent on growth.   19 *state:* i.e., elegant and drawn-out
courtship.

Deserts of vast eternity.
Thy beauty shall no more be found; 25
Nor, in thy marble vault, shall sound
My echoing song. Then worms shall try
That long preserved virginity:
And your quaint honour turn to dust;
And into ashes all my lust. 30
The grave's a fine and private place,
But none, I think, do there embrace.
   Now, therefore, while the youthful hue
Sits on thy skin like morning dew,
And while thy willing soul transpires 35
At every pore with instant fires,
Now let us sport us while we may;
And now, like amorous birds of prey,
Rather at once our time devour,
Than languish in his slow-chapped power. 40
Let us roll all our strength, and all
Our sweetness, up into one ball;
And tear our pleasures, with rough strife,
Thorough the iron gates of life.
   Thus, though we cannot make our sun 45
Stand still, yet we will make him run.

35 *transpires:* breathes out.   40 *slow-chapped:* slow jawed. Marvell
sees Time as slowly devouring the lovers and all the world.

THE DEFINITION OF LOVE

My love is of a birth as rare
  As 'tis for object strange and high:
It was begotten by Despair
  Upon Impossibility.

Magnanimous Despair alone 5
  Could show me so divine a thing,
Where feeble Hope could ne'er have flown
  But vainly flapped its tinsel wing.

And yet I quickly might arrive
    Where my extended soul is fixed;   10
But Fate does iron wedges drive,
    And always crowds itself betwixt.

For Fate with jealous eye doth see
    Two perfect loves; nor lets them close:
Their union would her ruin be   15
    And her tyrannic power depose.

And therefore her decrees of steel
    Us as the distant poles have placed,
(Though Love's whole world on us doth wheel)
    Not by themselves to be embraced: 20

Unless the giddy heaven fall,
    And earth some new convulsion tear,
And, us to join, the world should all
    Be cramped into a planisphere.

As lines, so loves oblique may well   25
    Themselves in every angle greet:
But ours, so truly parallel,
    Though infinite can never meet.

Therefore the love which us doth bind,
    But Fate so enviously debars,   30
Is the conjunction of the mind,
    And opposition of the stars.

24 *planisphere:* round map of the earth.

THE GARDEN

How vainly men themselves amaze
To win the palm, the oak, or bays;
And their incessant labours see
Crowned from some single herb or tree,

1 *amaze:* confuse, trouble.   2 . . . *or bays:* wreaths given for excellence in athletics, civic service, and the arts, in that order.

Whose short and narrow-verged shade 5
Does prudently their toils upbraid;
While all the flowers and trees do close
To weave the garlands of repose.

Fair Quiet, have I found thee here,
And Innocence, thy sister dear! 10
Mistaken long, I sought you then
In busy companies of men.
Your sacred plants, if here below,
Only among the plants will grow:
Society is all but rude 15
To this delicious solitude.

No white nor red was ever seen
So amorous as this lovely green.
Fond lovers, cruel as their flame,
Cut in these trees their mistress' name: 20
Little, alas, they know or heed,
How far these beauties her exceed!
Fair trees! wheres'e'er your barks I wound,
No name shall but your own be found.

When we have run our passion's heat, 25
Love hither makes his best retreat.
The gods, that mortal beauty chase,
Still in a tree did end their race:
Apollo hunted Daphne so,
Only that she might laurel grow; 30
And Pan did after Syrinx speed,
Not as a nymph, but for a reed.

What wondrous life in this I lead!
Ripe apples drop about my head;
The luscious clusters of the vine 35
Upon my mouth do crush their wine;
The nectarine, and curious peach,

17 *No white nor red:* of a woman's complexion; also conventional symbols of innocence and passion, respectively. 32 . . . *for a reed:* Apollo pursued Daphne until she was changed into a laurel; in the same circumstances Pan harried Syrinx until she became a clump of reeds from which Pan fashioned his musical pipes. 37 *curious:* marvelous.

Into my hands themselves do reach;
Stumbling on melons, as I pass,
Ensnared with flowers, I fall on grass.   40

Meanwhile the mind, from pleasure less,
Withdraws into its happiness:
The mind, that ocean where each kind
Does straight its own resemblance find;
Yet it creates, transcending these,   45
Far other worlds,. and other seas;
Annihilating all that's made
To a green thought in a green shade.

Here at the fountain's sliding foot,
Or at some fruit-tree's mossy root,   50
Casting the body's vest aside,
My soul into the boughs does glide:
There like a bird it sits and sings,
Then whets, and combs its silver wings;
And, till prepared for longer flight,   55
Waves in its plumes the various light.

Such was that happy garden-state,
While man there walked without a mate:
After a place so pure and sweet,
What other help could yet be meet?   60
But 'twas beyond a mortal's share
To wander solitary there:
Two Paradises 'twere in one,
To live in Paradise alone.

How well the skilful gardener drew   65
Of flowers and herbs this dial new!
Where, from above, the milder sun

---

41 . . . *from pleasure less:* i.e., because of pleasure with the garden the
mind shrinks away from intellectualizing.   44 . . . *resemblance find:* this
follows the folk belief that the ocean and the land were mirror kingdoms.
Marvell extends this to the notion that the mind holds counterparts of all
nature.   51 *body's vest:* the garment or vestment of the body. The soul
leaves it behind.   54 *whets:* preens.   66 *this dial:* the entire garden
is seen to be a clock, measuring time by growth, decay, and the seasons; or,
the gardener has planted a flower bed in the form of a sundial.

Does through a fragrant zodiac run;
And, as it works, the industrious bee
Computes its time as well as we.   70
How could such sweet and wholesome hours
Be reckoned but with herbs and flowers?

THE MOWER'S SONG

My mind was once the true survey
Of all these meadows fresh and gay,
And in the greenness of the grass
Did see its hopes as in a glass;
When Juliana came, and she,   5
What I do to the grass, does to my thoughts and me.

But these, while I with sorrow pine,
Grew more luxuriant still and fine,
That not one blade of grass you spied,
But had a flower on either side;   10
When Juliana came, and she,
What I do to the grass, does to my thoughts and me.

Unthankful meadows, could you so
A fellowship so true forgo,
And in your gaudy May-games meet,   15
While I lay trodden under feet?
When Juliana came, and she,
What I do to the grass, does to my thoughts and me.

But what you in compassion ought,
Shall now by my revenge be wrought;   20
And flowers, and grass, and I, and all,
Will in one common ruin fall;
For Juliana comes, and she,
What I do to the grass, does to my thoughts and me.

And thus, ye meadows, which have been   25
Companions of my thoughts more green,

1 *survey:* map.

Shall now the heraldry become
With which I shall adorn my tomb;
For Juliana comes, and she,
What I do to the grass, does to my thoughts and me.   30

THE MOWER TO THE GLOW-WORMS

Ye living lamps, by whose dear light
    The nightingale does sit so late,
And, studying all the summer night,
    Her matchless songs does meditate;

Ye country comets, that portend   5
    No war, nor prince's funeral,
Shining unto no higher end
    Than to presage the grasses' fall;

Ye glow-worms, whose officious flame
    To wandering mowers shows the way,   10
That in the night have lost their aim,
    And after foolish fires do stray;

Your courteous lights in vain you waste,
    Since Juliana here is come;
For she my mind hath so displaced   15
    That I shall never find my home.

THE FAIR SINGER

To make a final conquest of all me,
    Love did compose so sweet an enemy,
In whom both beauties to my death agree,
    Joining themselves in fatal harmony:
That while she with her eyes my heart doth bind,   5
She with her voice might captivate my mind.

I could have fled from one but singly fair:
    My disentangled soul itself might save,

97

Breaking the curled trammels of her hair:
   But how should I avoid to be her slave,   10
Whose subtle art invisibly can wreathe
My fetters of the very air I breathe?

It had been easy fighting in some plain
   Where victory might hang in equal choice;
But all resistance against her is vain,   15
   Who has the advantage both of eyes and voice:
And all my forces needs must be undone,
She having gained both the wind and sun.

AMETAS AND THESTYLIS MAKING HAY-ROPES

Ametas

Think'st thou that this love can stand
   Whilst thou still dost say me nay?
Love unpaid does soon disband:
   Love binds love, as hay binds hay.

Thestylis

Think'st thou that this rope would twine   5
   If we both should turn one way?
Where both parties so combine
   Neither love will twist, nor hay.

Ametas

Thus you vain excuses find,
   Which yourself and us delay: 10
And love ties a woman's mind
   Looser than with ropes of hay.

Thestylis

What you cannot constant hope
   Must be taken as you may.

Ametas

Then let 's both lay by our rope,   15
   And go and kiss within the hay.

THE PICTURE OF LITTLE T. C.
IN A PROSPECT OF FLOWERS

See with what simplicity
This nymph begins her golden days!
In the green grass she loves to lie,
And there with her fair aspect tames
The wilder flowers, and gives them names,   5
But only with the roses plays,
      And them does tell
What colour best becomes them, and what smell.

Who can foretell for what high cause
This darling of the gods was born?   10
Yet this is she whose chaster laws
The wanton Love shall one day fear,
And, under her command severe,
See his bow broke and ensigns torn.
      Happy, who can   15
Appease this virtuous enemy of man!

O then let me in time compound
And parley with those conquering eyes,
Ere they have tried their force to wound;
Ere with their glancing wheels they drive   20
In triumph over hearts that strive,
And them that yield but more despise:
      Let me be laid
Where I may see thy glories from some shade.

Meantime, whilst every verdant thing   25
Itself does at thy beauty charm,
Reform the errors of the Spring:
Make that the tulips may have share
Of sweetness, seeing they are fair;
And roses of their thorns disarm;   30

The Picture of Little T. C.: possibly Theophila Cornewall, born in 1644.
Darling of the Gods, line 10, is an approximate translation of Theophila.

But most procure
That violets may a longer age endure.

But O, young beauty of the woods,
Whom Nature courts with fruits and flowers,
Gather the flowers, but spare the buds,   35
Lest Flora, angry at thy crime
To kill her infants in their prime,
Do quickly make the example yours;
      And, ere we see,
Nip in the blossom all our hopes and thee.   40

ON PARADISE LOST

When I beheld the poet blind, yet bold,
In slender book his vast design unfold,
Messiah crowned, God's reconciled decree,
Rebelling angels, the forbidden tree,
Heaven, hell, earth, chaos, all; the argument   5
Held me a while misdoubting his intent,
That he would ruin (for I saw him strong)
The sacred truths to fable and old song
(So Sampson groped the temples in spite)
Thet world o'erwhelming to revenge his sight.   10
  Yet as I read, soon growing less severe,
I liked his project, the success did fear;
Through that wide field how he his way should find
O're which lame faith leads understanding blind;
Lest he perplexed the things he would explain,   15
And what was easy he should render vain.
  Or if a work so infinite he spanned,
Jealous I was that some less skilful hand
(Such as disquiet always what is well,
And by ill imitating would excel)   20
Might hence presume the whole creation's day
To change in scenes, and show it in a play.
  Pardon me, mighty poet, nor despise
My causeless, yet not impious surmise.

But I am now convinced, and none will dare   25
Within thy labors to pretend a share.
Thou hast not missed one thought that could be fit,
And all that was improper dost omit:
So that no room is here for writers left,
But to detect their ignorance or theft.   30
    That majesty which through thy work doth reign
Draws the devout, deterring the profane.
And things divine thou treatst of in such state
As them preserves, and thee inviolate.
At once delight and horror on us seize,   35
Thou singst with so much gravity and ease;
And above human flight dost soar aloft
With plume so strong, so equal, and so soft.
The bird named from that paradise you sing
So never flags, but always keeps on wing.   40
    Where couldst thou words of such a compass find?
Whence furnish such a vast expense of mind?
Just Heaven thee like Tiresias to requite
Rewards with prophecy thy loss of sight.
    Well mightst thou scorn thy readers to allure   45
With tinkling rhyme, of thy own sense secure;
While the Town-Bayes writes all the while and spells,
And like a pack-horse tires without his bells:
Their fancies like our bushy-points appear,
The poets tag them, we for fashion wear.   50
I too transported by the mode offend,
And while I meant to praise thee must commend.
Thy verse created like thy theme sublime,
In number, weight, and measure, needs not rhyme.

40 *but always keeps on wing:* the feet were removed from bird-of-paradise
skins before they were shipped to Europe, and it was popularly supposed
that they had none; hence they lived always in the air.   47 *Town-Bayes:*
Dryden. The Duke of Buckingham satirized Dryden in *The Rehearsal,* giving
him the name of Mr. Bayes.   49 *bushy-points:* ornamented and tasseled
laces for fastening men's stockings.

JOHN DRYDEN

[1631–1700]

Marvell's contemporary, John Dryden, was also deeply involved in the political vagaries of seventeenth-century England. Dryden was born to a Puritan family in Aldwinkle, Northamptonshire, on August 9, 1631. He attended Westminster school as a King's scholar and in 1650 entered Trinity College, Cambridge. By 1654 he had earned his B.A., and the inheritance of his family property enabled him to leave for London to find work as a writer. His first employment was as secretary to his cousin, Sir Gilbert Pickering, after which he worked for the publisher Henry Herringman. Dryden's first substantial poem was in praise of Cromwell ("Heroique Stanzas on the Death of Cromwell," 1659), but he was quick to change with the political tide, publishing ASTRAEA REDUX *in 1660,* TO HIS SACRED MAJESTY . . . ON HIS CORONATION *in 1661, and* TO MY LORD CHANCELLOR *in 1662. Dryden rapidly became the professional poet of the new court. In 1663 he married Lady Elizabeth Howard. He wrote the progovernment* ANNUS MIRABILIS *in 1667 and the following year was appointed historiographer royal and poet laureate. He held these appointments until 1688.*

Dryden concentrated on the lucrative genre of drama between 1664 and 1681 when playgoing was most popular with the pleasure-loving court of Charles II. While under contract to various London theaters he produced nearly thirty plays in as many years. Many of these productions were reworkings of English or French favorites, such as THE STATE OF INNOCENCE *(1674) (from Milton's* PARADISE LOST), ALL FOR LOVE: OR, THE WORLD WELL LOST *(1677) (from Shakespeare's* ANTONY AND CLEOPATRA), TROILUS AND CRESSIDA *(1679), and many matched the rather low standards of the audiences they were written to please. The prefaces to many of Dryden's plays were devoted to criticism; his* OF DRAMATICK POESIE, AN ESSAY *(1668) was a defense of English drama against the French tradition. In* MAC FLECKNOE *(1678) Dryden discovered his strength in verse satire. In his* ABSALOM AND ACHITOPHEL *(1681),* HIS MAJESTIES DECLARATION DEFENDED *(1681),* RELIGIO LAICI OR A LAYMAN'S FAITH *(1682), and* THE HIND AND THE PANTHER *(1687), he joined in the political and religious controversies of the day. His reputation as the leading man of letters in England was established.*

The end of Dryden's life was devoted primarily to criticism and translation of the classics. In 1697 he translated THE WORKS OF VIRGIL, *and in 1700 he published* FABLES ANCIENT AND MODERN . . . FROM HOMER, OVID, BOCCACE, AND CHAUCER. *He died on May 1, 1700, and was buried in Westminster Abbey.*

John Dryden's works were published by Walter Scott in eighteen volumes (1808) and revised by G. Saintsbury (1882–1893). J. Kinsley edited his POETICAL WORKS *in four volumes in 1958. In 1940 J. M. Osborn published* JOHN DRYDEN: SOME BIOGRAPHICAL FACTS AND PROBLEMS. *Other recent criticism on Dryden includes T. S. Eliot's* SELECTED ESSAYS *(1932); D. Nichol Smith's* JOHN DRYDEN *(1950); Mark Van Doren's* JOHN DRYDEN *(1946), a spendid analysis of the poet; and the most thorough analysis of Dryden's religious, political, and philosophical thought, Louis I. Bredvold's* THE INTELLECTUAL MILIEU OF JOHN DRYDEN *(1934).*

A SONG FOR ST. CECILIA'S DAY, 1687

I

From harmony, from heavenly harmony
    This universal frame began:
    When Nature underneath a heap
      Of jarring atoms lay,
    And could not heave her head,   5
The tuneful voice was heard from high:
    "Arise, ye more than dead."
Then cold, and hot, and moist, and dry,
In order to their stations leap,
      And music's power obey.   10
From harmony, from heavenly harmony

8 . . . *and dry:* the four supposed elements of Nature: earth, fire, water, and air.

This universal frame began:
From harmony to harmony
Through all the compass of the notes it ran,
The diapason closing full in Man.   15

II

What passion cannot music raise and quell!
    When Jubal struck the corded shell,
    His listening brethren stood around,
    And, wondering, on their faces fell
    To worship that celestial sound.   20
Less than a god they thought there could not dwell
    Within the hollow of that shell
    That spoke so sweetly and so well.
What passion cannot music raise and quell!

III

    The trumpet's loud clangor   25
        Excites us to arms,
    With shrill notes of anger,
        And mortal alarms.
    The double double double beat
        Of the thundering drum   30
Cries: "Hark! the foes come;
Charge, charge, 'tis too late to retreat."

IV

    The soft complaining flute
    In dying notes discovers
    The woes of hopeless lovers,   35
Whose dirge is whispered by the warbling lute.

V

    Sharp violins proclaim
    Their jealous pangs, and desperation,

15 *The diapason* . . . :the full chromatic range of tone in the musical scale. The figure suggests all-inclusiveness, harmony, and a graduated order. 17 *Jubal:* "The father of all such as handle the harp and organ" (Genesis 4:21).

Fury, frantic indignation,
Depth of pains, and height of passion,   40
  For the fair, disdainful dame.

VI

  But O! what art can teach,
  What human voice can reach,
The sacred organ's praise?
  Notes inspiring holy love,   45
Notes that wing their heavenly ways
  To mend the choirs above.

VII

Orpheus could lead the savage race;
And trees unrooted left their place,
  Sequacious of the lyre;   50
But bright Cecilia raised the wonder higher:
When to her organ vocal breath was given,
An angel heard, and straight appeared,
  Mistaking earth for heaven.

GRAND CHORUS

As from the power of sacred lays   55
  The spheres began to move,
And sung the great Creator's praise
  To all the blest above;
So, when the last and dreadful hour
This crumbling pageant shall devour,   60
The trumpet shall be heard on high,
The dead shall live, the living die,
And music shall untune the sky.

---

48 *Orpheus:* legendary Greek musician, son of the Muse of epic poetry, Calliope, whose skill was so great that he entranced animals (*the savage race*) and rocks and trees followed him (line 49).   50 *Sequacious:* following. 60 *crumbling pageant:* created Nature.

ALEXANDER'S FEAST

OR, THE POWER OF MUSIC;
AN ODE IN HONOR OF ST. CECILIA'S DAY

I

'Twas at the royal feast, for Persia won
    By Philip's warlike son:
  Aloft in awful state
  The godlike hero sat
    On his imperial throne: 5
  His valiant peers were placed around;
Their brows with roses and with myrtles bound:
  (So should desert in arms be crowned.)
The lovely Thais, by his side,
Sat like a blooming Eastern bride   10
In flower of youth and beauty's pride.
  Happy, happy, happy pair!
  None but the brave,
  None but the brave,
  None but the brave deserves the fair.   15

CHORUS

Happy, happy, happy pair!
None but the brave,
None but the brave,
None but the brave deserves the fair.

II

Timotheus, placed on high   20
  Amid the tuneful choir,
  With flying fingers touched the lyre:
The trembling notes ascend the sky,
          And heavenly joys inspire.

2 *warlike son:* Alexander the Great.
who went with Alexander into Persia.
vorite musician.

9 *Thais:* an Athenian courtesan
20 *Timotheus:* Alexander's fa-

The song began from Jove,   25
Who left his blissful seats above,
(Such is the power of mighty love.)
A dragon's fiery form belied the god:
Sublime on radiant spires he rode,
    When he to fair Olympia pressed;   30
    And while he sought her snowy breast:
Then, round her slender waist he curled,
And stamped an image of himself, a sovereign of the world.
The listening crowd admire the lofty sound;
"A present deity," they shout around;   35
"A present deity," the vaulted roofs rebound:
    With ravished ears
    The monarch hears,
    Assumes the god,
    Affects to nod,   40
And seems to shake the spheres.

CHORUS

*   With ravished ears*
*   The monarch hears,*
*   Assumes the god,*
*   Affects to nod,*   45
And seems to shake the spheres.

III

The praise of Bacchus then the sweet musician sung,
    Of Bacchus ever fair and ever young:
      "The jolly god in triumph comes;
      Sound the trumpets; beat the drums: 50
        Flushed with a purple grace
        He shows his honest face:
Now give the hautboys breath; he comes, he comes.
      Bacchus, ever fair and young,
        Drinking joys did first ordain;   55
      Bacchus' blessings are a treasure,
        Drinking is the soldier's pleasure:

25 *from Jove:* the song begins by asserting Alexander's divine parentage: Jove, in the guise of a dragon, uniting with Olympias, Alexander's mortal mother.   29 *on radiant spires:* spirals, coils.   34 *admire:* regards with wonder.   47 *Bacchus:* the god of wine.   53 *hautboys:* oboes.

Rich the treasure,
Sweet the pleasure,
Sweet is pleasure after pain." 60

CHORUS

Bacchus' blessings are a treasure,
Drinking is the soldier's pleasure:
Rich the treasure,
Sweet the pleasure,
Sweet is pleasure after pain. 65

IV

Soothed with the sound, the king grew vain;
Fought all his battles o'er again;
And thrice he routed all his foes; and thrice he slew the slain.
The master saw the madness rise;
His glowing cheeks, his ardent eyes; 70
And, while he heaven and earth defied,
Changed his hand, and checked his pride.
He chose a mournful Muse,
Soft pity to infuse:
He sung Darius great and good, 75
By too severe a fate,
Fallen, fallen, fallen, fallen,
Fallen from his high estate,
And weltering in his blood;
Deserted, at his utmost need, 80
By those his former bounty fed;
On the bare earth exposed he lies,
With not a friend to close his eyes.
With downcast looks the joyless victor sat,
Revolving in his altered soul 85
The various turns of chance below;
And, now and then, a sigh he stole;
And tears began to flow.

69 *master:* Timotheus.   71 *he:* Alexander.   72 . . . *hand* . . .
pride: Timotheus' *hand* and Alexander's *pride*.   75 *Darius:* Darius III,
emperor of Persia 336–331 B.C. He was killed by his own guard.   85
Revolving: carefully considering.

CHORUS

Revolving in his altered soul
  The various turns of chance below;   90
And, now and then, a sigh he stole;
  And tears began to flow.

V

The mighty master smiled, to see
That love was in the next degree:
'Twas but a kindred sound to move,   95
For pity melts the mind to love.
  Softly sweet, in Lydian measures,
  Soon he soothed his soul to pleasures.
  "War," he sung, "is toil and trouble;
  Honor, but an empty bubble;   100
    Never ending, still beginning,
  Fighting still, and still destroying:
    If the world be worth thy winning,
  Think, O think it worth enjoying;
    Lovely Thais sits beside thee,   105
    Take the good the gods provide thee."
The many rend the skies with loud applause;
So Love was crowned, but Music won the cause.
  The prince, unable to conceal his pain,
      Gazed on the fair   110
      Who caused his care,
    And sighed and looked, sighed and looked,
  Sighed and looked, and sighed again:
At length with love and wine at once oppressed,
The vanquished victor sunk upon her breast.   115

CHORUS

The prince, unable to conceal his pain,
    Gazed on the fair
    Who caused his care,
  And sighed and looked, sighed and looked,
Sighed and looked, and sighed again: 120

97 *Lydian measures:* the Lydian mode is sweet and sad.

At length, with love and wine at once oppressed,
The vanquished victor sunk upon her breast.

VI

Now strike the golden lyre again:
A louder yet, and yet a louder strain.
Break his bands of sleep asunder,   125
And rouse him, like a rattling peal of thunder.
   Hark, hark, the horrid sound
    Has raised up his head:
    As awaked from the dead,
    And amazed, he stares around.   130
"Revenge, revenge!" Timotheus cries,
  "See the Furies arise!
 See the snakes that they rear,
 How they hiss in their hair,
 And the sparkles that flash from their eyes!   135
  Behold a ghastly band,
  Each a torch in his hand!
Those are Grecian ghosts, that in battle were slain,
    And unburied remain
    Inglorious on the plain: 140
  Give the vengeance due
  To the valiant crew.
Behold how they toss their torches on high,
  How they point to the Persian abodes,
And glittering temples of their hostile gods!"   145
The princes applaud, with a furious joy;
And the king seized a flambeau with zeal to destroy;
   Thais led the way,
   To light him to his prey,
And, like another Helen, fired another Troy.   150

CHORUS
And the king seized a flambeau with zeal to destroy;
   Thais led the way,
   To light him to his prey,
And, like another Helen, fired another Troy.

---

132 *the Furies:* the Greek spirits of vengeance. 144 *the Persian*
abodes: the city of Persepolis. 147 *flambeau:* torch.

VII

Thus, long ago, 155
Ere heaving bellows learned to blow,
While organs yet were mute;
Timotheus, to his breathing flute,
And sounding lyre,
Could swell the soul to rage, or kindle soft desire. 160
At last, divine Cecilia came,
Inventress of the vocal frame;
The sweet enthusiast, from her sacred store,
Enlarged the former narrow bounds,
And added length to solemn sounds, 165
With nature's mother wit, and arts unknown before.
Let old Timotheus yield the prize,
Or both divide the crown;
He raised a mortal to the skies;
She drew an angel down. 170

GRAND CHORUS

At last, divine Cecilia came,
Inventress of the vocal frame;
The sweet enthusiast, from her sacred store,
Enlarged the former narrow bounds,
And added length to solemn sounds, 175
With nature's mother wit, and arts unknown before.
Let old Timotheus yield the prize,
Or both divide the crown;
He raised a mortal to the skies;
She drew an angel down. 180

162 *the vocal frame:* organ. 163 *The sweet enthusiast:* divinely possessed.

TO THE MEMORY OF MR. OLDHAM

Farewell, too little, and too lately known,
Whom I began to think and call my own:
For sure our souls were near allied, and thine

To the Memory of Mr. Oldham: John Oldham (1653–1683), an energetic political satirist.

Cast in the same poetic mold with mine.
One common note on either lyre did strike,   5
And knaves and fools we both abhorred alike.
To the same goal did both our studies drive;
The last set out the soonest did arrive.
Thus Nisus fell upon the slippery place,
While his young friend performed and won the race.   10
O early ripe! to thy abundant store
What could advancing age have added more?
It might (what nature never gives the young)
Have taught the numbers of thy native tongue.
But satire needs not those, and wit will shine   15
Through the harsh cadence of a rugged line:
A noble error, and but seldom made,
When poets are by too much force betrayed.
Thy generous fruits, though gathered ere their prime,
Still showed a quickness; and maturing time   20
But mellows what we write to the dull sweets of rhyme.
Once more, hail and farewell; farewell, thou young,
But ah too short, Marcellus of our tongue;
Thy brows with ivy, and with laurels bound;
But fate and gloomy night encompass thee around.   25

10 . . . *and won the race:* the race lost by Nisus to his friend Euryalus is
an incident in Virgil's *Aeneid,* Bk. V.   14 *thy native tongue:* English
metrics.   23 *Marcellus:* the nephew, adopted son, and heir of the emperor Augustus. He died at the age of twenty and Virgil laments his death
as one of Rome's greatest losses (*Aeneid,* Bk. VI, 861 ff).

EPIGRAM ON MILTON

Three poets, in three distant ages born,
Greece, Italy, and England did adorn.
The first in loftiness of thought surpassed,
The next in majesty, in both the last:
The force of nature could no farther go;   5
To make a third, she joined the former two.

1 *Three poets:* Homer, Virgil, and Milton.

TRANSLATION OF HORACE'S
"THE NINTH ODE OF THE FIRST BOOK"

I

Behold yon mountain's hoary height,
  Made higher with new mounts of snow;
Again behold the winter's weight
  Oppress the laboring woods below;
And streams, with icy fetters bound,   5
Benumbed and cramped to solid ground.

II

With well-heaped logs dissolve the cold,
  And feed the genial hearth with fires;
Produce the wine, that makes us bold,
  And sprightly wit and love inspires: 10
For what hereafter shall betide,
God, if it is worth his care, provide.

III

Let him alone, with what he made,
  To toss and turn the world below;
At his command the storms invade;   15
  The winds by his commission blow;
Till with a nod he bids 'em cease,
And then the calm returns, and all is peace.

IV

To-morrow and her works defy,
  Lay hold upon the present hour,   20
And snatch the pleasures passing by,
  To put them out of Fortune's power:
Nor love, nor love's delights disdain;
Whate'er thou gets to-day is gain.

V

Secure those golden early joys   25
  That youth unsoured with sorrow bears,
Ere withering time the taste destroys,

With sickness and unwieldly years.
For active sports, for pleasing rest,
This is the time to be possessed;   30
The best is but in season best.

VI

The pointed hour of promised bliss,
    The pleasing whisper in the dark,
The half-unwilling willing kiss,
    The laugh that guides thee to the mark,   35
When the kind nymph would coyness feign,
And hides but to be found again;
These, these are joys the gods for youth ordain.

TO MY DEAR FRIEND, MR. CONGREVE

ON HIS COMEDY CALLED THE DOUBLE-DEALER

Well then, the promised hour is come at last;
The present age of wit obscures the past:
Strong were our sires, and as they fought they writ,
Conquering with force of arms, and dint of wit;
Theirs was the giant race, before the flood;   5
And thus, when Charles returned, our empire stood.
Like Janus he the stubborn soil manured,
With rules of husbandry the rankness cured;
Tamed us to manners, when the stage was rude;
And boisterous English wit with art inbued.   10
Our age was cultivated thus at length,

To My Dear Friend, Mr. Congreve, on His Comedy Called the Double-Dealer: William Congreve (1670–1729), playwright. *The Double-Dealer* was produced in 1694.   2 *age of wit:* creative intelligence.   5 . . . *before the flood: Our sires* (line 3) and the *giant race* refer to the Elizabethan playwrights John Fletcher (1579–1625), Ben Jonson (1573–1637), and Shakespeare who lived before the flood of the Civil War and the Commonwealth as did the "giants in the earth" before Noah's Flood (Genesis 6:4). 6 *Charles:* Charles II, restored to the English throne in 1660.   7 *Janus:* the god of entrance and beginnings. His role as culture hero in the founding of Rome is an obscure one.

But what we gained in skill we lost in strength.
Our builders were with want of genius cursed;
The second temple was not like the first:
Till you, the best Vitruvius, come at length;   15
Our beauties equal, but excel our strength.
Firm Doric pillars found your solid base;
The fair Corinthian crowns the higher space:
Thus all below is strength, and all above is grace.
In easy dialogue is Fletcher's praise;   20
He moved the mind, but had not power to raise.
Great Jonson did by strength of judgment please;
Yet, doubling Fletcher's force, he wants his ease.
In differing talents both adorned their age;
One for the study, t'other for the stage: 25
But both to Congreve justly shall submit,
One matched in judgment, both o'ermatched in wit.
In him all beauties of this age we see,
Etherege his courtship, Southerne's purity,
The satire, wit, and strength of Manly Wycherley.   30
All this in blooming youth you have achieved,
Nor are your foiled contemporaries grieved.
So much the sweetness of your manners move,
We cannot envy you, because we love.
Fabius might joy in Scipio, when he saw   35
A beardless consul made against the law;
And join his suffrage to the votes of Rome,
Though he with Hannibal was overcome.
Thus old Romano bowed to Raphael's fame,
And scholar to the youth he taught became.   40

---

14 . . . *like the first:* the restoration was not like the Renaissance. The
analogy is to the makeshift rebuilding of the Temple of Israel after the
Babylonian exile ca. 520–516 B.C. (Ezra 1–6).   15 *Vitruvius:* Roman
architect; the sole classical author on the subject whose writing survived.
30 . . . *Wycherley:* Sir George Etherege (ca. 1634–1691), Thomas Southerne
(1659–1746), and William Wycherley (1641–1715) were Restoration playwrights. Manly is the protagonist in Wycherley's *Plain Dealer*.   35 . . . *in
Scipio* . . . : Fabius was the Roman leader displaced by the younger Scipio
Africanus after the latter's victory over Hannibal.   39 *old Romano:* In-
correctly assumed by Dryden to be the teacher of the Italian Renaissance
painter Raphael.

O that your brows my laurel had sustained;
Well had I been deposed, if you had reigned!
The father had descended for the son;
For only you are lineal to the throne.
Thus, when the state one Edward did depose,   45
A greater Edward in his room arose.
But now, not I, but poetry is cursed;
For Tom the Second reigns like Tom the First.
But let 'em not mistake my patron's part,
Nor call his charity their own desert.   50
Yet this I prophesy: thou shalt be seen
(Though with some short parenthesis between)
High on the throne of wit; and, seated there,
Not mine—that's little—but thy laurel wear.
Thy first attempt an early promise made;   55
That early promise this has more than paid.
So bold, yet so judiciously you dare,
That your least praise is to be regular.
Time, place, and action, may with pains be wrought;
But genius must be born, and never can be taught.   60
This is your portion; this your native store;
Heaven, that but once was prodigal before,
To Shakespeare gave as much; she could not give him more.
    Maintain your post: that's all the fame you need;
For 'tis impossible you should proceed.   65
Already I am worn with cares and age,
And just abandoning the ungrateful stage;
Unprofitably kept at Heaven's expense,
I live a rent-charge on his providence:
But you, whom every Muse and Grace adorn,   70
Whom I foresee to better fortune born,
Be kind to my remains; and O defend,
Against your judgment, your departed friend!
Let not the insulting foe my fame pursue,

---

46 . . . *A greater Edward* . . . : Edward II was assassinated in 1327. He
was followed by Edward III who crushed the French in the battle of Crecy
(1346) and reigned until 1377.   48 . . . *Tom the First:* Thomas Rymer
and Thomas Shadwell, respectively. Shadwell was poet laureate (replacing
Dryden) from 1688–1692; Rymer had the post from 1692 until his death in
1713.   55 *an early promise made:* Congreve's *The Old Bachelor* (1693).

But shade those laurels which descend to you;   75
And take for tribute what these lines express:
You merit more; nor could my love do less.

MAC FLECKNOE

OR, A SATIRE UPON THE TRUE-BLUE-PROTESTANT POET T. S.

All human things are subject to decay,
And when fate summons, monarchs must obey
This Flecknoe found, who, like Augustus, young
Was called to empire, and had governed long;
In prose and verse, was owned, without dispute,   5
Through all the realms of Nonsense, absolute.
This aged prince, now flourishing in peace,
And blessed with issue of a large increase;
Worn out with business, did at length debate
To settle the succession of the State;   10
And, pondering which of all his sons was fit
To reign and wage immortal war with wit,
Cried: "'Tis resolved; for nature pleads, that he
Should only rule, who most resembles me.
Sh—— alone my perfect image bears,   15
Mature in dullness from his tender years:
Sh—— alone, of all my sons, is he
Who stands confirmed in full stupidity.
The rest to some faint meaning make pretense,
But Sh—— never deviates into sense.   20
Some beams of wit on other souls may fall,
Strike through, and make a lucid interval;
But Sh——'s genuine night admits no ray,
His rising fogs prevail upon the day.

Mac Flecknoe, or, a Satire upon the True-Blue-Protestant Poet T. S.: T.S.:
Thomas Shadwell (1642?–1692), poet laureate.   3 *Augustus:* the first
emperor of Rome.   12 *wit:* verbal skill; intelligence.   15 *Sh——:*
a common device of the time, not intended to conceal the name but to
intensify the tone of personal reference, and often (as here) to leave open
the opportunity for double meaning.

Besides, his goodly fabric fills the eye,   25
And seems designed for thoughtless majesty;
Thoughtless as monarch oaks that shade the plain,
And, spread in solemn state, supinely reign.
Heywood and Shirley were but types of thee,
Thou last great prophet of tautology.   30
Even I, a dunce of more renown than they,
Was sent before but to prepare thy way;
And, coarsely clad in Norwich drugget, came
To teach the nations in thy greater name.
My warbling lute, the lute I whilom strung,   35
When to King John of Portugal I sung,
Was but the prelude to that glorious day,
When thou on silver Thames didst cut thy way,
With well-timed oars before the royal barge,
Swelled with the pride of thy celestial charge;   40
And big with hymn, commander of a host,
The like was ne'er in Epsom blankets tossed.
Methinks I see the new Arion sail,
The lute still trembling underneath thy nail.
At thy well-sharpened thumb from shore to shore   45
The treble squeaks for fear, the basses roar;
Echoes from Pissing Alley Sh—— call,
And Sh—— they resound from Aston Hall.

25 *his goodly fabric fills the eye:* Shadwell was fat.   29 *Heywood and Shirley:* Thomas Heywood (1570, 1575?–1641?) and James Shirley (1596–1666), seventeenth-century dramatists whose style was "Elizabethan" and whose reputations were, at the time of "Mac Flecknoe," in a severe decline. 33 *Norwich drugget:* a rough woolen fabric. This and the next line convey Flecknoe's analogy of himself to John the Baptist.   35 *whilom:* formerly; at one time.   36 *to King John of Portugal I sung:* Flecknoe had been received at the court of John IV.   42 *Epsom:* one of Shadwell's comedies was *Epsom Wells*. There is an incident of blanket tossing in another, *The Virtuoso*.   43 *Arion:* a Greek poet and musician (ca. 700 B.C.). According to legend he was robbed by sailors and thrown overboard while on a voyage. A dolphin, following the ship and charmed by music Arion had played, took him on his back and carried him safely home. Shadwell considered himself to be a talented musician and in 1647 had produced a highly successful operatic version of Dryden's reworking of *The Tempest*. The allusion here seems to be to Shadwell's involvement with some musical pageant on the Thames.   47 *Pissing Alley:* a narrow street in London leading off the Strand.   48 *Aston Hall:* has not been identified.

About thy boat the little fishes throng,
As at the morning toast that floats along.   50
Sometimes, as prince of thy harmonious band,
Thou wield'st thy papers in thy threshing hand.
St. André's feet ne'er kept more equal time,
Not even the feet of thy own *Psyche's* rhyme;
Though they in number as in sense excel: 55
So just, so like tautology, they fell,
That, pale with envy, Singleton forswore
The lute and sword, which he in triumph bore,
And vowed he ne'er would act Villerius more."
Here stopped the good old sire, and wept for joy   60
In silent raptures of the hopeful boy.
All arguments, but most his plays, persuade,
That for anointed dullness he was made.
   Close to the walls which fair Augusta bind,
(The fair Augusta much to fears inclined,)   65
An ancient fabric raised t' inform the sight,
There stood of yore, and Barbican it hight:
A watchtower once; but now, so fate ordains,
Of all the pile an empty name remains.
From its old ruins brothel-houses rise,   70
Scenes of lewd loves, and of polluted joys,
Where their vast courts the mother-strumpets keep,
And, undisturbed by watch, in silence sleep.
Near these a Nursery erects its head,
Where queens are formed, and future heroes bred;   75
Where unfledged actors learn to laugh and cry,

---

50 *the morning toast:* sewage. The Thames had long since become an
open sewer.   53 *St. Andre's:* a French dancing master who designed the
choreography of Shadwell's *Psyche* (1675), an opera.   57 *Singleton:* John
Singleton (d. 1686), opera singer at the Theatre Royal.   59 *Villerius:*
character in Sir William D'avenant's *The Siege of Rhodes* (1656), the first
English opera.   63 *anointed dullness:* English kings are anointed with
oil. The expectation here would be "anointed majesty."   64 *Augusta:*
London.   65 *fears:* the hysteria stimulated by the Popish Plot (1678) in
which it was believed that Jesuits had organized to assassinate Charles II,
burn London, massacre all Protestants, and re-establish the Roman Church
in England.   67 *hight:* was called. This was a conscious archaism on
Dryden's part and is a convention of mock-heroic style.   74 *Nursery:*
a school for young actors.

Where infant punks their tender voices try,
And little Maximins, the gods defy.
Great Fletcher never treads in buskins here,
Nor greater Jonson dares in socks appear;   80
But gentle Simkin just reception finds
Amidst this monument of vanished minds:
Pure clinches the suburbian Muse affords,
And Panton waging harmless war with words.
Here Flecknoe, as a place to fame well known,   85
Ambitiously designed his Sh——'s throne;
For ancient Dekker prophesied long since,
That in this pile should reign a mighty prince,
Born for a scourge of wit, and flail of sense;
To whom true dullness should some *Psyches* owe,   90
But worlds of Misers from his pen should flow;
Humorists and *Hypocrites* it should produce,
Whole Raymond families, and tribes of Bruce.
    Now Empress Fame had published the renown
Of Sh——'s coronation through the town.   95
Roused by report of Fame, the nations meet,
From near Bunhill, and distant Watling Street.
No Persian carpets spread the imperial way,
But scattered limbs of mangled poets lay;
From dusty shops neglected authors come,   100

77 *punks:* prostitutes. Many of the actresses of the period used the stage as a steppingstone to becoming the mistress of a courtier and occasionally of Charles II himself.   78 *Maximins:* the Roman emperor in Dryden's *Tyrannic Love* (1669), a character who epitomizes turgid and inflated speech. 79 *Fletcher:* John Fletcher (1579–1625). Renaissance playwright.   79 *buskins:* the laced boots emblematic of tragedy.   80 *socks:* emblematic of comedy.   81 *Simkin:* a clown's conventional name.   83 *clinches:* puns.   84 *Panton:* probably Thomas Panton (d. 1685), a gambler and *bon vivant* who had a reputation for witty and punning conversation.
87 *Dekker:* Thomas Dekker (ca. 1572–1632). Renaissance playwright, satirized by Ben Jonson in *The Poetaster* (1601).   92 . . . *Hypocrites:* three plays by Shadwell. *The Miser* was adapted from Molière. *The Hypocrite* failed and was not published.   93 *Raymond . . . Bruce:* characters in, respectively, *The Humorists* and *The Virtuoso.*   97 *Watling Street:* Shadwell is crowned at the Nursery. Bunhill and Watling Street are approximately one-quarter and one-half mile away. Shadwell's fame does not seem widespread. The locations are in the city's center as well, the part of London considered by the "best" people of Dryden's time to be vulgarly middle class.

Martyrs of pies, and relics of the bum.
Much Heywood, Shirley, Ogleby there lay,
But loads of Sh—— almost choked the way.
Bilked stationers for yeomen stood prepared,
And Herringman was captain of the guard.   105
The hoary prince in majesty appeared,
High on a throne of his own labors reared.
At his right hand our young Ascanius sat,
Rome's other hope, and pillar of the State.
His brows thick fogs, instead of glories, grace,   110
And lambent dullness played around his face.
As Hannibal did to the altars come,
Sworn by his sire a mortal foe to Rome;
So Sh—— swore, nor should his vow be vain,
That he till death true dullness would maintain;   115
And, in his father's right, and realm's defense,
Ne'er to have peace with wit, nor truce with sense.
The king himself the sacred unction made,
As king by office, and as priest by trade.
In his sinister hand, instead of ball,   120
He placed a mighty mug of potent ale;
Love's Kingdom to his right he did convey,
At once his scepter, and his rule of sway;
Whose righteous lore the prince had practiced young,
And from whose loins recorded *Psyche* sprung.   125
His temples, last, with poppies were o'erspread,
That nodding seemed to consecrate his head.
Just at that point of time, if fame not lie,
On his left hand twelve reverend owls did fly.
So Romulus, 'tis sung, by Tiber's brook,   130

101 . . . *relics of the bum:* books which could not be sold were bought
for next to nothing by bakers to line pans and by the populous for use as
toilet paper.   102 *Ogleby:* John Ogilby (d. 1676) translated Homer and
Virgil. He was also a victim of Alexander Pope.   104 *Bilked stationers . . . :* publishers who found themselves with unsalable books, led by
Henry Herringman, who was for years the leading publisher in London.
He published both Dryden and Shadwell until 1679.   108 *Ascanius:* the
son of Aeneas in Virgil's *Aeneid.*   120 *ball:* the globe held in the left
hand of a British king during his coronation. It is a symbol of the world
over which he holds the power symbolized by the scepter which he holds in
his right hand.   122 *Love's Kingdom:* a dreary play of Flecknoe's.

Presage of sway from twice six vultures took.
The admiring throng loud acclamations make,
And omens of his future empire take.
The sire then shook the honors of his head,
And from his brows damps of oblivion shed   135
Full on the filial dullness: long he stood,
Repelling from his breast the raging god;
At length burst out in this prophetic mood:
   "Heavens bless my son, from Ireland let him reign
To far Barbadoes on the western main;   140
Of his dominion may no end be known,
And greater than his father's be his throne;
Beyond *Love's Kingdom* let him stretch his pen!"
He paused, and all the people cried, "Amen."
Then thus continued he: "My son, advance   145
Still in new impudence, new ignorance.
Success let others teach, learn thou from me
Pangs without birth, and fruitless industry.
Let *Virtuosos* in five years be writ;
Yet not one thought accuse thy toil of wit.   150
Let gentle George in triumph tread the stage,
Make Dorimant betray, and Loveit rage;
Let Cully, Cockwood, Fopling, charm the pit,
And in their folly show the writer's wit.
Yet still thy fools shall stand in thy defense,   155
And justify their author's want of sense.
Let 'em be all by thy own model made
Of dullness, and desire no foreign aid;
That they to future ages may be known,
Not copies drawn, but issue of thy own.   160
Nay, let thy men of wit too be the same,
All full of thee, and differing but in name.
But let no alien S—dl—y interpose,
To lard with wit thy hungry *Epsom* prose.

---

137 *the raging god:* Apollo, god of poetic inspiration.   151 *gentle
George:* Sir George Etherege (d. 1691), a witty Restoration playwright. The
characters named in the two lines below are his.   163 *S-dl-y:* Sir Charles
Sedley (1638–1701), courtier, playboy, poet, and playwright. Dryden suggests here that Sedley had a hand in Shadwell's *Epsom Wells* beyond the
straightforward contribution of its prologue.

And when false flowers of rhetoric thou wouldst cull,   165
Trust nature, do not labor to be dull;
But write thy best, and top; and, in each line,
Sir Formal's oratory will be thine:
Sir Formal, though unsought, attends thy quill,
And does thy northern dedications fill.   170
Nor let false friends seduce thy mind to fame,
By arrogating Jonson's hostile name.
Let father Flecknoe fire thy mind with praise,
And uncle Ogleby thy envy raise.
Thou art my blood, where Jonson has no part: 175
What share have we in nature, or in art?
Where did his wit on learning fix a brand,
And rail at arts he did not understand?
Where made he love in Prince Nicander's vein,
Or swept the dust in *Psyche's* humble strain?   180
Where sold he bargains, 'whip-stitch, kiss my arse,'
Promised a play and dwindled to a farce?
When did his Muse from Fletcher scenes purloin,
As thou whole Etherege dost transfuse to thine?
But so transfused, as oil on water's flow,   185
His always floats above, thine sinks below.
This is thy province, this thy wondrous way
New humors to invent for each new play:
This is that boasted bias of thy mind,
By which one way, to dullness, 'tis inclined;   190
Which makes thy writings lean on one side still,
And, in all changes, that way bends thy will.
Nor let thy mountain-belly make pretense
Of likeness; thine 's a tympany of sense.
A tun of man in thy large bulk is writ,   195
But sure thou art but a kilderkin of wit.

---

168 *Sir Formal:* Sir Formal Trifle, a character in *The Virtuoso* whose style is pompous and whose mind is empty.   170 *northern dedications:* a reference to Shadwell's frequent dedication of plays to the Duke of New-castle and his family.   179 *Prince Nicander:* a character in *Psyche.* 181 *Where sold he bargains . . . :* If one asks a simple question and receives an insulting answer, one has been "sold a bargain"; *whip stitch* in the answer means "quick."   194 *tympany:* a bodily swelling caused by gas. 195 *tun:* a very large wine cask.   196 *kilderkin:* a very small wine cask.

Like mine, thy gentle numbers feebly creep;
Thy tragic Muse gives smiles, thy comic sleep.
With whate'er gall thou settest thyself to write,
Thy inoffensive satires never bite.   200
In thy felonious heart though venom lies,
It does but touch thy Irish pen, and dies.
Thy genius calls thee not to purchase fame
In keen iambics, but mild anagram.
Leave writing plays, and choose for thy command   205
Some peaceful province in acrostic land.
There thou mayest wings display and altars raise,
And torture one poor word ten thousand ways.
Or, if thou wouldst thy different talents suit,
Set thy own songs, and sing them to thy lute."   210
    He said: but his last words were scarcely heard;
For Bruce and Longvil had a trap prepared,
And down they sent the yet declaiming bard.
Sinking he left his drugget robe behind,
Borne upwards by a subterranean wind.   215
The mantle fell to the young prophet's part,
With double portion of his father's art.

202 . . . *and dies:* there are no snakes in Ireland according to the tradition. Flecknoe was Irish as must be his son.   207 . . . *and altars raise:* a reference to the brief seventeenth-century vogue of shaping poems to appear as objects on the page, as in George Herbert's "Easter Wings" and "The Atlas." Dryden considered the practice to be tortured and trivial.   212 *Bruce and Longvil:* characters in *The Virtuoso* in which Sir Formal Trifle has a trap sprung beneath him as he is orating.   217 . . . *his father's art:* as the prophet Elijah ascended to heaven in a fiery chariot, his mantle fell on his successor, the young Elisha, together with a double portion of his spirit (2 Kings 2:9:15). Flecknoe, of course, goes down, not up.

WILLIAM BLAKE

[1757-1827]

William Blake was born in London, on November 28, 1757. Throughout his life he was both a dedicated poet and a gifted artist. His father, James Blake, was a hosier of limited means, but he recognized his son's early artistic ability and gave William every opportunity he could afford. At the age of ten the boy was sent to Henry Pars' drawing school in the Strand. When he was twelve, William was apprenticed to the engraver Basire, under whom the young man developed a deep attraction to Gothic style in sculpture and architecture. During this part of his life Blake also wrote poetry; these early writings were published privately in the volume POETICAL SKETCHES in 1783.

Following the end of his apprenticeship Blake earned his living by engraving for booksellers and publishers. In his work he was assisted by his wife Catherine (Boucher), whom he had married in 1783. During this time he also published many of his own works: SONGS OF INNOCENCE (1789), THE BOOK OF THEL (1789), THE MARRIAGE OF HEAVEN AND HELL (1793), SONGS OF EXPERIENCE (1794), URIZEN (1794), THE BOOK OF LOS (1795), THE BOOK OF AHANIA (1795), and THE SONG OF LOS (1795). The appearance of these volumes marked Blake's progression from simple lyrical poetry to writings dominated by a vigorous and imaginative mysticism. Blake illustrated these books himself, and it was while working with them that he developed a new method of copper etching.

Blake was never able to earn a living from his own works, which were too obscure to be appreciated by the public. Under the patronage of William Butts, however, he found sufficient work engraving for other writers. Meanwhile, he continued to express his strong spiritual and creative nature in visionary poems such as MILTON (1808) and JERUSALEM (1818). Many of his contemporaries regarded Blake's visionary style and his tendency to withdraw from society as signs of madness, but those who knew him have testified to the poet's sanity. *The last ten years of Blake's life were his happiest. He became a close friend of John Linnell, the landscape painter, and through him he was able to move more freely in London society. A group of young artists gathered around him. In 1826, Blake published his* ILLUSTRATIONS OF THE BOOK OF JOB. *He died on August 12, 1827, and was buried in an unmarked grave in Bunhill Fields Cemetery.*

Sir Geoffrey Keynes has edited Blake's works in WILLIAM BLAKE, COMPLETE WRITINGS *(1957). Three influential volumes of criticism are N. Frye,* FEARFUL SYMMETRY *(1947), Mark Schorer,* WILLIAM BLAKE: THE POLITICS OF VISION *(1946), and Robert F. Gleckner's study of the* SONGS OF INNOCENCE *and* SONGS OF EXPERIENCE *entitled* THE PIPER AND THE BARD *(1959).*

TO SPRING

O thou with dewy locks, who lookest down
Through the clear windows of the morning, turn
Thine angel eyes upon our western isle,
Which in full choir hails thy approach, O Spring!

The hills tell each other, and the listening   5
Valleys hear; all our longing eyes are turned
Up to thy bright pavillions: issue forth,
And let thy holy feet visit our clime.

Come o'er the eastern hills, and let our winds
Kiss thy perfumed garments; let us taste   10
Thy morn and evening breath; scatter thy pearls
Upon our love-sick land that mourns for thee.

O deck her forth with thy fair fingers; pour
Thy soft kisses on her bosom; and put
Thy golden crown upon her languished head,   15
Whose modest tresses were bound up for thee!

TO SUMMER

O thou, who passest through our valleys in
Thy strength, curb thy fierce steeds, allay the heat
That flames from their large nostrils! thou, O Summer,
Oft pitched'st here thy golden tent, and oft
Beneath our oaks hast slept, while we beheld   5
With joy thy ruddy limbs and flourishing hair.

Beneath our thickest shades we oft have heard
Thy voice, when noon upon his fervid car
Rode o'er the deep of heaven; beside our springs
Sit down, and in our mossy valleys, on   10
Some bank beside a river clear, throw thy
Silk draperies off, and rush into the stream:
Our valleys love the Summer in his pride.

Our bards are famed who strike the silver wire:
Our youth are bolder than the southern swains: 15
Our maidens fairer in the sprightly dance:
We lack not songs, nor instruments of joy,
Nor echoes sweet, nor waters clear as heaven,
Nor laurel wreaths against the sultry heat.

TO AUTUMN

O Autumn, laden with fruit, and stained
With the blood of the grape, pass not, but sit
Beneath my shady roof; there thou may'st rest,
And tune thy jolly voice to my fresh pipe;
And all the daughters of the year shall dance!   5
Sing now the lusty song of fruits and flowers.

"The narrow bud opens her beauties to
The sun, and love runs in her thrilling veins;
Blossoms hang round the brows of morning, and

127

Flourish down the bright cheek of modest eve,   10
Till clustering Summer breaks forth into singing,
And feathered clouds strew flowers round her head.

"The spirits of the air live on the smells
Of fruit; and joy, with pinions light, roves round
The gardens, or sits singing in the trees."   15
Thus sang the jolly Autumn as he sat;
Then rose, girded himself, and o'er the bleak
Hills fled from our sight; but left his golden load.

TO WINTER

O Winter! bar thine adamantine doors:
The north is thine; there hast thou built thy dark
Deep-founded habitation. Shake not thy roofs,
Nor bend thy pillars with thine iron car.

He hears me not, but o'er the yawning deep   5
Rides heavy; his storms are unchained, sheathed
In ribbed steel; I dare not lift mine eyes,
For he hath reared his sceptre o'er the world.

Lo! now the direful monster, whose skin clings
To his strong bones, strides o'er the groaning rocks: 10
He withers all in silence, and his hand
Unclothes the earth, and freezes up frail life.

He takes his seat upon the cliffs; the mariner
Cries in vain. Poor little wretch! that dealest
With storms, till heaven smiles, and the monster   15
Is driven yelling to his caves beneath mount Hecla.

16 *Hecla:* a peak in the Outer Hebrides, off the western coast of Scotland.

PIPING DOWN THE VALLEYS WILD

Piping down the valleys wild,
Piping songs of pleasant glee,
On a cloud I saw a child,
And he laughing said to me:

"Pipe a song about a Lamb!"   5
So I piped with merry cheer.
"Piper, pipe that song again;"
So I piped: he wept to hear.

"Drop thy pipe, thy happy pipe;
Sing thy songs of happy cheer:"   10
So I sung the same again,
While he wept with joy to hear.

"Piper, sit thee down and write
In a book that all may read."
So he vanished from my sight,   15
And I plucked a hollow reed,

And I made a rural pen,
And I stained the water clear,
And I wrote my happy songs
Every child may joy to hear.   20

THE LAMB

Little Lamb, who made thee?
  Dost thou know who made thee?
Gave thee life, & bid thee feed
By the stream & o'er the mead;
Gave thee clothing of delight,   5
Softest clothing, wooly, bright;
Gave thee such a tender voice,
Making all the vales rejoice?

Little Lamb, who made thee?
Dost thou know who made thee?   10

Little Lamb, I'll tell thee,
Little Lamb, I'll tell thee:
He is called by thy name,
For he calls himself a Lamb.
He is meek & he is mild;   15
He became a little child.
I a child & thou a lamb,
We are called by his name.
Little Lamb, God bless thee!
Little Lamb, God bless thee!   20

THE LITTLE BLACK BOY

My mother bore me in the southern wild,
And I am black, but O! my soul is white;
White as an angel is the English child,
But I am black as if bereaved of light.

My mother taught me underneath a tree,   5
And sitting down before the heat of day,
She took me on her lap and kissed me,
And pointing to the east, began to say:

"Look on the rising sun: there God does live,
And gives his light, and gives his heat away;   10
And flowers and trees and beasts and men receive
Comfort in morning, joy in the noonday.

"And we are put on earth a little space,
That we may learn to bear the beams of love;
And these black bodies and this sunburnt face   15
Is but a cloud, and like a shady grove.

"For when our souls have learned the heat to bear
The cloud will vanish; we shall hear his voice,
Saying: 'Come out from the grove, my love & care,
And round my golden tent like lambs rejoice.'"   20

Thus did my mother say, and kissed me;
And thus I say to little English boy:
When I from black and he from white cloud free,
And round the tent of God like lambs we joy:

I'll shade him from the heat till he can bear   25
To lean in joy upon our father's knee;
And then I'll stand and stroke his silver hair,
And be like him and he will then love me.

THE CHIMNEY SWEEPER

When my mother died I was very young,
And my father sold me while yet my tongue
Could scarcely cry " 'weep! 'weep! 'weep! 'weep!"
So your chimneys I sweep, & in soot I sleep.

There's little Tom Dacre, who cried when his head   5
That curled like a lamb's back, was shaved: so I said
"Hush, Tom! never mind it, for when your head's bare
You know that the soot cannot spoil your white hair."

And so he was quiet, & that very night,
As Tom was a-sleeping, he had such a sight!   10
That thousands of sweepers, Dick, Joe, Ned, & Jack,
Were all of them locked up in coffins of black.

And by came an Angel who had a bright key,
And he opened the coffins & set them all free;
Then down a green plain leaping, laughing, they run,   15
And wash in a river and shine in the sun.

Then naked & white, all their bags left behind,
They rise upon clouds and sport in the wind;
And the Angel told Tom, if he'd be a good boy,
He'd have God for his father & never want joy.   20

And so Tom awoke and we rose in the dark,
And got with our bags & our brushes to work.
Tho' the morning was cold, Tom was happy & warm;
So if all do their duty they need not fear harm.

THE DIVINE IMAGE

To Mercy, Pity, Peace, and Love
All pray in their distress;
And to these virtues of delight
Return their thankfulness.

For Mercy, Pity, Peace, and Love   5
Is God, our father dear,
And Mercy, Pity, Peace, and Love
Is Man, his child and care.

For Mercy has a human heart,
Pity a human face,   10
And Love, the human form divine,
And Peace, the human dress.

Then every man of every clime,
That prays in his distress,
Prays to the human form divine,   15
Love, Mercy, Pity, Peace.

And all must love the human form,
In heathen, turk, or jew;
Where Mercy, Love, & Pity dwell
There God is dwelling too.   20

'TWAS ON A HOLY THURSDAY

'Twas on a Holy Thursday, their innocent faces clean,
The children walking two & two in red & blue & green,
Grey-headed beadles walked before, with wands as white as snow,
Till into the high dome of Paul's they like Thames' waters flow.

O what a multitude they seemed, these flowers of London town!   5
Seated in companies they sit with radiance all their own.

The hum of multitudes was there, but multitudes of lambs,
Thousands of little boys & girls raising their innocent hands.

Now like a mighty wind they raise to heaven the voice of song,
Or like harmonious thunderings the seats of Heaven among.　10
Beneath them sit the aged men, wise guardians of the poor;
Then cherish pity, lest you drive an angel from your door.

IS THIS A HOLY THING TO SEE

Is this a holy thing to see
In a rich and fruitful land,
Babes reduced to misery,
Fed with cold and usurous hand?

Is that trembling cry a song?　　　　5
Can it be a song of joy?
And so many children poor?
It is a land of poverty!

And their sun does never shine,
And their fields are bleak & bare,　　10
And their ways are filled with thorns:
It is eternal winter there.

For where-e'er the sun does shine,
And where-e'er the rain does fall:
Babe can never hunger there,　　　15
Nor poverty the mind appall.

THE TIGER

Tiger! Tiger! burning bright,
In the forests of the night:
What immortal hand or eye
Could frame thy fearful symmetry?

In what distant deeps or skies   5
Burnt the fire of thine eyes?
On what wings dare he aspire?
What the hand dare seize the fire?

And what shoulder, & what art,
Could twist the sinews of thy heart?   10
And when thy heart began to beat,
What dread hand? & what dread feet?

What the hammer? what the chain?
In what furnace was thy brain?
What the anvil? what dread grasp,   15
Dare its deadly terrors clasp?

When the stars threw down their spears
And watered heaven with their tears:
Did he smile his work to see?
Did he who made the Lamb make thee?   20

Tiger! Tiger! burning bright,
In the forests of the night:
What immortal hand or eye,
Dare frame thy fearful symmetry?

AH! SUN-FLOWER

Ah, sun-flower! weary of time,
Who countest the steps of the sun,
Seeking after that sweet golden clime
Where the traveller's journey is done:

Where the youth pined away with desire,   5
And the pale virgin shrouded in snow
Arise from their graves, and aspire
Where my sun-flower wishes to go.

THE GARDEN OF LOVE

I went to the Garden of Love,
And saw what I never had seen:
A chapel was built in the midst,
Where I used to play on the green.

And the gates of this chapel were shut,   5
And "Thou shalt not" writ over the door;
So I turned to the Garden of Love
That so many sweet flowers bore;

And I saw it was filled with graves,
And tomb-stones where flowers should be;   10
And priests in black gowns were walking their rounds,
And binding with briars my joys & desires.

LONDON

I wander thro' each chartered street,
Near where the chartered Thames does flow,
And mark in every face I meet
Marks of weakness, marks of woe.

In every cry of every man,   5
In every infant's cry of fear,
In every voice, in every ban,
The mind-forged manacles I hear.

How the chimney-sweeper's cry
Every black'ning church appalls;   10
And the hapless soldier's sigh
Runs in blood down palace walls.

1 *chartered:* incorporated, under civil law and order; also, restricted, narrow, confined.

But most through midnight streets I hear
How the youthful harlot's curse
Blasts the new born infant's tear,   15
And blights with plagues the marriage hearse.

THE HUMAN ABSTRACT

Pity would be no more
If we did not make somebody poor,
And mercy no more could be
If all were as happy as we.

And mutual fear brings peace,   5
Till the selfish loves increase:
Then cruelty knits a snare,
And spreads his baits with care.

He sits down with holy fears,
And waters the ground with tears;   10
Then humility takes its root
Underneath his foot.

Soon spreads the dismal shade
Of mystery over his head;
And the caterpiller and fly   15
Feed on the mystery.

And it bears the fruit of deceit,
Ruddy and sweet to eat;
And the raven his nest has made
In its thickest shade.   20

The gods of the earth and sea
Sought through nature to find this tree;
But their search was all in vain:
There grows one in the human brain.

A POISON TREE

I was angry with my friend:
I told my wrath, my wrath did end.
I was angry with my foe:
I told it not, my wrath did grow.

And I watered it in fears,   5
Night & morning with my tears;
And I sunned it with smiles,
And with soft deceitful wiles.

And it grew both day and night,
Till it bore an apple bright;   10
And my foe beheld it shine,
And he knew that it was mine,

And into my garden stole
When the night had veiled the pole;
In the morning glad I see   15
My foe outstretched beneath the tree.

NEVER PAIN TO TELL THY LOVE

Never pain to tell thy love
Love that never told can be;
For the gentle wind does move
Silently, invisibly.

I told my love, I told my love,   5
I told her all my heart;
Trembling, cold, in ghastly fears—
Ah, she doth depart.

Soon as she was gone from me
A traveller came by   10
Silently, invisibly—
He took her with a sigh.

137

MOCK ON, MOCK ON

Mock on, mock on Voltaire, Rousseau.
Mock on, mock on: 'tis all in vain!
You throw the sand against the wind,
And the wind blows it back again.

And every sand becomes a gem   5
Reflected in the beams divine.
Blown back they blind the mocking eye,
But still in Israel's paths they shine.

The atoms of Democritus
And Newton's particles of light   10
Are sands upon the Red sea shore
Where Israel's tents do shine so bright.

AUGURIES OF INNOCENCE

To see a world in a grain of sand
And a heaven in a wild flower
Hold infinity in the palm of your hand
And eternity in an hour.

A robin red breast in a cage   5
Puts all heaven in a rage.
A dove house filled with doves & pigeons
Shudders hell thro' all its regions.
A dog starved at his master's gate
Predicts the ruin of the state.   10
A horse misused upon the road
Calls to heaven for human blood.
Each outcry of the hunted hare
A fibre from the brain does tear.
A skylark wounded in the wing   15
A cherubim does cease to sing.
The game cock clipped & armed for fight

Does the rising sun affright.
Every wolf's & lion's howl
Raises from hell a human soul. 20
The wild deer wandering here & there
Keeps the human soul from care.
The lamb misused breeds public strife
And yet forgives the butcher's knife.
The bat that flits at close of eve 25
Has left the brain that won't believe.
The owl that calls upon the night
Speaks the unbeliever's fright.
He who shall hurt the little wren
Shall never be beloved by men. 30
He who the ox to wrath has moved
Shall never be by woman loved.
The wanton boy that kills the fly
Shall feel the spider's enmity.
He who torments the chafer's sprite 35
Weaves a bower in endless night.
The caterpiller on the leaf
Repeats to thee thy mother's grief.
Kill not the moth nor butterfly
For the Last Judgment draweth nigh. 40
He who shall train the horse to war
Shall never pass the polar bar.
The beggar's dog & widow's cat,
Feed them & thou wilt grow fat.
The gnat that sings his summer's song 45
Poison gets from slander's tongue.
The poison of the snake & newt
Is the sweat of envy's foot.
The poison of the honey bee
Is the artist's jealousy. 50
The prince's robes & beggar's rags
Are toadstools on the miser's bags.
A truth that's told with bad intent
Beats all the lies you can invent.
It is right it should be so; 55

35 *chafer:* a beetle.

Man was made for joy & woe;
And when this we rightly know
Thro' the world we safely go.
Joy & woe are woven fine,
A clothing for the Soul divine;   60
Under every grief & pine
Runs a joy with silken twine.
The babe is more than swaddling bands,
Throughout all these human lands
Tools were made, & born were hands,   65
Every farmer understands.
Every tear from every eye
Becomes a babe in eternity;
This is caught by females bright
And returned to its own delight.   70
The bleat, the bark, bellow & roar
Are waves that beat on heaven's shore.
The babe that weeps the rod beneath
Writes revenge in realms of death.
The beggar's rags fluttering in air   75
Does to rags the heavens tear.
The soldier armed with sword & gun
Palsied strikes the summer's sun.
The poor man's farthing is worth more
Than all the gold on Afric's shore.   80
One mite wrung from the laborer's hands
Shall buy & sell the miser's lands:
Or if protected from on high,
Does that whole nation sell & buy.
He who mocks the infant's faith   85
Shall be mocked in age & death.
He who shall teach the child to doubt
The rotting grave shall ne'er get out.
He who respects the infant's faith
Triumphs over hell & death.   90
The child's toys & the old man's reasons
Are the fruits of the two seasons.
The questioner, who sits so sly,
Shall never know how to reply.
He who replies to words of doubt   95

Doth put the light of knowledge out.
The strongest poison ever known
Came from Caesar's laurel crown.
Nought can deform the human race
Like to the armor's iron brace.   100
When gold & gems adorn the plow
To peaceful arts shall envy bow.
A riddle or the cricket's cry
Is to doubt a fit reply.
The emmet's inch & eagle's mile   105
Make lame philosophy to smile.
He who doubts from what he sees
Will ne'er believe, do what you please.
If the sun & moon should doubt,
They'd immediately go out.   110
To be in a passion you good may do,
But no good if a passion is in you.
The whore & gambler by the state
Licensed build that nation's fate.
The harlot's cry from street to street   115
Shall weave old England's winding sheet.
The winner's shout, the loser's curse,
Dance before dead England's hearse.
Every night & every morn
Some to misery are born.   120
Every morn & every night
Some are born to sweet delight.
Some are born to sweet delight,
Some are born to endless night.
We are led to believe a lie   125
When we see not through the eye
Which was born in a night to perish in a night
When the soul slept in beams of light.
God appears & God is light
To those poor Souls who dwell in night,   130
But does a human form display
To those who dwell in realms of day.

105 *The emmet's:* an ant.

GEORGE GORDON, LORD BYRON

[1788–1824]

Captain John Byron was in France in January of 1788 when his son, George, was born in London; he died three years later, and the boy was then reared by his Scottish mother and a nurse. George was a beautiful child, save for a club foot, a deformity to which he was extremely sensitive all his life. He was sent to Aberdeen grammar school, and later attended Harrow. When he was ten, he inherited the title and estates of his great-uncle, Lord Byron. In 1805 he went to Trinity College, Cambridge, where he led a dissolute life. During his second year at Cambridge his early poems were published privately as FUGITIVE PIECES, *and in 1807 he published* HOURS OF IDLENESS. *Unfavorable criticism of this latter book in the* EDINBURGH REVIEW *brought a counterattack in Byron's first important work,* ENGLISH BARDS AND SCOTCH REVIEWERS *(1809).*

In 1809 Byron left England to travel in Greece with his Trinity friend, John Cam Hobhouse. His experiences abroad are related in CHILDE HAROLD'S PILGRIMAGE, *two cantos of which were published in 1812, making him instantly famous. Upon his return to England, Byron wrote the Oriental tales* THE BRIDE OF ABYDOS *(1813),* THE CORSAIR, *and* LARA *(1814). In 1815 he married Anne Isabella, daughter of Sir Ralph and Lady Judith Milbanke. The marriage lasted only one year: Lady Byron left her husband with the charge that he had an incestuous relationship with his half sister, Augusta Leigh. Byron left again for Europe, never to return to England.*

The poet spent eight or nine months with Shelley in Geneva, then went on to Italy. During 1819 he wrote the first two cantos of DON JUAN *and met the Countess Teresa Guiccioli. He fell passionately in love with her and became her cavalier with the permission of her elderly husband, a common arrangement in the noble Italian society of the time. He became involved with Teresa's family, the Gambas, in a revolutionary society, the* Carbonari, *which sought to free northern Italy from Austrian control and for the rest of his life Byron traveled with Teresa as she and her family sought asylum from political enemies. In Ravenna in 1821 he wrote* THE PROPHECY OF DANTE, *cantos three, four, and five of* DON JUAN, *the closet tragedies* MARINO FALIERO, SARDANAPALUS, THE TWO FOSCARI, CAIN, *and the verse satire* THE VISION OF JUDGMENT. *In Pisa, Leigh Hunt persuaded Shelley and Byron to help him in the publication of* THE LIBERAL, *a periodical which produced only four numbers. In 1823, Byron left to help the Greeks in their war for independence against the Turks. He died of fever in Greece in April 1824.*

The standard edition of Lord Byron's letters and journals was published in six volumes by R. E. Prothero (1898–1901). His poetry was edited in seven volumes by E. H. Coleridge (1898–1904). Leslie A. Marchand has written BYRON, A BIOGRAPHY *(3 vols., 1957), and Doris Langley Moore has recorded and evaluated Byron's posthumous reputation and its bases in* THE LATE LORD BYRON *(1961). Among the critical works published on the poet are: Elizabeth F. Boyd's* BYRON'S DON JUAN, A CRITICAL STUDY *(1945), Ernest J. Lovell, Jr.'s* BYRON, THE RECORD OF A QUEST *(1950), and Paul West's* BYRON AND THE SPOILER'S ART *(1960).*

WHEN WE TWO PARTED

When we two parted
  In silence and tears,
Half broken-hearted
  To sever for years,
Pale grew thy cheek and cold,   5
  Colder thy kiss;
Truly that hour foretold
  Sorrow to this.

The dew of the morning
  Sunk chill on my brow—   10
It felt like the warning
  Of what I feel now.
Thy vows are all broken,
  And light is thy fame:
I hear thy name spoken,   15
  And share in its shame.

14 *fame:* reputation.

They name thee before me,
  A knell to mine ear;
A shudder comes o'er me—
  Why wert thou so dear?   20
They know not I knew thee,
  Who knew thee too well:
Long, long shall I rue thee,
  Too deeply to tell.

In secret we met—   25
  In silence I grieve,
That thy heart could forget,
  Thy spirit deceive.
If I should meet thee
  After long years,   30
How should I greet thee?
  With silence and tears.

SHE WALKS IN BEAUTY

1

She walks in beauty, like the night
  Of cloudless climes and starry skies;
And all that's best of dark and bright
  Meet in her aspect and her eyes:
Thus mellowed to that tender light   5
  Which heaven to gaudy day denies.

2

One shade the more, one ray the less,
  Had half impaired the nameless grace
Which waves in every raven tress,
  Or softly lightens o'er face;   10
Where thoughts serenely sweet express
  How pure, how dear their dwelling-place.

3

And on that cheek, and o'er that brow,
  So soft, so calm, yet eloquent,

The smiles that win, the tints that glow, 15
But tell of days in goodness spent,
A mind at peace with all below,
A heart whose love is innocent!

THE DESTRUCTION OF SENNACHERIB

1

The Assyrian came down like the wolf on the fold,
And his cohorts were gleaming in purple and gold;
And the sheen of their spears was like stars on the sea,
When the blue wave rolls nightly on deep Galilee.

2

Like the leaves of the forest when Summer is green, 5
That host with their banners at sunset were seen:
Like the leaves of the forest when Autumn hath blown,
That host on the morrow lay withered and strown.

3

For the Angel of Death spread his wings on the blast,
And breathed in the face of the foe as he passed; 10
And the eyes of the sleepers waxed deadly and chill,
And their hearts but once heaved, and for ever grew still!

4

And there lay the steed with his nostril all wide,
But through it there rolled not the breath of his pride;
And the foam of his gasping lay white on the turf, 15
And cold as the spray of the rock-bearing surf.

5

And there lay the rider distorted and pale,
With the dew on his brow, and the rust on his mail:
And the tents were all silent, the banners alone,
The lances unlifted, the trumpet unblown. 20

6

And the widows of Ashur are loud in their wail,
And the idols are broke in the temple of Baal;

And the might of the Gentile, unsmote by the sword,
Hath melted like snow in the glance of the Lord!

STANZAS FOR MUSIC:
THERE BE NONE OF BEAUTY'S DAUGHTERS

There be none of Beauty's daughters
  With a magic like thee;
And like music on the waters
  Is thy sweet voice to me:
When, as if its sound were causing   5
The charmed ocean's pausing,
The waves lie still and gleaming
And the lulled winds seem dreaming:

And the midnight moon is weaving
  Her bright chain o'er the deep;   10
Whose breast is gently heaving,
  As an infant's asleep:
So the spirit bows before thee,
To listen and adore thee;   15
With a full but soft emotion,
Like the swell of Summer's ocean.

DARKNESS

I had a dream, which was not all a dream.
The bright sun was extinguished, and the stars
Did wander darkling in the eternal space,
Rayless, and pathless, and the icy earth
Swung blind and blackening in the moonless air;   5
Morn came and went—and came, and brought no day,
And men forgot their passions in the dread
Of this their desolation; and all hearts
Were chilled into a selfish prayer for light:
And they did live by watchfires—and the thrones,   10
The palaces of crowned kings—the huts,
The habitations of all things which dwell,
Were burnt for beacons; cities were consumed,

And men were gather'd round their blazing homes
To look once more into each other's face; 15
Happy were those who dwelt within the eye
Of the volcanos, and their mountain-torch:
A fearful hope was all the world contained;
Forests were set on fire—but hour by hour
They fell and faded—and the crackling trunks 20
Extinguished with a crash—and all was black.
The brows of men by the despairing light
Wore an unearthly aspect, as by fits
The flashes fell upon them; some lay down
And hid their eyes and wept; and some did rest 25
Their chins upon their clenched hands, and smiled;
And others hurried to and fro, and fed
Their funeral piles with fuel, and looked up
With mad disquietude on the dull sky,
The pall of a past world; and then again 30
With curses cast down upon the dust,
And gnashed their teeth and howled: the wild birds shrieked
And, terrified, did flutter on the ground,
And flap their useless wings; the wildest brutes
Came tame and tremulous; and vipers crawled 35
And twined themselves among the multitude,
Hissing, but stingless—they were slain for food.
And War, which for a moment was no more,
Did glut himself again:—a meal was bought
With blood, and each sat sullenly apart 40
Gorging himself in gloom: no love was left;
All earth was but one thought—and that was death
Immediate and inglorious; and the pang
Of famine fed upon all entrails—men
Died, and their bones were tombless as their flesh; 45
The meagre by the meagre were devoured,
Even dogs assailed their masters, all save one,
And he was faithful to a corse, and kept
The birds and beasts and famished men at bay,
Till hunger clung them, or the dropping dead 50
Lured their lank jaws; himself sought out no food,
But with a piteous and perpetual moan,
And a quick desolate cry, licking the hand

Which answered not with a caress—he died.
The crowd was famished by degrees; but two   55
Of an enormous city did survive,
And they were enemies: they met beside
The dying embers of an altar-place
Where had been heaped a mass of holy things
For an unholy usage; they raked up,   60
And shivering scraped with their cold skeleton hands
The feeble ashes, and their feeble breath
Blew for a little life, and made a flame
Which was a mockery; then they lifted up
Their eyes as it grew lighter, and beheld   65
Each other's aspects—saw, and shrieked, and died—
Even of their mutual hideousness they died,
Unknowing who he was upon whose brow
Famine had written Fiend. The world was void,
The populous and the powerful was a lump,   70
Seasonless, herbless, treeless, manless, lifeless,
A lump of death—a chaos of hard clay.
The rivers, lakes, and ocean all stood still,
And nothing stirred within their silent depths;
Ships sailorless lay rotting on the sea,   75
And their masts fell down piecemeal: as they dropped
They slept on the abyss without a surge—
The waves were dead; the tides were in their grave,
The moon, their mistress, had expired before;
The winds were withered in the stagnant air,   80
And the clouds perished; Darkness had no need
Of aid from them—She was the Universe.

"I HAVE NOT LOVED THE WORLD"

I have not loved the world, nor the world me;
I have not flattered its rank breath, nor bowed
To its idolatries a patient knee,
Nor coined my cheek to smiles, nor cried aloud
In worship of an echo; in the crowd   5
They could not deem me one of such; I stood

Among them, but not of them; in a shroud
Of thoughts which were not their thoughts, and still could,
Had I not filed my mind, which thus itself subdued.

I have not loved the world, nor the world me,— 10
But let us part fair foes; I do believe,
Though I have found them not, that there may be
Words which are things, hopes which will not deceive,
And virtues which are merciful, nor weave
Snares for the failing; I would also deem 15
O'er others' griefs that some sincerely grieve;
That two, or one, are almost what they seem,
That goodness is no name, and happiness no dream.

FROM *Childe Harold's Pilgrimage* (Canto 3, stanzas 113, 114)

DON JUAN AND HAIDÉE

Return we to Don Juan. He begun
    To hear new words, and to repeat them; but
Some feelings, universal as the sun,
    Were such as could not in his breast be shut
More than within the bosom of a nun: 5
    He was in love,—as you would be, no doubt,
With a young benefactress,—so was she,
Just in the way we very often see.

And every day by daybreak—rather early
    For Juan, who was somewhat fond of rest— 10
She came into the cave, but it was merely
    To see her bird reposing in his nest;
And she would softly stir his locks so curly,
    Without disturbing her yet slumbering guest,
Breathing all gently o'er his cheek and mouth, 15
As o'er a bed of roses the sweet south.

And every morn his colour freshlier came,
    And every day helped on his convalescence;
'Twas well, because health in the human frame
    Is pleasant, besides being true love's essence, 20

For health and idleness to passion's flame
   Are oil and gunpowder; and some good lessons
Are also learnt from Ceres and from Bacchus,
Without whom Venus will not long attack us.

While Venus fills the heart (without heart really   25
   Love, though good always, is not quite so good),
Ceres presents a plate of vermicelli,—
   For love must be sustain'd like flesh and blood,
While Bacchus pours out wine, or hands a jelly:
   Eggs, oysters, too, are amatory food;   30
But who is their purveyor from above
Heaven knows,—it may be Neptune, Pan, or Jove.

When Juan woke he found some good things ready,
   A bath, a breakfast, and the finest eyes
That ever made a youthful heart less steady,   35
   Besides her maid's, as pretty for their size;
But I have spoken of all this already—
   And repetition's tiresome and unwise,—
Well—Juan, after bathing in the sea,
Came always back to coffee and Haidée.   40

Both were so young, and one so innocent,
   That bathing passed for nothing: Juan seemed
To her, as 'twere, the kind of being sent,
   Of whom these two years she had nightly dreamed,
A something to be loved, a creature meant   45
   To be her happiness, and whom she deemed
To render happy: all who joy would win
Must share it,—Happiness was born a twin.

It was such pleasure to behold him, such
   Enlargement of existence to partake   50
Nature with him, to thrill beneath his touch,
   To watch him slumbering, and to see him wake;
To live with him for ever were too much;
   But then the thought of parting made her quake:

---

23 . . . *from Bacchus:* the goddess of grain and the god of wine respectively.

He was her own, her ocean-treasure, cast   55
Like a rich wreck—her first love, and her last.

And thus a moon rolled on, and fair Haidée
   Paid daily visits to her boy, and took
Such plentiful precautions, that still he
   Remained unknown within his craggy nook;   60
At last her father's prows put out to sea,
   For certain merchantmen upon the look,
Not as of yore to carry off an Io,
But three Ragusan vessels bound for Scio.

Then came her freedom, for she had no mother,   65
   So that, her father being at sea, she was
Free as a married woman, or such other
   Female, as where she likes may freely pass,
Without even the encumbrance of a brother,
   The freest she that ever gazed on glass: 70
I speak of Christian lands in this comparison,
Where wives, at least, are seldom kept in garrison.

Now she prolonged her visits and her talk
   (For they must talk), and he had learnt to say
So much as to propose to take a walk,—   75
   For little had he wandered since the day
On which, like a young flower snapped from the stalk,
   Drooping and dewy on the beach he lay,—
And thus they walked out in the afternoon,
And saw the sun set opposite the moon.   80

It was a wild and breaker-beaten coast,
   With cliffs above, and a broad sandy shore,
Guarded by shoals and rocks as by an host,
   With here and there a creek, whose aspect wore
A better welcome to the tempest-tost;   85
   And rarely ceased the haughty billow's roar,

63 . . . an Io: the beautiful daughter of the river god Inachus. Zeus turned
her into a white heifer and pursued her; after many wanderings she was
captured by Phoenician merchants and part-time cattle thieves. As the next
line indicates, Haidée's father was not a cattle thief but a pirate.

Save on the dead long summer days, which make
The outstretched ocean glitter like a lake.

And the small ripple spilt upon the beach
   Scarcely o'erpassed the cream of your champagne, 90
When o'er the brim the sparkling bumpers reach,
   That spring-dew of the spirit! the heart's rain!
Few things surpass old wine; and they may preach
   Who please,—the more because they preach in vain,—
Let us have wine and women, mirth and laughter, 95
Sermons and soda-water the day after.

Man, being reasonable, must get drunk;
   The best of life is but intoxication:
Glory, the grape, love, gold, in these are sunk
   The hopes of all men, and of every nation; 100
Without their sap, how branchless were the trunk
   Of life's strange tree, so fruitful on occasion!
But to return,—Get very drunk; and when
You wake with headache, you shall see what then.

Ring for your valet—bid him quickly bring 105
   Some hock and soda-water, then you'll know
A pleasure worthy Xerxes the great king;
   For not the blessed sherbet, sublimed with snow,
Nor the first sparkle of the desert spring,
   Nor Burgundy in all its sunset glow, 110
After long travel, ennui, love, or slaughter,
Vie with that draught of hock and soda-water.

The coast—I think it was the coast that I
   Was just describing—Yes, it *was* the coast—
Lay at this period quiet as the sky, 115
   The sands untumbled, the blue waves untossed,
And all was stillness, save the sea-bird's cry,
   And dolphin's leap, and little billow crossed
By some low rock or shelf that made it fret
Against the boundary it scarcely wet. 120

---

91 *sparkling bumpers:* overflowing glasses or cups. 106 *hock:* white
Rhine wine. 107 *Xerxes:* King of Persia (ca. 486–465 B.C.).

And forth they wandered, her sire being gone,
  As I have said, upon an expedition;
And mother, brother, guardian, she had none,
  Save Zoe, who, although with due precision
She waited on her lady with the sun,   125
  Thought daily service was her only mission,
Bringing warm water, wreathing her long tresses,
And asking now and then for cast-off dresses.

It was the cooling hour, just when the rounded
  Red sun sinks down behind the azure hill,   130
Which then seems as if the whole earth it bounded,
  Circling all nature, hushed, and dim, and still,
With the far mountain-crescent half surrounded
  On one side, and the deep sea calm and chill,
Upon the other, and the rosy sky,   135
With one star sparkling through it like an eye.

And thus they wandered forth, and hand in hand,
  Over the shining pebbles and the shells,
Glided along the smooth and hardened sand,
  And in the worn and wild receptacles   140
Worked by the storms, yet worked as it were planned,
  In hollow halls, with sparry roofs and cells,
They turned to rest; and, each clasped by an arm,
Yielded to the deep twilight's purple charm.

They looked up to the sky, whose floating glow   145
  Spread like a rosy ocean, vast and bright;
They gazed upon the glittering sea below,
  Whence the broad moon rose circling into sight;
They heard the waves splash, and the wind so low,
  And saw each other's dark eyes darting light   150
Into each other—and, beholding this,
Their lips drew near, and clung into a kiss;

A long, long kiss, a kiss of youth, and love,
  And beauty, all concentrating like rays
Into one focus, kindled from above;   155
  Such kisses as belong to early days,
Where heart, and soul, and sense, in concert move,

And the blood's lava, and the pulse a blaze,
Each kiss a heart-quake,—for a kiss's strength,
I think it must be reckoned by its length.   160

By length I mean duration; theirs endured
    Heaven knows how long—no doubt they never reckoned;
And if they had, they could not have secured
    The sum of their sensations to a second:
They had not spoken; but they felt allured,   165
    As if their souls and lips each other beckoned,
Which, being joined, like swarming bees they clung—
Their hearts the flowers from whence the honey sprung.

They were alone, but not alone as they
    Who shut in chambers think it loneliness;   170
The silent ocean, and the starlight bay,
    The twilight glow, which momently grew less,
The voiceless sands, and dropping caves, that lay
    Around them, made them to each other press,
As if there were no life beneath the sky   175
Save theirs, and that their life could never die.

They feared no eyes nor ears on that lone beach,
    They felt no terrors from the night; they were
All in all to each other; though their speech
    Was broken words, they *thought* a language there,—   180
And all the burning tongues the passions teach
    Found in one sigh the best interpreter
Of nature's oracle—first love,—that all
Which Eve has left her daughters since her fall.

Haidée spoke not of scruples, asked no vows,   185
    Nor offered any; she had never heard
Of plight and promises to be a spouse,
    Or perils by a loving maid incurred;
She was all which pure ignorance allows,
    And flew to her young mate like a young bird,   190
And never having dreamt of falsehood, she
Had not one word to say of constancy.

She loved, and was beloved—she adored,
    And she was worshipped; after nature's fashion.

Their intense souls, into each other poured,   195
 If souls could die, had perished in that passion,—
But by degrees their senses were restored,
 Again to be o'ercome, again to dash on;
And, beating 'gainst *his* bosom, Haidée's heart
Felt as if never more to beat apart.   200

Alas! they were so young, so beautiful,
 So lonely, loving, helpless, and the hour
Was that in which the heart is always full,
 And, having o'er itself no further power,
Prompts deeds eternity cannot annul,   205
 But pays off moments in an endless shower
Of hell-fire—all prepared for people giving
Pleasure or pain to one another living.

Alas! for Juan and Haidée! they were
 So loving and so lovely—till then never,   210
Excepting our first parents, such a pair
 Had run the risk of being damned for ever;
And Haidée, being devout as well as fair,
 Had, doubtless, heard about the Stygian river,
And hell and purgatory—but forgot   215
Just in the very crisis she should not.

They look upon each other, and their eyes
 Gleam in the moonlight; and her white arm clasps
Round Juan's head, and his around her lies
 Half buried in the tresses which it grasps: 220
She sits upon his knee, and drinks his sighs,
 He hers, until they end in broken gasps;
And thus they form a group that's quite antique,
Half naked, loving, natural, and Greek.

And when those deep and burning moments passed,   225
 And Juan sunk to sleep within her arms,
She slept not, but all tenderly, though fast,
 Sustained his head upon her bosom's charms;
And now and then her eye to heaven is cast,

214 *the Stygian river:* the Styx, the underground river which separates
the underworld from the land of the living.

And then on the pale cheek her breast now warms,   230
Pillowed on her o'erflowing heart, which pants
With all it granted, and with all it grants.

An infant when it gazes on a light,
   A child the moment when it drains the breast,
A devotee when soars the Host in sight,   235
   An Arab with a stranger for a guest,
A sailor when the prize has struck in fight,
   A miser filling his most hoarded chest,
Feel rapture; but not such true joy are reaping
As they who watch o'er what they love while sleeping.   240

For there it lies so tranquil, so beloved,
   All that it hath of life with us is living;
So gentle, stirless, helpless, and unmoved,
   And all unconscious of the joy 'tis giving;
All it hath felt, inflicted, passed, and proved,   245
   Hushed into depths beyond the watcher's diving;
There lies the thing we love with all its errors
And all its charms, like death without its terrors.

The lady watched her lover—and that hour
   Of Love's, and Night's, and Ocean's solitude,   250
O'erflowed her soul with their united power;
   Amidst the barren sand and rocks so rude
She and her wave-worn love had made their bower,
   Where nought upon their passion could intrude,
And all the stars that crowded the blue space   255
Saw nothing happier than her glowing face.

Alas! the love of women! it is known
   To be a lovely and a fearful thing;
For all of theirs upon that die is thrown,
   And if 'tis lost, life hath no more to bring   260
To them but mockeries of the past alone,
   And their revenge is as the tiger's spring,
Deadly, and quick, and crushing; yet, as real
Torture is theirs, what they inflict they feel.

They are right; for man, to man so oft unjust,   265
   Is always so to women; one sole bond

Awaits them, treachery is all their trust;
    Taught to conceal, their bursting hearts despond
Over their idol, till some wealthier lust
    Buys them in marriage—and what rests beyond?   270
A thankless husband, next a faithless lover,
Then dressing, nursing, praying, and all's over.

Some take a lover, some take drams or prayers,
    Some mind their household, others dissipation,
Some run away, and but exchange their cares,   275
    Losing the advantage of a virtuous station;
Few changes e'er can better their affairs,
    Theirs being an unnatural situation,
From the dull palace to the dirty hovel:
Some play the devil, and then write a novel.   280

Haidée was Nature's bride, and knew not this:
    Haidée was Passion's child, born where the sun
Showers triple light, and scorches even the kiss
    Of his gazelle-eyed daughters; she was one
Made but to love, to feel that she was his   285
    Who was her chosen: what was said or done
Elsewhere was nothing. She had nought to fear,
Hope, care, nor love beyond,—her heart beat *here*.

And oh! that quickening of the heart, that beat!
    How much it costs us! yet each rising throb   290
Is in its cause as its effect so sweet,
    That Wisdom, ever on the watch to rob
Joy of its alchemy, and to repeat
    Fine truths; even Conscience, too, has a tough job
To make us understand each good old maxim,   295
So good—I wonder Castlereagh don't tax 'em.

And now 'twas done—on the lone shore were plighted
    Their hearts; the stars, their nuptial torches, shed
Beauty upon the beautiful they lighted:
    Ocean their witness, and the cave their bed,   300
By their own feelings hallowed and united,

296 *Castlereagh:* Viscount Castlereagh, a British minister of state, Foreign Secretary from 1812 to 1822.

Their priest was Solitude, and they were wed:
And they were happy, for to their young eyes
Each was an angel, and earth paradise.

FROM *Don Juan* (Canto 2, stanzas 167–204)

THE ISLES OF GREECE

I

The isles of Greece, the isles of Greece!
  Where burning Sappho loved and sung,
Where grew the arts of war and peace,
  Where Delos rose, and Phoebus sprung!
Eternal summer gilds them yet,   5
But all, except their sun, is set.

II

The Scian and the Teian muse,
  The hero's harp, the lover's lute,
Have found the fame your shores refuse:
  Their place of birth alone is mute   10
To sounds which echo further west
Than your sires' "Islands of the Blessed."

III

The mountains look on Marathon—
  And Marathon looks on the sea;
And musing there an hour alone,   15
  I dreamed that Greece might still be free;
For standing on the Persians' grave,
I could not deem myself a slave.

---

2 *Sappho:* Greek lyric poetess.   4 . . . *Delos* . . . *Phoebus* . . . : an island off the east coast of Greece and the god of poetry and the other arts, respectively.   7 . . . *muse:* Homer was reputed to have been from the island of Scio, and Amacreon, a lyric poet of the fifth century B.C. was from Teos, in Asia Minor.   "12 . . . *Blessed":* legendary eternal dwelling place of mortals most favored by the gods.   13 *Marathon:* a plain near Athens, site of Greek army victory over Persians in 490 B.C.

IV

A king sat on the rocky brow
   Which looks o'er sea-born Salamis;   20
And ships, by thousands, lay below,
   And men in nations;—all were his!
He counted them at break of day—
And when the sun set where were they?

V

And where are they? and where art thou,   25
   My country? On thy voiceless shore
The heroic lay is tuneless now—
   The heroic bosom beats no more!
And must thy lyre, so long divine,
Degenerate into hands like mine?   30

VI

'Tis something, in the dearth of fame,
   Though linked among a fettered race,
To feel at least a patriot's shame,
   Even as I sing, suffuse my face;
For what is left the poet here?   35
For Greeks a blush—for Greece a tear.

VII

Must *we* but weep o'er days more blest?
   Must *we* but blush?—Our fathers bled.
Earth! render back from out thy breast
   A remnant of our Spartan dead!   40
Of the three hundred grant but three,
To make a new Thermopylae!

VIII

What, silent still? and silent all?
   Ah! no;—the voices of the dead
Sound like a distant torrent's fall,   45

19 *king:* Xerxes, king of Persia (ca. 486–465 B.C.).   20 *Salamis:* an island near Athens, site of Greek naval victory over Persians in 450 B.C. 42 *Thermopylae:* a pass in northern Greece, site of battle between 300 Spartans and the Persian army in 480 B.C.

And answer, "Let one living head,
But one arise,—we come, we come!"
'Tis but the living who are dumb.

IX

In vain—in vain: strike other chords;
   Fill high the cup with Samian wine!   50
Leave battles to the Turkish hordes,
   And shed the blood of Scio's vine!
Hark! rising to the ignoble call—
How answers each bold Bacchanal!

X

You have the Pyrrhic dance as yet;   55
   Where is the Pyrrhic phalanx gone?
Of two such lessons, why forget
   The nobler and the manlier one?
You have the letters Cadmus gave—
Think ye he meant them for a slave?   60

XI

Fill high the bowl with Samian wine.
   We will not think of themes like these!
It made Anacreon's song divine:
   He served—but served Polycrates—
A tyrant; but our masters then   65
Were still, at least, our countrymen.

XII

The tyrant of the Chersonese
   Was freedom's best and bravest friend;
That tyrant was Miltiades!
   Oh! that the present hour would lend   70

50 *Samian:* from Samos, an island in the Aegean Sea.   55 *Pyrrhic dance:* a Greek war dance.   56 *Pyrrhic phalanx:* a military formation developed by the general, Pyrrhus, in the third century B.C.   59 . . . *Cadmus:* legendary founder of the Greek city of Thebes. He was credited with introducing the sixteen letters from the Phoenician alphabet into the Greek.   64 *Polycrates:* ruler of Samos (535–522? B.C.).   67 *Chersonese:* a peninsula; modern Gallipoli.   69 *Miltiades:* Athenian general in the fifth century B.C.

Another despot of the kind!
Such chains as his were sure to bind.

XIII

Fill high the bowl with Samian wine!
   On Suli's rock, and Parga's shore,
Exists the remnant of a line   75
   Such as the Doric mothers bore;
And there, perhaps, some seed is sown,
The Heracleidan blood might own.

XIV

Trust not for freedom to the Franks—
   They have a king who buys and sells;   80
In native swords, and native ranks,
   The only hope of courage dwells:
But Turkish force, and Latin fraud,
Would break your shield, however broad.

XV

Fill high the bowl with Samian wine!   85
   Our virgins dance beneath the shade—
I see their glorious black eyes shine;
   But gazing on each glowing maid,
My own the burning tear-drop laves,
To think such breasts must suckle slaves.   90

XVI

Place me on Sunium's marbled steep,
   Where nothing, save the waves and I,
May hear our mutual murmurs sweep;
   There, swan-like, let me sing and die:
A land of slaves shall ne'er be mine—   95
Dash down yon cup of Samian wine!

FROM *Don Juan* (Canto 3, stanza 86)

74 *Suli . . . Parga:* the former is a mountainous area, the latter a seaport, both in Asia Minor.   76 *Doric:* from Doris, a province of ancient Greece. 78 *Heracleidan:* literally, "of the line of Heracles," i.e., "ancient Greek." 79 *Franks:* eastern Mediterranean term for Europeans.   91 *Sunium:* headland southeast of Athens.

ALFRED, LORD TENNYSON

[1809–1892]

Alfred Tennyson was born in Somersby, Lincolnshire, fourth of the twelve children of the Anglican rector, George Clayton Tennyson. The family was a gifted one: two of Alfred's brothers, Frederick and Charles, became poets of some distinction. Alfred himself began writing prose and verse early in his life. At seven he was sent to grammar school at Louth, but he received his most basic education after he returned home five years later. There, at the rectory, he had the run of Somersby Rectory's excellent library, and in it from his father he gained a thorough knowledge of the classics and English literature. When he was seventeen he published POEMS BY TWO BROTHERS, together with Frederick and Charles.

In 1828 Tennyson matriculated at Trinity College, Cambridge. The following year he won the Chancellor's prize for his poem "Timbuctoo," and in 1830 he published his POEMS, CHIEFLY LYRICAL. In February of 1831 he returned home to be with his ailing father. The next few years, which he spent in Somersby, were among the happiest in his life. The end of this idyllic period came with the death of his closest friend, Arthur Hallam (1833), and the eviction of the Tennysons from the rectory (1837).

In 1842 a two-volume edition of his POEMS appeared, and Tennyson quickly became both a popular and a critical success. By the age of thirty-three he had become one of the leading poets of England. Among his friends were Dickens and Elizabeth Barrett. Unwise speculation led to the loss of his inheritance, but his Cambridge friends persuaded Prime Minister Sir Robert Peel to grant the poet a pension. In 1850 Tennyson married Emily Sellwood and published one of his best-known works, IN MEMORIAM, in honor of Hallam. In that same year Wordsworth died, and Tennyson was designated poet laureate by Queen Victoria. Tennyson's next two important works, "Ode on the Death of the Duke of Wellington" (1852), and "The Charge of the Light Brigade" (1854), were po-

litically inspired. His MAUD *(1855) was not well received, but the public was delighted with his poems in the Arthurian tradition: the* IDYLLS OF THE KING *(1859), the* HOLY GRAIL *(1869),* GARETH AND LYNETTE *and* THE LAST TOURNAMENT *(1872). From 1875 to 1884 he tried his hand unsuccessfully at drama. In 1883 he was offered a peerage by Prime Minister William Gladstone and the following year took his seat in the House of Lords. His last major works were* LOCKSLEY HALL SIXTY YEARS AFTER *(1886) and* DEMETER AND OTHER POEMS *(1889). On October 6, 1892, he died at Aldworth. He was buried in Westminster Abbey.*

The standard biography of Tennyson is his son Hallam's ALFRED, LORD TENNYSON, *in two volumes (1897). Hallam Tennyson also edited his father's* WORKS *in nine volumes (1913). There are good modern biographies of the poet, and he has attracted contemporary critics as well: H. Nicolson's* TENNYSON: ASPECTS OF HIS LIFE, CHARACTER, AND POETRY *(1949), Paul F. Baum's* TENNYSON SIXTY YEARS AFTER *(1948), W. H. Auden's "Introduction" to* A SELECTION FROM THE POEMS OF ALFRED, LORD TENNYSON *(1944), Jerome Buckley's* TENNYSON: THE GROWTH OF A POET *(1960), are representative. A useful anthology in paperback is* ALFRED, LORD TENNYSON, SELECTED POEMS, *edited by Herbert Marshall McLuhan.*

THE LADY OF SHALOTT

(Part I)

On either side the river lie
Long fields of barley and of rye,
That clothe the wold and meet the sky;
And through the field the road runs by
    To many-towered Camelot;   5
And up and down the people go,
Gazing where the lilies blow
Round an island there below,
    The island of Shalott.

Willows whiten, aspens quiver,   10
Little breezes dusk and shiver
Through the wave that runs for ever

By the island in the river
    Flowing down to Camelot.
Four gray walls, and four gray towers,   15
Overlook a space of flowers,
And the silent isle imbowers
    The Lady of Shalott.

By the margin, willow-veiled,
Slide the heavy barges trailed   20
By slow horses; and unhailed
The shallop flitteth silken-sailed
    Skimming down to Camelot:
But who hath seen her wave her hand?
Or at the casement seen her stand?   25
Or is she known in all the land,
    The Lady of Shalott?

Only reapers, reaping early
In among the bearded barley,
Hear a song that echoes cheerly   30
From the river winding clearly,
    Down to towered Camelot;
And by the moon the reaper weary,
Piling sheaves in uplands airy,
Listening, whispers " 'Tis the fairy   35
    Lady of Shalott."

(Part II)

There she weaves by night and day
A magic web with colors gay.
She has heard a whisper say,
A curse is on her if she stay   40
    To look down to Camelot.
She knows not what the curse may be,
And so she weaveth steadily,
And little other care hath she,
    The Lady of Shalott.   45

And moving through a mirror clear
That hangs before her all the year,
Shadows of the world appear.
There she sees the highway near

Winding down to Camelot;   50
There the river eddy whirls,
And there the surly village-churls,
And the red cloaks of market girls,
    Pass onward from Shalott.

Sometimes a troop of damsels glad,   55
An abbot on an ambling pad,
Sometimes a curly shepherd-lad,
Or long-haired page in crimson clad,
    Goes by to towered Camelot;
And sometimes through the mirror blue   60
The knights come riding two and two:
She hath no loyal knight and true,
    The Lady of Shalott.

But in her web she still delights
To weave the mirror's magic sights,   65
For often through the silent nights
A funeral, with plumes and lights
    And music, went to Camelot;
Or when the moon was overhead,
Came two young lovers lately wed: 70
"I am half sick of shadows," said
    The Lady of Shalott.

(Part III)

A bow-shot from her bower-eaves,
He rode between the barley-sheaves,
The sun came dazzling through the leaves,   75
And flamed upon the brazen greaves
    Of bold Sir Lancelot.
A red-cross knight for ever kneeled
To a lady in his shield,
That sparkled on the yellow field,   80
    Beside remote Shalott.

The gemmy bridle glittered free,
Like to some branch of stars we see

---

56 *an ambling pad:* a road horse, as distinguished from a work horse or a
hunter.

Hung in the golden galaxy.
The bridle bells rang merrily   85
    As he rode down to Camelot;
And from his blazoned baldric slung
A mighty silver bugle hung,
And as he rode his armor rung,
    Beside remote Shalott.   90

All in the blue unclouded weather
Thick-jewelled shone the saddle-leather,
The helmet and the helmet-feather
Burned like one burning flame together,
    As he rode down to Camelot;   95
As often through the purple night,
Below the starry clusters bright,
Some bearded meteor, trailing light,
    Moves over still Shalott.

His broad clear brow in sunlight glowed;   100
On burnished hooves his war-horse trode;
From underneath his helmet flowed
His coal-black curls as on he rode,
    As he rode down to Camelot.
From the bank and from the river   105
He flashed into the crystal mirror,
"Tirra lirra," by the river
    Sang Sir Lancelot.

She left the web, she left the loom,
She made three paces through the room,   110
She saw the water-lily bloom,
She saw the helmet and the plume,
    She looked down to Camelot.
Out flew the web and floated wide;
The mirror cracked from side to side;   115
"The curse is come upon me," cried
    The Lady of Shalott.

(*Part IV*)

In the stormy east-wind straining,
The pale yellow woods were waning,

The broad stream in his banks complaining,   120
Heavily the low sky raining
     Over towered Camelot;
Down she came and found a boat
Beneath a willow left afloat,
And round about the prow she wrote   125
     The Lady of Shalott.

And down the river's dim expanse
Like some bold seer in a trance,
Seeing all his own mischance—
With a glassy countenance   130
     Did she look to Camelot.
And at the closing of the day
She loosed the chain, and down she lay;
The broad stream bore her far away,
     The Lady of Shalott.   135

Lying, robed in snowy white
That loosely flew to left and right—
The leaves upon her falling light—
Through the noises of the night
     She floated down to Camelot;   140
And as the boat-head wound along
The willowy hills and fields among,
They heard her singing her last song,
     The Lady of Shalott.

Heard a carol, mournful, holy,   145
Chanted loudly, chanted lowly,
Till her blood was frozen slowly,
And her eyes were darkened wholly,
     Turned to towered Camelot.
For ere she reached upon the tide   150
The first house by the water-side,
Singing in her song she died,
     The Lady of Shalott.

Under tower and balcony,
By garden-wall and gallery,   155
A gleaming shape she floated by,
Dead-pale between the houses high,

Silent into Camelot.
Out upon the wharfs they came,
Knight and burgher, lord and dame, 160
And round the prow they read her name,
    The Lady of Shalott.

Who is this? and what is here?
And in the lighted palace near
Died the sound of royal cheer; 165
And they crossed themselves for fear,
    All the knights at Camelot:
But Lancelot mused a little space;
He said, "She has a lovely face;
God in his mercy lend her grace, 170
    The Lady of Shalott."

INTRODUCTION
TO THE LOTOS—EATERS

"Courage!" he said, and pointed toward the land,
"This mounting wave will roll us shoreward soon."
In the afternoon they came unto a land
In which it seemed always afternoon.
All round the coast the languid air did swoon, 5
Breathing like one that hath a weary dream.
Full-faced above the valley stood the moon;
And, like a downward smoke, the slender stream
Along the cliff to fall and pause and fall did seem.

A land of streams! some, like a downward smoke, 10
Slow-dropping veils of thinnest lawn, did go;
And some through wavering lights and shadows broke,
Rolling a slumbrous sheet of foam below.
They saw the gleaming river seaward flow
From the inner land; far off, three mountain-tops, 15
Three silent pinnacles of aged snow,
Stood sunset-flushed; and dewed with showery drops,

11 *lawn:* fine, thin linen.

Up-clomb the shadowy pine above the woven copse.
The charmed sunset lingered low adown
In the red West; through mountain clefts the dale   20
Was seen far inland, and the yellow down
Bordered with palm, and many a winding vale
And meadow, set with slender galingale;
A land where all things always seemed the same!
And round about the keel with faces pale,   25
Dark faces pale against that rosy flame,
The mild-eyed melancholy Lotos-eaters came.

Branches they bore of that enchanted stem,
Laden with flower and fruit, whereof they gave
To each, but whoso did receive of them   30
And taste, to him the gushing of the wave
Far far away did seem to mourn and rave
On alien shores; and if his fellow spake,
His voice was thin, as voices from the grave;
And deep-asleep he seemed, yet all awake,   35
And music in his ears his beating heart did make.

They sat them down upon the yellow sand,
Between the sun and moon upon the shore;
And sweet it was to dream of Fatherland,
Of child, and wife, and slave; but evermore   40
Most weary seemed the sea, weary the oar,
Weary the wandering fields of barren foam.
Then some one said, "We will return no more";
And all at once they sang, "Our island home
Is far beyond the wave; we will no longer roam."   45

23 *galingale:* a coarse English grass with aromatic roots.

ULYSSES

It little profits that an idle king,
By this still hearth, among these barren crags,
Matched with an aged wife, I mete and dole
Unequal laws unto a savage race,
That hoard, and sleep, and feed, and know not me.   5

I cannot rest from travel; I will drink
Life to the lees. All times I have enjoyed
Greatly, have suffered greatly, both with those
That loved me, and alone; on shore, and when
Through scudding drifts the rainy Hyades   10
Vexed the dim sea. I am become a name;
For always roaming with a hungry heart
Much have I seen and known,—cities of men
And manners, climates, councils, governments,
Myself not least, but honored of them all,—   15
And drunk delight of battle with my peers,
Far on the ringing plains of windy Troy.
I am a part of all that I have met;
Yet all experience is an arch wherethrough
Gleams that untravelled world whose margin fades   20
For ever and for ever when I move.
How dull it is to pause, to make an end,
To rust unburnished, not to shine in use!
As though to breathe were life! Life piled on life
Were all too little, and of one to me   25
Little remains; but every hour is saved
From that eternal silence, something more,
A bringer of new things; and vile it were
For some three suns to store and hoard myself,
And this gray spirit yearning in desire   30
To follow knowledge like a sinking star,
Beyond the utmost bound of human thought.
    This is my son, mine own Telemachus,
To whom I leave the sceptre and the isle,—
Well-loved of me, discerning to fulfil   35
This labor, by slow prudence to make mild
A rugged people, and through soft degrees
Subdue them to the useful and the good.
Most blameless is he, centred in the sphere
Of common duties, decent not to fail   40
In offices of tenderness, and pay
Meet adoration to my household gods,
When I am gone. He works his work, I mine.

10 *Hyades:* a group of stars which, upon rising, were thought to be followed by rain, the *scudding drifts.*

There lies the port; the vessel puffs her sail;
There gloom the dark, broad seas. My mariners,   45
Souls that have toiled, and wrought, and thought with me,—
That ever with a frolic welcome took
The thunder and the sunshine, and opposed
Free hearts, free foreheads,—you and I are old;
Old age hath yet his honor and his toil.   50
Death closes all; but something ere the end,
Some work of noble note, may yet be done,
Not unbecoming men that strove with Gods.
The lights begin to twinkle from the rocks;
The long day wanes; the slow moon climbs; the deep   55
Moans round with many voices. Come, my friends.
'Tis not too late to seek a newer world.
Push off, and sitting well in order smite
The sounding furrows; for my purpose holds
To sail beyond the sunset, and the baths   60
Of all the western stars, until I die.
It may be that the gulfs will wash us down;
It may be we shall touch the Happy Isles,
And see the great Achilles, whom we knew.
Though much is taken, much abides; and though   65
We are not now that strength which in old days
Moved earth and heaven, that which we are, we are,—
One equal temper of heroic hearts,
Made weak by time and fate, but strong in will
To strive, to seek, to find, and not to yield.   70

63 *Happy Isles:* Islands of the Blessed. See note, p. 171.

THE VISION OF SIN

I

I had a vision when the night was late;
A youth came riding toward a palace-gate.
He rode a horse with wings, that would have flown,
But that his heavy rider kept him down.
And from the palace came a child of sin,   5
And took him by the curls, and led him in,

Where sat a company with heated eyes,
Expecting when a fountain should arise.
A sleepy light upon their brows and lips—
As when the sun, a crescent of eclipse, 10
Dreams over lake and lawn, and isles and capes—
Suffused them, sitting, lying, languid shapes,
By heaps of gourds, and skins of wine, and piles of grapes.

II

Then methought I heard a mellow sound,
Gathering up from all the lower ground; 15
Narrowing in to where they sat assembled,
Low voluptuous music winding trembled,
Woven in circles. They that heard it sighed,
Panted hand-in-hand with faces pale,
Swung themselves, and in low tones replied; 20
Till the fountain spouted, showering wide
Sleet of diamond-drift and pearly hail.
Then the music touched the gates and died,
Rose again from where it seemed to fail,
Stormed in orbs of song, a growing gale; 25
Till thronging in and in, to where they waited,
As 'twere a hundred-throated nightingale,
The strong tempestuous treble throbbed and palpitated;
Ran into its giddiest whirl of sound,
Caught the sparkles, and in circles, 30
Purple gauzes, golden hazes, liquid mazes,
Flung the torrent rainbow round.
Then they started from their places,
Moved with violence, changed in hue,
Caught each other with wild grimaces, 35
Half-invisible to the view,
Wheeling with precipitate paces
To the melody, till they flew,
Hair and eyes and limbs and faces,
Twisted hard in fierce embraces, 40
Like to Furies, like to Graces,
Dashed together in blinding dew;
Till, killed with some luxurious agony,
The nerve-dissolving melody
Fluttered headlong from the sky. 45

III

And then I looked up toward a mountain-tract,
That girt the region with high cliff and lawn.
I saw that every morning, far withdrawn
Beyond the darkness and the cataract,
God made Himself an awful rose of dawn,   50
Unheeded; and detaching, fold by fold,
From those still heights, and, slowly drawing near,
A vapor heavy, hueless, formless, cold,
Came floating on for many a month and year,
Unheeded; and I thought I would have spoken,   55
And warned that madman ere it grew too late,
But, as in dreams, I could not. Mine was broken,
When that cold vapor touched the palace-gate,
And linked again. I saw within my head
A gray and gap-toothed man as lean as death,   60
Who slowly rode across a withered heath,
And lighted at a ruined inn, and said:

IV

"Wrinkled ostler, grim and thin!
    Here is custom come your way;
Take my brute, and lead him in,   65
    Stuff his ribs with mouldy hay.

"Bitter barmaid, waning fast!
    See that sheets are on my bed.
What! the flower of life is past;
    It is long before you wed.   70

"Slip-shod waiter, lank and sour,
    At the Dragon on the heath!
Let us have a quiet hour,
    Let us hob-and-nob with Death.

"I am old, but let me drink;   75
    Bring me spices, bring me wine;
I remember, when I think,
    That my youth was half divine.

"Wine is good for shrivelled lips,
    When a blanket wraps the day,   80

When the rotten woodland drips,
   And the leaf is stamped in clay.

"Sit thee down, and have no shame,
   Cheek by jowl, and knee by knee;
What care I for any name?   85
   What for order or degree?

"Let me screw thee up a peg;
   Let me loose thy tongue with wine;
Callest thou that thing a leg?
   Which is thinnest? thine or mine?   90

"Thou shalt not be saved by works,
   Thou hast been a sinner too;
Ruined trunks on withered forks,
   Empty scarecrows, I and you!

"Fill the cup and fill the can,   95
   Have a rouse before the morn;
Every moment dies a man,
   Every moment one is born.

"We are men of ruined blood;
   Therefore comes it we are wise.   100
Fish are we that love the mud,
   Rising to no fancy-flies.

"Name and fame! to fly sublime
   Through the courts, the camps, the schools,
Is to be the ball of Time,   105
   Bandied by the hands of fools.

"Friendship!—to be two in one—
   Let the canting liar pack!
Well I know, when I am gone,
   How she mouths behind my back.   110

"Virtue!—to be good and just—
   Every heart, when sifted well,
Is a clot of warmer dust,
   Mixed with cunning sparks of hell.

"O, we two as well can look   115
   Whited thought and cleanly life

As the priest, above his book
   Leering at his neighbor's wife.

"Fill the cup and fill the can,
   Have a rouse before the morn: 120
Every moment dies a man,
   Every moment one is born.

"Drink, and let the parties rave;
   They are filled with idle spleen,
Rising, falling, like a wave,   125
   For they know not what they mean.

"He that roars for liberty
   Faster binds a tyrant's power,
And the tyrant's cruel glee
   Forces on the freer hour.   130

"Fill the can and fill the cup;
   All the windy ways of men
Are but dust that rises up,
   And is lightly laid again.

"Greet her with applausive breath,   135
   Freedom, gaily doth she tread;
In her right a civic wreath,
   In her left a human head.

"No, I love not what is new;
   She is of an ancient house,   140
And I think we know the hue
   Of that cap upon her brows.

"Let her go! her thirst she slakes
   Where the bloody conduit runs,
Then her sweetest meal she makes   145
   On the first-born of her sons.

"Drink to lofty hopes that cool,—
   Visions of a perfect State;
Drink we, last, the public fool,
   Frantic love and frantic hate.   150

"Chant me now some wicked stave,
   Till thy drooping courage rise,

And the glow-worm of the grave
   Glimmer in thy rheumy eyes.

"Fear not thou to loose thy tongue,   155
   Set thy hoary fancies free;
What is loathsome to the young
   Savors well to thee and me.

"Change, reverting to the years,
   When thy nerves could understand   160
What there is in loving tears,
   And the warmth of hand in hand.

"Tell me tales of thy first love—
   April hopes, the fools of chance—
Till the graves begin to move,   165
   And the dead begin to dance.

"Fill the can and fill the cup;
   All the windy ways of men
Are but dust that rises up,
   And is lightly laid again.   170

"Trooping from their mouldy dens
   The chap-fallen circle spreads—
Welcome, fellow-citizens,
   Hollow hearts and empty heads!

"You are bones, and what of that?   175
   Every face, however full,
Padded round with flesh and fat,
   Is but modelled on a skull.

"Death is king, and Vivat Rex!
   Tread a measure on the stones,   180
Madam—if I know your sex
   From the fashion of your bones.

"No, I cannot praise the fire
   In your eye—nor yet your lip;
All the more do I admire   185
   Joints of cunning workmanship.

172 *chap-fallen:* fallen-jawed.   179 *Vivat Rex:* long live the king.

"Lo! God's likeness—the ground-plan—
   Neither modelled, glazed, nor framed;
Buss me, thou rough sketch of man,
   Far too naked to be shamed!   190

"Drink to Fortune, drink to Chance,
   While we keep a little breath!
Drink to heavy Ignorance!
   Hob-and-nob with brother Death!

"Thou art mazed, the night is long,   195
   And the longer night is near—
What! I am not all as wrong
   As a bitter jest is dear.

"Youthful hopes, by scores, to all,
   When the locks are crisp and curled;   200
Unto me my maudlin gall
   And my mockeries of the world.

"Fill the cup and fill the can;
   Mingle madness, mingle scorn!
Dregs of life, and lees of man;   205
   Yet we will not die forlorn."

V

The voice grew faint; there came a further change;
Once more uprose the mystic mountain-range.
Below were men and horses pierced with worms,
And slowly quickening into lower forms;   210
By shards and scurf of salt, and scum of dross,
Old plash of rains, and refuse patched with moss.
Then some one spake: "Behold! it was a crime
Of sense avenged by sense that wore with time."
Another said: "The crime of sense became   215
The crime of malice, and is equal blame."
And one: "He had not wholly quenched his power;
A little grain of conscience made him sour."
At last I heard a voice upon the slope
Cry to the summit, "Is there any hope?"   220

189 *Buss:* kiss.   195 *mazed:* drunk.   211 *scurf:* scaly incrustation.
212 *plash:* puddles.

To which an answer pealed from that high land,
But in a tongue no man could understand;
And on the glimmering limit far withdrawn
God made Himself an awful rose of dawn.

"BREAK, BREAK, BREAK"

Break, break, break,
  On thy cold gray stones, O Sea!
And I would that my tongue could utter
  The thoughts that arise in me.

O, well for the fisherman's boy,   5
  That he shouts with his sister at play!
O, well for the sailor lad,
  That he sings in his boat on the bay!

And the stately ships go on
  To their haven under the hill;   10
But O for the touch of a vanished hand,
  And the sound of a voice that is still!

Break, break, break,
  At the foot of thy crags, O Sea!
But the tender grace of a day that is dead   15
  Will never come back to me.

"TEARS, IDLE TEARS"

"Tears, idle tears, I know not what they mean,
Tears from the depth of some divine despair
Rise in the heart, and gather to the eyes,
In looking on the happy autumn-fields,
And thinking of the days that are no more.   5

"Fresh as the first beam glittering on a sail,
That brings our friends up from the underworld,
Sad as the last which reddens over one

That sinks with all we love below the verge;
So sad, so fresh, the days that are no more.   10

"Ah, sad and strange as in dark summer dawns
The earliest pipe of half-awakened birds
To dying ears, when unto dying eyes
The casement slowly grows a glimmering square;
So sad, so strange, the days that are no more.   15

"Dear as remembered kisses after death,
And sweet as those by hopeless fancy feigned
On lips that are for others; deep as love,
Deep as first love, and wild with all regret;
O Death in Life, the days that are no more!"   20

FROM *The Princess: A Medley*

"O SWALLOW, SWALLOW"

"O Swallow, Swallow, flying, flying south,
Fly to her, and fall upon her gilded eaves,
And tell her, tell her, what I tell to thee.

"O, tell her, Swallow, thou that knowest each,
That bright and fierce and fickle is the South,   5
And dark and true and tender is the North.

"O Swallow, Swallow, if I could follow, and light
Upon her lattice, I would pipe and trill,
And cheep and twitter twenty million loves.

"O, were I thou that she might take me in,   10
And lay me on her bosom, and her heart
Would rock the snowy cradle till I died!

"Why lingereth she to clothe her heart with love,
Delaying as the tender ash delays
To clothe herself, when all the woods are green?   15

"O, tell her, Swallow, that thy brood is flown;
Say to her, I do but wanton in the South,
But in the North long since my nest is made.

"O, tell her, brief is life but love is long,
And brief the sun of summer in the North, 20
And brief the moon of beauty in the South.

"O Swallow, flying from the golden woods,
Fly to her, and pipe and woo her, and make her mine,
And tell her, tell her, that I follow thee."

FROM *The Princess: A Medley*

"NOW SLEEPS THE CRIMSON PETAL"

"Now sleeps the crimson petal, now the white;
Nor waves the cypress in the palace walk;
Nor winks the gold fin in the porphyry font.
The fire-fly wakens; waken thou with me.

"Now droops the milk-white peacock like a ghost, 5
And like a ghost she glimmers on to me.

"Now lies the Earth all Danaë to the stars,
And all thy heart lies open unto me.

"Now slides the silent meteor on, and leaves
A shining furrow, as thy thoughts in me. 10

"Now folds the lily all her sweetness up,
And slips into the bosom of the lake.
So fold thyself, my dearest, thou, and slip
Into my bosom and be lost in me."

FROM *The Princess: A Medley*

7 *Danaë:* a princess to whom Zeus descended in a golden shower.

"COME DOWN, O MAID"

"Come down, O maid, from yonder mountain height.
What pleasure lives in height (the shepherd sang),
In height and cold, the splendor of the hills?

But cease to move so near the heavens, and cease
To glide a sunbeam by the blasted pine,   5
To sit a star upon the sparkling spire;
And come, for Love is of the valley, come,
For Love is of the valley, come thou down
And find him; by the happy threshold, he,
Or hand in hand with Plenty in the maize,   10
Or red with spirited purple of the vats,
Or foxlike in the vine; nor cares to walk
With Death and Morning on the Silver Horns,
Nor wilt thou snare him in the white ravine,
Nor find him dropped upon the firths of ice,   15
That huddling slant in furrow-cloven falls
To roll the torrent out of dusky doors.
But follow; let the torrent dance thee down
To find him in the valley; let the wild
Lean-headed eagles yelp alone, and leave   20
The monstrous ledges there to slope, and spill
Their thousand wreaths of dangling water-smoke,
That like a broken purpose waste in air.
So waste not thou, but come; for all the vales
Await thee; azure pillars of the hearth   25
Arise to thee; the children call, and I
Thy shepherd pipe, and sweet is every sound,
Sweeter thy voice, but every sound is sweet;
Myriads of rivulets hurrying through the lawn,
The moan of doves in immemorial elms,   30
And murmuring of innumerable bees."

FROM *The Princess: A Medley*

13 *Silver Horns:* mountains in the Alps.   15 *firths:* glaciers.

"SWEET AND LOW"

Sweet and low, sweet and low,
   Wind of the western sea,
Low, low, breathe and blow,
   Wind of the western sea!

Over the rolling waters go,   5
Come from the dying moon, and blow,
    Blow him again to me;
While my little one, while my pretty one sleeps.

Sleep and rest, sleep and rest,
    Father will come to thee soon;   10
Rest, rest, on mother's breast,
    Father will come to thee soon;
Father will come to his babe in the nest,
Silver sails all out of the west
    Under the silver moon;   15
Sleep, my little one, sleep, my pretty one, sleep.

FROM *The Princess: A Medley*

"THE SPLENDOR FALLS ON CASTLE WALLS"

The splendor falls on castle walls
    And snowy summits old in story;
The long light shakes across the lakes,
    And the wild cataract leaps in glory.
Blow, bugle, blow, set the wild echoes flying,   5
Blow, bugle; answer, echoes, dying, dying, dying.

O, hark, O hear! how thin and clear,
    And thinner, clearer, farther going!
O, sweet and far from cliff and scar
    The horns of Elfland faintly blowing!   10
Blow, let us hear the purple glens replying,
Blow, bugle; answer, echoes, dying, dying, dying.

O love, they die in yon rich sky,
    They faint on hill or field or river;
Our echoes roll from soul to soul,   15
    And grow for ever and for ever.
Blow, bugle, blow, set the wild echoes flying,
And answer, echoes, answer, dying, dying, dying.

FROM *The Princess: A Medley*

THE EAGLE: A FRAGMENT

He clasps the crag with crooked hands;
Close to the sun in lonely lands,
Ringed with the azure world, he stands.

The wrinkled sea beneath him crawls;
He watches from his mountain walls,   5
And like a thunderbolt he falls.

"I ENVY NOT IN ANY MOODS"

I envy not in any moods
    The captive void of noble rage,
    The linnet born within the cage,
That never knew the summer woods;

I envy not the beast that takes   5
    His license in the field of time,
    Unfettered by the sense of crime,
To whom a conscience never wakes;

Nor, what may count itself as blessed,
    The heart that never plighted troth   10
    But stagnates in the weeds of sloth;
Nor any want-begotten rest.

I hold it true, whate'er befall;
    I feel it, when I sorrow most;
    'Tis better to have loved and lost
Than never to have loved at all.

FROM *In Memoriam A.H.H.* (xxvii)

"COME INTO THE GARDEN, MAUD"

I

Come into the garden, Maud,
  For the black bat, night, has flown,
Come into the garden, Maud,
  I am here at the gate alone;
And the woodbine spices are wafted abroad,   5
  And the musk of the rose is blown.

II

For a breeze of morning moves,
  And the planet of Love is on high,
Beginning to faint in the light that she loves
  On a bed of daffodil sky,   10
To faint in the light of the sun she loves,
  To faint in his light, and to die.

III

All night have the roses heard
  The flute, violin, bassoon;
All night has the casement jessamine stirred   15
  To the dancers dancing in tune;
Till a silence fell with the waking bird,
  And a hush with the setting moon.

IV

I said to the lily, "There is but one,
  With whom she has heart to be gay.   20
When will the dancers leave her alone?
  She is weary of dance and play."
Now half to the setting moon are gone,
  And half to the rising day;
Low on the sand and loud on the stone   25
  The last wheel echoes away.

V

I said to the rose, "The brief night goes
  In babble and revel and wine.

O young lord-lover, what sighs are those,
  For one that will never be thine? 30
But mine, but mine," so I swore to the rose,
  "For ever and ever, mine."

VI

And the soul of the rose went into my blood,
  As the music clashed in the hall;
And long by the garden lake I stood, 35
  For I heard your rivulet fall
From the lake to the meadow and on to the wood,
  Our wood, that is dearer than all;

VII

From the meadow your walks have left so sweet
  That whenever a March-wind sighs 40
He sets the jewel-print of your feet
  In violets blue as your eyes,
To the woody hollows in which we meet
  And the valleys of Paradise.

VIII

The slender acacia would not shake 45
  One long milk-bloom on the tree;
The white lake-blossom fell into the lake
  As the pimpernel dozed on the lea;
But the rose was awake all night for your sake,
  Knowing your promise to me; 50
The lilies and roses were all awake,
  They sighed for the dawn and thee.

IX

Queen rose of the rosebud garden of girls,
  Come hither, the dances are done,
In gloss of satin and glimmer of pearls, 55
  Queen lily and rose in one;
Shine out, little head, sunning over with curls,
  To the flowers, and be their sun.

X

There has fallen a splendid tear
  From the passion-flower at the gate. 60

She is coming, my dove, my dear;
  She is coming, my life, my fate.
The red rose cries, "She is near, she is near;"
  And the white rose weeps, "She is late;"
The larkspur listens, "I hear, I hear;"   65
  And the lily whispers, "I wait."

XI

She is coming, my own, my sweet;
  Were it ever so airy a tread,
My heart would hear her and beat,
  Were it earth in an earthy bed;   70
My dust would hear her and beat,
  Had I lain for a century dead,
Would start and tremble under her feet,
  And blossom in purple and red.

FROM MAUD: *A Monodrama* (I, xxii)

THE CHARGE OF THE LIGHT BRIGADE

I

Half a league, half a league,
Half a league onward,
All in the valley of death
  Rode the six hundred.
"Forward the Light Brigade!   5
Charge for the guns!" he said.
Into the valley of death
  Rode the six hundred.

II

"Forward, the Light Brigade!"
Was there a man dismayed?   10
Not though the soldier knew
  Some one had blundered.
Theirs not to make reply,
Theirs not to reason why,

Theirs but to do and die.   15
Into the valley of death
  Rode the six hundred.

III

Cannon to right of them,
Cannon to left of them,
Cannon in front of them   20
  Volleyed and thundered;
Stormed at with shot and shell,
Boldly they rode and well,
Into the jaws of death,
Into the mouth of hell   25
  Rode the six hundred.

IV

Flashed all their sabres bare,
Flashed as they turned in air
Sabring the gunners there,
Charging an army, while   30
  All the world wondered.
Plunged in the battery-smoke
Right through the line they broke;
Cossack and Russian
Reeled from the sabre-stroke   35
  Shattered and sundered.
Then they rode back, but not,
  Not the six hundred.

V

Cannon to right of them,
Cannon to left of them,   40
Cannon behind them
  Volleyed and thundered;
Stormed at with shot and shell,
While horse and hero fell,
They that had fought so well   45
Came through the jaws of death,
Back from the mouth of hell,
All that was left of them,
  Left of six hundred.

VI

When can their glory fade? 50
O the wild charge they made!
  All the world wondered.
Honor the charge they made!
Honor the Light Brigade,
   Noble six hundred! 55

CROSSING THE BAR

This poem first appeared in the "Demeter" volume of 1889, and is placed here in accordance with Lord Tennyson's request that it might be put at the end of all editions of his poems.

Sunset and evening star, 22
  And one clear call for me!
And may there be no moaning of the bar,
  When I put out to sea,

But such a tide as moving seems asleep, 5
  Too full for sound and foam,
When that which drew from out the boundless deep
  Turns again home.

Twilight and evening bell,
  And after that the dark! 10
And may there be no sadness of farewell,
  When I embark;

For though from out our bourne of time and place
  The flood may bear me far,
I hope to see my Pilot face to face 15
  When I have crossed the bar.

THOMAS HARDY

[1840–1928]

Thomas Hardy was born near Stinsford, in Dorset, on June 2, 1840. He attended school in the village and in Dorchester; his formal education was augmented by extensive private reading. Hardy's father was a master-builder (contractor), and the boy set out to become an architect. At 15 he was apprenticed to John Hicks; six years later, in 1861, he left for London to practice architecture. Meanwhile, he discovered his ability in writing prose and verse. His dual interests and talents are reflected in the fact that in 1863 he won both the medal of the Royal Institute for an essay on architecture and the Architectural Association's prize for design. Hardy soon became disillusioned with city life, and in 1867 he returned to Dorset.

Although he resumed his association with Hicks, Hardy had decided in favor of a literary career. He was unable to find a publisher for his first novel, but by 1873 he had published three works. He married Emma Lavinia Gifford in 1874, and his first popular success, FAR FROM THE MADDING CROWD, appeared that same year. One of his finest novels, THE RETURN OF THE NATIVE, was written in 1876; it was followed by four lesser works, and then another triumph, THE MAYOR OF CASTERBRIDGE (1886). Hardy's reputation was established, and he found a ready audience for his writings which usually appeared in serial form. A second attempt at London life resulted in a permanent return to his Dorset countryside. He designed his home, "Max Gate," himself. Hardy's most famous novel, TESS OF THE D'URBERVILLES, was written in 1891; JUDE THE OBSCURE, in 1896. By 1900, Hardy had turned from prose to verse writing. THE DYNASTS, an epic drama relating England's struggle against Napoleon, was published in three parts in 1903–1904, 1906, and 1908. In July of 1910 he received the Order of Merit. Two years later his wife died, and in 1914 he married Florence Emily Dugdale. Hardy devoted the remainder of his life primarily to lyric poetry.

TIME'S LAUGHING STOCKS *was published in 1909*, SATIRES OF CIRCUM-
STANCE *in 1914*, MONUMENTS OF VISION *in 1917*, LATE LYRICS AND
EARLIER *in 1922, and* HUMAN SHOWS, FAR PHANTASIES *in 1925. On
January 11, 1928, Thomas Hardy died at "Max Gate"; he was
buried in Westminster Abbey.*

The complete WORKS OF THOMAS HARDY *is published in the Library
Edition (1953–   ). These are numerous editions of the* COLLECTED
POETRY. *Florence Hardy wrote* THE EARLY LIFE OF THOMAS HARDY
(1928), and THE LATER YEARS OF THOMAS HARDY *(1930). Critical
studies of Hardy's work include, among others, C. Day Lewis'*
THE LYRICAL POETRY OF THOMAS HARDY *(1953) and J. Holloways'*
THE VICTORIAN SAGE *(1953). An excellent discussion of Hardy's
lyricism is in R. P. Blackmur's "The Shorter Poems of Hardy" in
his* LANGUAGE AS GESTURE *(1952).*

HAP

If some vengeful god would call to me
From up the sky, and laugh: "Thou suffering thing,
Know that thy sorrow is my ecstasy,
That thy love's loss is my hate's profiting!"

Then would I bear it, clench myself, and die,   5
Steeled by the sense of ire unmerited;
Half-eased in that a Powerfuller than I
Had willed and meted me the tears I shed.

But not so. How arrives it joy lies slain,
And why unblooms the best hope ever sown?   10
—Crass Casualty obstructs the sun and rain,
And dicing Time for gladness casts a moan. . . .
These purblind doomsters had as readily strown
Blisses about my pilgrimage as pain.

NEUTRAL TONES

We stood by a pond that winter day,
And the sun was white, as though chidden of God,
And a few leaves lay on the starving sod;
    —They had fallen from an ash, and were gray.

Your eyes on me were as eyes that rove   5
Over tedious riddles of years ago;
And some words played between us to and fro
    On which lost the more by our love.

The smile on your mouth was the deadest thing
Alive enough to have strength to die;   10
And a grin of bitterness swept thereby
    Like an ominous bird a-wing. . . .

Since then, keen lessons that love deceives,
And wrings with wrong, have shaped to me
Your face, and the God-cursed sun, and a tree,   15
    And a pond edged with grayish leaves.

2 *chidden of:* scolded by.

NATURE'S QUESTIONING

Upon them stirs in lippings mere
    (As if once clear in call,
    But now scarce breathed at all)—
"We wonder, ever wonder, why we find us here!

    "Has some Vast Imbecility,   5
        Mighty to build and blend,
        But impotent to tend,
Framed us in jest, and left us now to hazardry?

    "Or come we of an Automaton
        Unconscious of our pains? . . .   10

Or are we live remains
Of Godhead dying downwards, brain and eye now gone?

"Or is it that some high plan betides,
　　As yet not understood,
　　Of Evil stormed by Good,
We the Forlorn Hope over which Achievement strides?" 　15

Thus things around. No answerer I. . . .
　　Meanwhile the winds, and rains,
　　And Earth's old glooms and pains
Are still the same, and Life and Death are neighbours nigh. 　20

DRUMMER HODGE

I

They throw in Drummer Hodge, to rest
　　Uncoffined—just as found:
His landmark is a kopje-crest
　　That breaks the veldt around;
And foreign constellations west 　5
　　Each night above his mound.

II

Young Hodge the Drummer never knew—
　　Fresh from his Wessex home—
The meaning of the broad Karoo,
　　The Bush, the dusty loam, 　10
And why uprose to nightly view
　　Strange stars amid the gloom.

III

Yet portion of that unknown plain
　　Will Hodge for ever be;
His homely Northern breast and brain 　15
　　Grow to some Southern tree,
And strange-eyed constellations reign
　　His stars eternally.

3 *kopje-crest:* South African word meaning stony knob or small hill.
4 *veldt:* prairie.　9 *the broad Karoo:* a large arid plateau in South Africa.

THE DARKLING THRUSH

I leant upon a coppice gate
    When frost was spectre-gray,
And winter's dregs made desolate
    The weakening eye of day.
The tangled bine-stems scored the sky   5
    Like strings of broken lyres,
And all mankind that haunted nigh
    Had sought their household fires.

The land's sharp features seemed to be
    The century's corpse outleant,   10
His crypt the cloudy canopy,
    The wind his death-lament.
The ancient pulse of germ and birth
    Was shrunken hard and dry,
And every spirit upon earth   15
    Seemed fervourless as I.

At once a voice arose among
    The bleak twigs overhead
In a full-hearted evensong
    Of joy illimited;   20
An aged thrush, frail, gaunt, and small,
    In blast-beruffled plume,
Had chosen thus to fling his soul
    Upon the growing gloom.

So little cause for carolings   25
    Of such ecstatic sound
Was written on terrestrial things
    Afar or nigh around,
That I could think there trembled through
    His happy good-night air   30
Some blessed hope, whereof he knew
    And I was unaware.

THE MAN HE KILLED

"Had he and I but met
By some old ancient inn,
We should have sat us down to wet
Right many a nipperkin!

"But ranged as infantry,   5
And staring face to face,
I shot at him as he at me,
And killed him in his place.

"I shot him dead because—
Because he was my foe,   10
Just so: my foe of course he was;
That's clear enough; although

"He thought he'd 'list, perhaps,
Off-hand like—just as I—
Was out of work—had sold his traps—   15
No other reason why.

"Yes; quaint and curious war is!
You shoot a fellow down
You'd treat if met where any bar is,
Or help to half-a-crown."   20

4 *nipperkin:* small tankard.   15 *traps:* personal belongings.

IN TIME OF "THE BREAKING OF NATIONS"

I

Only a man harrowing clods
In a slow silent walk
With an old horse that stumbles and nods
Half asleep as they stalk.

II

Only thin smoke without flame   5
  From the heaps of couch-grass;
Yet this will go onward the same
  Though dynasties pass.

III

Yonder a maid and her wight
  Come whispering by: 10
War's annals will fade into night
  Ere their story die.

"AH, ARE YOU DIGGING ON MY GRAVE?"

"Ah, are you digging on my grave
  My loved one?—planting rue?"
—"No: yesterday he went to wed
One of the brightest wealth has bred.
'It cannot hurt her now,' he said,   5
  'That I should not be true.'"

"Then who is digging on my grave?
  My nearest dearest kin?"
—"Ah, no: they sit and think, 'What use!
What good will planting flowers produce?   10
No tendance of her mound can loose
  Her spirit from Death's gin.'"

"But some one digs upon my grave?
  My enemy?—prodding sly?"
—"Nay: when she heard you had passed the Gate   15
That shuts on all flesh soon or late,
She thought you no more worth her hate,
  And cares not where you lie."

"Then, who is digging on my grave?
  Say—since I have not guessed!"   20
—"O it is I, my mistress dear,
Your little dog, who still lives near,

12 *gin:* engine, i.e., force.

195

And much I hope my movements here
    Have not disturbed your rest?"

"Ah, yes! *You* dig upon my grave . . .   25
    Why flashed it not on me
That one true heart was left behind!
What feeling do we ever find
To equal among human kind
    A dog's fidelity!"   30

"Mistress, I dug upon your grave
    To bury a bone, in case
I should be hungry near this spot
When passing on my daily trot.
I am sorry, but I quite forgot   35
    It was your resting-place."

THE DARK-EYED GENTLEMAN

I

I pitched my day's leazings in Crimmercrock Lane,
To tie up my garter and jog on again,
When a dear dark-eyed gentleman passed there and said,
In a way that made all o' me colour rose-red,
      "What do I see—   5
      O pretty knee!"
And he came and he tied up my garter for me.

II

'Twixt sunset and moonrise it was, I can mind:
Ah, 'tis easy to lose what we nevermore find!—
Of the dear stranger's home, of his name, I knew nought, 10
But I soon knew his nature and all that it brought.
      Then bitterly
      Sobbed I that he
Should ever have tied up my garter for me!

III

Yet now I've beside me a fine lissom lad,   15
And my slip's nigh forgot, and my days are not sad;

1 *leazings:* gleanings

My own dearest joy is he, comrade, and friend,
He it is who safe-guards me, on him I depend;
    No sorrow brings he,
    And thankful I be   20
That his daddy once tied up my garter for me!

A BEAUTY'S SOLILOQUY
DURING HER HONEYMOON

Too late, too late! I did not know my fairness
    Would catch the world's keen eyes so!
How the men look at me! My radiant rareness
    I deemed not they would prize so!

That I was a peach for any man's possession   5
    Why did not some one say
Before I leased myself in an hour's obsession
    To this dull mate for aye!

His days are mine. I am one who cannot steal her
    Ahead of his plodding pace: 10
As he is, so am I. One doomed to feel her
    A wasted form and face!

I was so blind! It did sometimes just strike me
    All girls were not as I,
But, dwelling much alone, how few were like me   15
    I could not well descry;

Till, at this Grand Hotel, all looks bend on me
    In homage as I pass
To take my seat at breakfast, dinner,—con me
    As poorly spoused, alas!   20

I was too young. I dwelt too much on duty:
    If I had guessed my powers
Where might have sailed this cargo of choice beauty
    In its unanchored hours!

8 *for aye:* forever.   19 *con:* think.

Well, husband, poor plain man; I've lost life's battle!— 25
    Come—let them look at me.
O damn, don't show in your looks that I'm your chattel
    Quite so emphatically!

27 *chattel:* movable piece of property.

SHE

AT HIS FUNERAL

They bear him to his resting-place—
In slow procession sweeping by;
I follow at a stranger's space;
His kindred they, his sweetheart I.
Unchanged my gown of garish dye, 5
Though sable-sad is their attire;
But they stand round with griefless eye,
Whilst my regret consumes like fire!

HER SECRET

That love's dull smart distressed my heart
    He shrewdly learned to see,
But that I was in love with a dead man
    Never suspected he.

He searched for the trace of a pictured face, 5
    He watched each missive come,
And a sheet that seemed like a love-line
    Wrought his look lurid and numb.

He dogged my feet to the city street,
    He followed me to the sea,
But not to the nigh, still churchyard 10
    Did he dream of following me!

SATIRES OF CIRCUMSTANCE: AT TEA

The kettle descants in a cosy drone,
And the young wife looks in her husband's face,
And then at her guest's, and shows in her own
Her sense that she fills an envied place;
And the visiting lady is all abloom,   5
And says there was never so sweet a room.

And the happy young housewife does not know
That the woman beside her was first his choice,
Till the fates ordained it could not be so. . . .
Betraying nothing in look or voice   10
The guest sits smiling and sips her tea,
And he throws her a stray glance yearningly.

SATIRES OF CIRCUMSTANCE: IN CHURCH

"And now to God the Father," he ends,
And his voice thrills up to the topmost tiles:
Each listener chokes as he bows and bends,
And emotion pervades the crowded aisles.
Then the preacher glides to the vestry-door,   5
And shuts it, and thinks he is seen no more.

The door swings softly ajar meanwhile,
And a pupil of his in the Bible class,
Who adores him as one without gloss or guile,
Sees her idol stand with a satisfied smile   10
And re-enact at the vestry-glass
Each pulpit gesture in deft dumb-show
That had moved the congregation so.

SATIRES OF CIRCUMSTANCE:
BY HER AUNT'S GRAVE

"Sixpence a week," says the girl to her lover,
"Aunt used to bring me, for she could confide
In me alone, she vowed. 'Twas to cover
The cost of her headstone when she died.
And that was a year ago last June;   5
I've not yet fixed it. But I must soon."

"And where is the money now, my dear?"
"O, snug in my purse . . . Aunt was *so* slow
In saving it—eighty weeks, or near." . . .
"Let's spend it," he hints. "For she won't know.   10
There's a dance to-night at the Load of Hay."
She passively nods. And they go that way.

SATIRES OF CIRCUMSTANCE:
IN THE RESTAURANT

"But hear. If you stay, and the child be born,
It will pass as your husband's with the rest,
While, if we fly, the teeth of scorn
Will be gleaming at us from east to west;
And the child will come as a life despised;   5
I feel an elopement is ill-advised!"

"O you realize not what it is, my dear,
To a woman! Daily and hourly alarms
Lest the truth should out. How can I stay here,
And nightly take him into my arms!   10
Come to the child no name or fame,
Let us go, and face it, and bear the shame."

SATIRES OF CIRCUMSTANCE:
AT THE DRAPER'S

"I stood at the back of the shop, my dear,
    But you did not perceive me.
Well, when they deliver what you were shown
    I shall know nothing of it, believe me!"

And he coughed and coughed as she paled and said,   5
    "O, I didn't see you come in there—
Why couldn't you speak?"—"Well, I didn't. I left
    That you should not notice I'd been there.

"You were viewing some lovely things. *'Soon required*
    For a widow, of latest fashion';   10
And I knew 'twould upset you to meet the man
    Who had to be cold and ashen

"And screwed in a box before they could dress you
    'In the last new note in mourning,'
As they defined it. So, not to distress you,   15
    I left you to your adorning."

AT A COUNTRY FAIR

At a bygone Western country fair
I saw a giant led by a dwarf
With a red string like a long thin scarf;
How much he was the stronger there
    The giant seemed unaware.   5

And then I saw that the giant was blind,
And the dwarf a shrewd-eyed little thing;
The giant, mild, timid, obeyed the string
As if he had no independent mind,
    Or will of any kind.   10

Wherever the dwarf decided to go
At his heels the other trotted meekly,
(Perhaps—I know not—reproaching weakly)
Like one Fate bade that it must be so,
    Whether he wished or no.   15

Various sights in various climes
I have seen, and more I may see yet,
But that sight never shall I forget,
And have thought it the sorriest of pantomimes,
    If once, a hundred times!   20

"THE CURTAINS NOW ARE DRAWN"

(SONG)

I

The curtains now are drawn,
And the spindrift strikes the glass,
Blown up the jagged pass
By the surly salt sou'-west,
And the sneering glare is gone   5
Behind the yonder crest,
    While she sings to me:
"O the dream that thou art my Love, be it thine,
And the dream that I am thy Love, be it mine,
And death may come, but loving is divine."   10

II

I stand here in the rain,
With its smite upon her stone,
And the grasses that have grown
Over women, children, men,
And their texts that "Life is vain";   15
But I hear the notes as when
    Once she sang to me:
"O the dream that thou art my Love, be it thine,
And the dream that I am thy Love, be it mine,
And death may come, but loving is divine."   20

IN A LONDON FLAT

I

"You look like a widower," she said
Through the folding-doors with a laugh from the bed,
As he sat by the fire in the outer room,
Reading late on a night of gloom,
And a cab-hack's wheeze, and the clap of its feet   5
In its breathless pace on the smooth wet street,
Were all that came to them now and then. . . .
"You really do!" she quizzed again.

II

And the Spirits behind the curtains heard,
And also laughed, amused at her word,   10
And at her light-hearted view of him.
"Let's get him made so—just for a whim!"
Said the Phantom Ironic. " 'Twould serve her right
If we coaxed the Will to do it some night."
"O pray not!" pleaded the younger one,   15
The Sprite of the Pities. "She said it in fun!"

III

But so it befell, whatever the cause,
That what she had called him he next year was;
And on such a night, when she lay elsewhere,
He, watched by those Phantoms, again sat there,   20
And gazed, as if gazing on far faint shores,
At the empty bed through the folding-doors
As he remembered her words; and wept
That she had forgotten them where she slept.

CIRCUS-RIDER TO RINGMASTER

When I am riding round the ring no longer,
    Tell a tale of me;
Say, no steed-borne woman's nerve was stronger

Then used mine to be.
, Let your whole soul say it; do: 5
    O it will be true!

Should I soon no more be mistress found in
    Feats I've made my own,
Trace the tan-laid track you'd whip me round in
    On the cantering roan: 10
    There may cross your eyes again
    My lithe look as then.

Show how I, when clay became my cover,
    Took the high-hoop leap
Into your arms, who coaxed and grew my lover,—   15
    Ah, to make me weep
    Since those claspings cared for so
    Ever so long ago!

Though not now as when you freshly knew me,
    But a fading form,   20
Shape the kiss you'd briskly blow up to me
    While our love was warm,
    And my cheek unstained by tears,
    As in these last years!

9 *tan-laid track:* track surfaced with tanbark.

PAYING CALLS

I went by footpath and by stile
    Beyond where bustle ends,
Strayed here a mile and there a mile
    And called upon some friends.

On certain ones I had not seen   5
    For years past did I call,
And then on others who had been
    The oldest friends of all.

It was the time of midsummer
    When they had used to roam;   10

But now, though tempting was the air,
    I found them all at home.

I spoke to one and other of them
    By mound and stone and tree
Of things we had done ere days were dim   15
    But they spoke not to me.

MIDNIGHT ON THE GREAT WESTERN

In the third-class seat sat the journeying boy,
    And the roof-lamp's only flame
Played down on his listless form and face,
Bewrapt past knowing to what he was going,
    Or whence he came.   5

In the band of his hat the journeying boy
    Had a ticket stuck; and a string
Around his neck bore the key of his box,
That twinkled gleams of the lamp's sad beams
    Like a living thing.   10

What past can be yours, O journeying boy
    Towards a world unknown,
Who calmly, as if incurious quite
On all at stake, can undertake
    This plunge alone?   15

Knows your soul a sphere, O journeying boy,
    Our rude realms far above,
Whence with spacious vision you mark and mete
This region of sin that you find you in,
    But are not of?   20

AN UPBRAIDING

Now I am dead you sing to me
    The songs we used to know,
But while I lived you had no wish
    Or care for doing so.

Now I am dead you come to me 5
In the moonlight, comfortless;
Ah, what would I have given alive
To win such tenderness!

When you are dead, and stand to me
Not differenced, as now, 10
But like again, will you be cold
As when we lived, or how?

THE CHILDREN AND SIR NAMELESS

Sir Nameless, once of Athelhall, declared:
"These wretched children romping in my park
Trample the herbage till the soul is bared,
And yap and yell from early morn till dark!
Go keep them harnessed to their set routines: 5
Thank God I've none to hasten my decay;
For green remembrance there are better means
Than offspring, who but wish their sires away."

Sir Nameless of that mansion said anon:
"To be perpetuate for my mightiness 10
Sculpture must image me when I am gone."
—He forthwith summoned carvers there express
To shape a figure stretching seven-odd feet
(For he was tall) in alabaster stone,
With shield, and crest, and casque, and sword complete: 15
When done a statelier work was never known.

Three hundred years hied; Church-restorers came,
And, no one of his lineage being traced,
They thought an effigy so large in frame
Best fitted for the floor. There it was placed, 20
Under the seats for schoolchildren. And they
Kicked out his name, and hobnailed off his nose;
And, as they yawn through sermon-time, they say,
"Who was this old stone man beneath our toes?"

HER APOTHEOSIS

"Secretum meum mihi"

(FADED WOMAN'S SONG)

There were years vague of measure
    Needless the asking when;
No honours, praises, pleasure
    Reached common maids from men.

And hence no lures bewitched them,   5
    No hand was stretched to raise,
No gracious gifts enriched them,
    No voices sang their praise.

Yet an iris at that season
    Amid the accustomed slight   10
From denseness, dull unreason,
    Ringed me with living light.

Secretum meum mihi: "My secret is my own."

A WOMAN DRIVING

How she held up the horses' heads,
    Firm-lipped, with steady rein,
Down that grim steep the coastguard treads,
    Till all was safe again!

With form erect and keen contour   5
    She passed against the sea,
And, dipping into the chine's obscure,
    Was seen no more by me.

To others she appeared anew
    At times of dusky light,   10
But always, so they told, withdrew
    From close and curious sight.

7 *the chine's obscure:* the steep ravine's obscurity.

Some said her silent wheels would roll
    Ruthless on softest loam,
And even that her steeds' footfall   15
    Sank not upon the foam.

Where drives she now? It may be where
    No mortal horses are,
But in a chariot of the air
    Towards some radiant star.   20

A CATHEDRAL FACADE AT MIDNIGHT

Along the sculptures of the western wall
    I watched the moonlight creeping:
It moved as if it hardly moved at all,
    Inch by inch thinly peeping
Round on the pious figures of freestone, brought   5
And poised there when the Universe was wrought
To serve its centre, Earth, in mankind's thought.

The lunar look skimmed scantly toe, breast, arm,
    Then edged on slowly, slightly,
To shoulder, hand, face; till each austere form   10
    Was blanched its whole length brightly
Of prophet, king, queen, cardinal in state,
That dead men's tools had striven to simulate;
And the stiff images stood irradiate.

A frail moan from the martyred saints there set   15
    Mid others of the erection
Against the breeze, seemed sighings of regret
    At the ancient faith's rejection
Under the sure, unhasting, steady stress
Of Reason's movement, making meaningless   20
The coded creeds of old-time godliness.

LAST WEEK IN OCTOBER

The trees are undressing, and fling in many places—
On the gray road, the roof, the window-sill—
Their radiant robes and ribbons and yellow laces;
A leaf each second so is flung at will,
Here, there, another and another, still and still.   5

A spider's web has caught one while downcoming,
That stays there dangling when the rest pass on;
Like a suspended criminal hangs he, mumming
In golden garb, while one yet green, high yon,
Trembles, as fearing such a fate for himself anon.   10

8 *mumming:* disguised or dressed fantastically.

THE GRAVEYARD OF DEAD CREEDS

I lit upon the graveyard of dead creeds
In wistful wanderings through old wastes of thought,
Where bristled fennish fungi, fruiting nought,
Amid the sepulchres begirt with weeds,

Which stone by stone recorded sanct, deceased   5
Catholicons that had, in centuries flown,
Physicked created man through his long groan,
Ere they went under, all their potence ceased.

When in a breath-while, lo, their spectres rose
Like wakened winds that autumn summons up:—   10
"Out of us cometh an heir, that shall disclose
New promise!" cried they. "And the caustic cup

3 *fennish:* swampish.   5 *sanct:* holy, virtuous.   6 *Catholicons:*
creeds.   7 *Physicked:* nursed.

We ignorantly upheld to men, be filled
With draughts more pure than those we ever distilled,
That shall make tolerable to sentient seers   15
The melancholy marching of the years."

THE SIX BOARDS

Six boards belong to me:
I do not know where they may be;
If growing green, or lying dry
    In a cockloft nigh.

Some morning I shall claim them,   5
And who may then possess will aim them
To bring to me those boards I need
    With thoughtful speed.

But though they hurry so
To yield me mine, I shall not know   10
How well my want they'll have supplied
    When notified.

4 *cockloft:* hayloft.

EPITAPH ON A PESSIMIST

I'm Smith of Stoke, aged sixty-odd,
    I've lived without a dame
From youth-time on; and would to God
    My dad had done the same.

CYNIC'S EPITAPH

A race with the sun as he downed
    I ran at evetide,
Intent who should first gain the ground
    And there hide.

He beat me by some minutes then,   5
    But I triumphed anon,
For when he'd to rise up again
    I stayed on.

THE CAGED GOLDFINCH

Within a churchyard, on a recent grave,
    I saw a little cage
That jailed a goldfinch. All was silence save
    Its hops from stage to stage.

There was inquiry in its wistful eye,   5
    And once it tried to sing;
Of him or her who placed it there, and why,
    No one knew anything.

THE GARDEN SEAT

Its former green is blue and thin,
And its once firm legs sink in and in;
Soon it will break down unaware,
Soon it will break down unaware.

At night when reddest flowers are black   5
Those who once sat thereon come back;
Quite a row of them sitting there,
Quite a row of them sitting there.

With them the seat does not break down,
Nor winter freeze them, nor floods down,   10
For they are as light as upper air,
They are as light as upper air!

I LOOKED UP FROM MY WRITING

I looked up from my writing,
  And gave a start to see,
As if rapt in my inditing,
  The moon's full gaze on me.

Her meditative misty head   5
  Was spectral in its air,
And I involuntarily said,
  "What are you doing there?"

"Oh, I've been scanning pond and hole
  And waterway hereabout   10
For the body of one with a sunken soul
  Who has put his life-light out.

"Did you hear his frenzied tattle?
  It was sorrow for his son
Who is slain in brutish battle,   15
  Though he has injured none.

"And now I am curious to look
  Into the blinkered mind
Of one who wants to write a book
  In a world of such a kind."   20

Her temper overwrought me,
  And I edged to shun her view,
For I felt assured she thought me
  One who should drown him too.

OLD FURNITURE

I know not how it may be with others
  Who sit amid relics of householdry
That date from the days of their mothers' mothers,

But well I know how it is with me
    Continually.   5

I see the hands of the generations
    That owned each shiny familiar thing
In play on its knobs and indentations,
    And with its ancient fashioning
        Still dallying: 10

Hands behind hands, growing paler and paler,
    As in a mirror a candle-flame
Shows images of itself, each frailer
    As it recedes, though the eye may frame
        Its shape the same.   15

On the clock's dull dial a foggy finger,
    Moving to set the minutes right
With tentative touches that lift and linger
    In the wont of a month on a summer night,
        Creeps to my sight.   20

On this old viol, too, fingers are dancing—
    As whilom—just over the strings by the nut,
The tip of a bow receding, advancing
    In airy quivers, as if it would cut
        The plaintive gut.   25

And I see a face by that box for tinder,
    Glowing forth in fits from the dark,
And fading again, as the linten cinder
    Kindles to red at the flinty spark,
        Or goes out stark.   30

Well, well. It is best to be up and doing,
    The world has no use for one to-day
Who eyes things thus—no aim pursuing!
    He should not continue in this stay,
        But sink away.   35

22 *whilom:* formerly.

THE RECALCITRANTS

Let us off and search, and find a place
Where yours and mine can be natural lives,
Where no one comes who dissects and dives
And proclaims that ours is a curious case,
Which its touch of romance can scarcely grace, 5

You would think it strange at first, but then
Everything has been strange in its time.
When some one said on a day of the prime
He would bow to no brazen god again
He doubtless dazed the mass of men. 10

None will see in us a pair whose claims
To righteous judgment we care not making;
Who have doubted if breath be worth the taking,
And have no respect for the current fames
Whence the saviour has flown while abide the names. 15

We have found us already shunned, disdained,
And for re-acceptance have not once striven;
Whatever offense our course has given
The brunt thereof we have long sustained.
Well, let us away, scorned, unexplained. 20

8 *of the prime:* in ancient or early times.

CHANNEL FIRING

That night your great guns, unawares,
Shook all our coffins as we lay,
And broke the chancel window-squares,
We thought it was the Judgment-day

And sat upright. While drearisome 5
Arose the howl of wakened hounds:

The mouse let fall the altar-crumb,
The worms drew back into the mounds,

The glebe cow drooled. Till God called, "No;
It's gunnery practice out at sea   10
Just as before you went below;
The world is as it used to be:

"All nations striving strong to make
Red war yet redder. Mad as hatters
They do no more for Christ's sake   15
Than you who are helpless in such matters.

"That this is not the judgment-hour
For some of them's a blessed thing,
For if it were they'd have to scour
Hell's floor for so much threatening. . . .   20

"Ha, ha. It will be warmer when
I blow the trumpet (if indeed
I ever do; for you are men,
And rest eternal sorely need)."

So down we lay again. "I wonder,   25
Will the world ever saner be,"
Said one, "than when He sent us under
In our indifferent century!"

And many a skeleton shook his head.
"Instead of preaching forty year,"   30
My neighbour Parson Thirdly said,
"I wish I had stuck to pipes and beer."

Again the guns disturbed the hour,
Roaring their readiness to avenge,
As far inland as Stourton Tower,   35
And Camelot, and starlit Stonehenge.

9 *glebe:* owned by the church.

THE CONVERGENCE OF THE TWAIN

(*Lines on the loss of the "Titanic"*)

I

In a solitude of the sea
Deep from human vanity,
And the Pride of Life that planned her, stilly couches she.

II

Steel chambers, late the pyres
Of her salamandrine fires,   5
Cold currents thrid, and turn to rhythmic tidal lyres.

III

Over the mirrors meant
To glass the opulent
The sea-worm crawls—grotesque, slimed, dumb, indifferent.

IV

Jewels in joy designed   10
To ravish the sensuous mind
Lie lightless, all their sparkles bleared and black and blind.

V

Dim moon-eyed fishes near
Gaze at the gilded gear
And query: "What does this vaingloriousness down here?" . . . 15

VI

Well: while was fashioning
This creature of cleaving wing,
The Immanent Will that stirs and urges everything

VII

Prepared a sinister mate
For her—so gaily great—   20
A Shape of Ice, for the time far and dissociate.

5 *salamandrine:* awesome, eternal. The salamander was a legendary lizard
which lived eternally in flames.   6 *thrid:* dialectic form of "thread."

VIII

And as the smart ship grew
In stature, grace, and hue,
In shadowy silent distance grew the Iceberg too.

IX

Alien they seemed to be: 25
No mortal eye could see
The intimate welding of their later history.

X

Or sign that they were bent
By paths coincident
On being anon twin halves of one august event,   30

XI

Till the Spinner of the Years
Said "Now!" And each one hears,
And consummation comes, and jars two hemispheres.

JOHN CROWE RANSOM

[*1888–*]

John Crowe Ransom was born in Pulaski, Tennessee, the son of a Methodist minister. After graduation from Vanderbilt University he was awarded a Rhodes Scholarship and enrolled at Christ College, Oxford, from which he received a B.A. in Classics.

Ransom taught for a year in a Mississippi high school and then became a member of the English department at Vanderbilt where he helped to start, in 1922, THE FUGITIVE, *a literary magazine also associated with the youthful Allen Tate and Robert Penn Warren. Ransom left Vanderbilt in 1937 to become Professor of English at Kenyon College and to found and edit the* KENYON REVIEW.

His first volume of verse, entitled POEMS ABOUT GOD, *was published in 1919. It was followed in 1924 by* CHILLS AND FEVER *and, in 1926, by* TWO GENTLEMEN IN BONDS. *His* SELECTED POEMS *appeared in 1945, and he was awarded the Bollingen Prize in 1951.*

During the 1930s Ransom devoted much of his writing to social and literary criticism. GOD WITHOUT THUNDER, *an indictment of the deification of science, was published in 1930, and* THE WORLD'S BODY, *an argument for the richness or "body" of poetry's delineation of experience (as against that of science), was published in 1938.*

In 1941 he published his influential collection of essays, THE NEW CRITICISM, *a rigorous analysis of the work of T. S. Eliot, William Empson, Yvor Winters, and I. A. Richards.*

There is no collected edition of Ransom's works and no full-length treatment of the man or his work has yet been published. His influence can be measured by the constant reference to him in critical journals and he is prominent in most contemporary literary histories and anthologies. A useful article of a general nature is "Homage to John Ransom: Essays on His Work as Poet and Critic," in the Summer 1948 issue of the SEWANEE REVIEW.

WINTER REMEMBERED

Two evils, monstrous either one apart,   23
Possessed me, and were long and loath at going:
A cry of Absence, Absence, in the heart,
And in the wood the furious winter blowing.

Think not, when fire was bright upon my bricks,   5
And past the tight boards hardly a wind could enter,
I glowed like them, the simple burning sticks,
Far from my cause, my proper heat and center.

Better to walk forth in the frozen air
And wash my wound in the snows; that would be healing; 10
Because my heart would throb less painful there,
Being caked with cold, and past the smart of feeling.

And where I walked, the murderous winter blast
Would have this body bowed, these eyeballs streaming,
And though I think this heart's blood froze not fast   15
It ran too small to spare one drop for dreaming.

Dear love, these fingers that had known your touch,
And tied our separate forces first together,
Were ten poor idiot fingers not worth much,
Ten frozen parsnips hanging in the weather.   20

MIRIAM TAZEWELL

When Miriam Tazewell heard the tempest bursting
And his wrathy whips across the sky drawn crackling
She stuffed her ears for fright like a young thing
And with heart full of the flowers took to weeping.

But the earth shook dry his old back in good season,   5
He had weathered storms that drenched him deep as
      this one,

And the sun, Miriam, ascended to his dominion,
The storm was withered against his empyrean.

After the storm she went forth with skirts kilted
To see in the strong sun her lawn deflowered,   10
Her tulip, iris, peony strung and pelted,
Pots of geranium spilled and the stalks naked.

The spring transpired in that year with no flowers
But the regular stars went busily on their courses,
Suppers and cards were calendared, and some bridals,   15
And the birds demurely sang in the bitten poplars.

To Miriam Tazewell the whole world was villain
To prosper when the fragile babes were fallen,
And not to unstop her own storm and be maudlin,
For weeks she went untidy, she went sullen.   20

DEAD BOY

The little cousin is dead, by foul subtraction,
A green bough from Virginia's aged tree,
And none of the county kin like the transaction,
Nor some of the world of outer dark, like me.

A boy not beautiful, nor good, nor clever,   5
A black cloud full of storms too hot for keeping,
A sword beneath his mother's heart—yet never
Woman bewept her babe as this is weeping.

A pig with a pasty face, so I had said,
Squealing for cookies, kinned by poor pretense   10
With a noble house. But the little man quite dead,
I see the forbears' antique lineaments.

The elder men have strode by the box of death
To the wide flag porch, and muttering low send round
The bruit of the day. O friendly waste of breath!   15
Their hearts are hurt with a deep dynastic wound.

He was pale and little, the foolish neighbors say;
The first-fruits, saith the Preacher, the Lord hath taken;
But this was the old tree's late branch wrenched away,
Grieving the sapless limbs, the shorn and shaken.   20

SPECTRAL LOVERS

By night they haunted a thicket of April mist,
Out of that black ground suddenly come to birth,
Else angels lost in each other had fallen on earth.
Lovers they knew they were, but why unclasped, un-
    kissed?
Why should two lovers go frozen apart in fear?   5
And yet they were, they were.

Over the shredding of an April blossom
Scarcely her fingers touched him, quick with care,
Yet of evasions even she made a snare.
The heart was bold that clanged within her bosom,   10
The moment perfect, the time stopped for them,
Still her face turned from him.

Strong were the batteries of the April night
And the stealthy emanations of the field;
Should the walls of her prison undefended yield   15
And open her treasure to the first clamorous knight?
"This is the mad moon, and shall I surrender all?
If he but ask it I shall."

And gesturing largely to the moon of Easter,
Mincing his steps and swishing the jubilant grass,   20
Beheading some field-flowers that had come to pass,
He had reduced his tributaries faster
Had not considerations pinched his heart
Unfitly for his art.

"Am I reeling with the sap of April like a drunkard?   25
Blessed is he that taketh this richest of cities;
But it is so stainless the sack were a thousand pities.
This is that marble fortress not to be conquered,

Lest its white peace in the black flame turn to tinder
And an unutterable cinder." 30

They passed me once in April, in the mist.
No other reason is it when one walks and discovers
Two tall and wandering, like spectral lovers,
White in the season's moon-gold and amethyst,
Who touch their quick fingers fluttering like a bird 35
Whose songs shall never be heard.

NECROLOGICAL

The friar had said his paternosters duly
And scourged his limbs, and afterwards would have slept;
But with much riddling his head became unruly,
He arose, from the quiet monastery he crept.

Dawn lightened the place where the battle had been
    won. 5
The people were dead—it is easy he thought to die—
These dead remained, but the living all were gone,
Gone with the wailing trumps of victory.

The dead wore no rainment against the air,
Bartholomew's men had spoiled them where they fell; 10
In defeat the heroes' bodies were whitely bare,
The field was white like meads of asphodel.

Not all were white; some gory and fabulous
Whom the sword had pierced and then the grey wolf
    eaten;
But the brother reasoned that heroes' flesh was thus. 15
Flesh fails, and the postured bones lie weather-beaten.

The lords of chivalry lay prone and shattered.
The gentle and the bodyguard of yeomen;
Bartholomew's stroke went home—but little it mattered,
Bartholomew went to be stricken of other foemen. 20
Beneath the blue ogive of the firmament

10 *Bartholomew:* a fictitious name.   21 *ogive:* pointed arch.

Was a dead warrior, clutching whose mighty knees
Was a leman, who with her flame had warmed his tent,
For him enduring all men's pleasantries.

Close by the sable stream that purged the plain   25
Lay the white stallion and his rider thrown,
The great beast had spilled there his little brain,
And the little groin of the knight was spilled by a stone.

The youth possessed him then of a crooked blade
Deep in the belly of a lugubrious wight;   30
He fingered it well, and it was cunningly made;
But strange apparatus was it for a Carmelite.

Then he sat upon a hill and bowed his head
As under a riddle, and in a deep surmise
So still that he likened himself unto those dead   35
Whom the kites of Heaven solicited with sweet cries.

BELLS FOR JOHN WHITESIDE'S DAUGHTER

There was such speed in her little body,
And such lightness in her footfall,
It is no wonder her brown study
Astonishes us all.

Her wars were bruited in our high window.   5
We looked among orchard trees and beyond
Where she took arms against her shadow,
Or harried unto the pond

The lazy geese, like a snow cloud
Dripping their snow on the green grass,   10
Tricking and stopping, sleepy and proud,
Who cried in goose, Alas,

For the tireless heart within the little
Lady with rod that made them rise
From their noon apple-dreams and scuttle   15
Goose-fashion under the skies!

But now go the bells, and we are ready,
In one house we are sternly stopped
To say we are vexed at her brown study,
Lying so primly propped.   20

HERE LIES A LADY

Here lies a lady of beauty and high degree.
Of chills and fever she died, of fever and chills,
The delight of her husband, her aunt, an infant of three,
And of medicos marveling sweetly on her ills.

For either she burned, and her confident eyes would blaze,   5
And her fingers fly in a manner to puzzle their heads—
What was she making? Why, nothing; she sat in a maze
Of old scraps of laces, snipped into curious shreds—

Or this would pass, and the light of her fire decline
Till she lay discouraged and cold, like a thin stalk white
            and blown,   10
And would not open her eyes, to kisses, to wine;
The sixth of these states was her last; the cold settled down.

Sweet ladies, long may ye bloom, and toughly I hope ye may
            thole,
But was she not lucky? In flowers and lace and mourning,
In love and great honor we bade God rest her soul   15
After six little spaces of chill, and six of burning.

13 *thole:* endure.

JUDITH OF BETHULIA

Beautiful as the flying legend of some leopard
She had not yet chosen her great captain or prince
Depositary to her flesh, and our defense;

Judith of Bethulia: for the full story, see the Book of Judith in the
Douay version (Catholic) Bible.

And a wandering beauty is a blade out of its scabbard.
You know how dangerous, gentlemen of threescore?   5
May you know it yet ten more.

Nor by process of veiling she grew the less fabulous.
Grey or blue veils, we were desperate to study
The invincible emanations of her white body,
And the winds at her ordered raiment were ominous.   10
Might she walk in the market, sit in the council of soldiers?
Only of the extreme elders.

But a rare chance was the girl's then, when the Invader
Trumpeted from the south, and rumbled from the north,
Beleaguered the city from four quarters of the earth,   15
Our soldiery too craven and sick to aid her—
Where were the arms could countervail this horde?
Her beauty was the sword.

She sat with the elders, and proved on their blear visage
How bright was the weapon unrusted in her keeping,   20
While he lay surfeiting on their harvest heaping,
Wasting the husbandry of their rarest vintage—
And dreaming of the broad-breasted dames for concubine?
These floated on his wine.

He was lapped with bay-leaves, and grass and fumiter weed, 25
And from under the wine-film encountered his mortal vision,
For even within his tent she accomplished his derision;
She loosed one veil and another, standing unafraid;
And he perished. Nor brushed her with even so much as a
    daisy?
She found his destruction easy.   30

The heathen are all perished. The victory was furnished,
We smote them hiding in our vineyards, barns, annexes,
And now their white bones clutter the holes of foxes,
And the chieftain's head, with grinning sockets, and
    varnished—
Is it hung on the sky with a hideous epitaphy?   35
No, the woman keeps the trophy.

21 *he:* Holofernes, general of Nebuchadnezzar.

May God send unto our virtuous lady her prince.
It is stated she went reluctant to that orgy,
Yet a madness fevers our young men, and not the clergy
Nor the elders have turned them unto modesty since.   40
Inflamed by the thought of her naked beauty with desire?
Yes, and chilled with fear and despair.

BLUE GIRLS

Twirling your blue skirts, travelling the sward
Under the towers of your seminary,
Go listen to your teachers old and contrary
Without believing a word.

Tie the white fillets then about your hair   5
And think no more of what will come to pass
Than bluebirds that go walking on the grass
And chattering on the air.

Practise your beauty, blue girls, before it fail;
And I will cry with my loud lips and publish   10
Beauty which all our power shall never establish,
It is so frail.

For I could tell you a story which is true;
I know a lady with a terrible tongue,
Blear eyes fallen from blue,   15
All her perfections tarnished—yet it is not long
Since she was lovelier than any of you.

CAPTAIN CARPENTER

Captain Carpenter rose up in his prime
Put on his pistols and went riding out
But had got wellnigh nowhere at that time
Till he fell in with ladies in a rout.

It was a pretty lady and all her train
That played with him so sweetly but before
An hour she'd taken a sword with all her main
And twined him of his nose for evermore.

Captain Carpenter mounted up one day
And rode straightway into a stranger rogue
That looked unchristian but be that as may
The Captain did not wait upon prologue.

But drew upon him out of his great heart
The other swung against him with a club
And cracked his two legs at the shinny part
And let him roll and stick like any tub.

Captain Carpenter rode many a time
From male and female took he sundry harms
He met the wife of Satan crying "I'm
The she-wolf bids you shall bear no more arms."

Their strokes and counters whistled in the wind
I wish he had delivered half his blows
But where she should have made off like a hind
The bitch bit off his arms at the elbows.

And Captain Carpenter parted with his ears
To a black devil that used him in this wise
O Jesus ere his threescore and ten years
Another had plucked out his sweet blue eyes.

Captain Carpenter got up on his roan
And sallied from the gate in hell's despite
I heard him asking in the grimmest tone
If any enemy yet there was to fight?

"To any adversary it is fame
If he risk to be wounded by my tongue
Or burnt in two beneath my red heart's flame
Such are the perils he is cast among.

"But if he can he has a pretty choice
From an anatomy with little to lose
Whether he cut my tongue and take my voice
Or whether it be my round red heart he choose."

It was the neatest knave that ever was seen
Stepping in perfume from his lady's bower
Who at this word put in his merry mien
And fell on Captain Carpenter like a tower.

I would not knock old fellows in the dust   45
But there lay Captain Carpenter on his back
His weapons were the old heart in his bust
And a blade shook between rotten teeth alack.

The rogue in scarlet and grey soon knew his mind
He wished to get his trophy and depart   50
With gentle apology and touch refined
He pierced him and produced the Captain's heart.

God's mercy rest on Captain Carpenter now
I thought him Sirs an honest gentleman
Citizen husband soldier and scholar enow   55
Let jangling kites eat of him if they can.

But God's deep curses follow after those
That shore him of his goodly nose and ears
His legs and strong arms at the two elbows
And eyes that had not watered seventy years.   60

The curse of hell upon the sleek upstart
That got the Captain finally on his back
And took the red vitals of his heart
And made the kites to whet their beaks clack clack.

PIAZZA PIECE

—I am a gentleman in a dustcoat trying
To make you hear. Your ears are soft and small
And listen to an old man not at all,
They want the young men's whispering and sighing.
But see the roses on your trellis dying   5
And hear the spectral singing of the moon;
For I must have my lovely lady soon,
I am a gentleman in a dustcoat trying.

—I am a lady young in beauty waiting
Until my truelove comes, and then we kiss. 10
But what grey man among the vines is this
Whose words are dry and faint as in a dream?
Back from my trellis, Sir, before I scream!
I am a lady young in beauty waiting.

PARTING, WITHOUT A SEQUEL

She has finished and sealed the letter
At last, which he so richly has deserved,
With characters venomous and hatefully curved,
And nothing could be better.

But even as she gave it 5
Saying to the blue-capped functioner of doom,
"Into his hands," she hoped the leering groom
Might somewhere lose and leave it.

Then all the blood
Forsook the face. She was too pale for tears, 10
Observing the ruin of her younger years.
She went and stood

Under her father's vaunting oak
Who kept his peace in wind and sun, and glistened
Stoical in the rain; to whom she listened 15
If he spoke.

And now the agitation of the rain
Rasped his sere leaves, and he talked low and gentle
Reproaching the wan daughter by the lintel;
Ceasing and beginning again. 20

Away went the messenger's bicycle,
His serpent's track went up the hill forever,
And all the time she stood there hot as fever
And cold as any icicle.

JANET WAKING

Beautifully Janet slept
Till it was deeply morning. She woke then
And thought about her dainty-feathered hen,
To see how it had kept.

One kiss she gave her mother.   5
Only a small one gave she to her daddy
Who would have kissed each curl of his shining baby;
No kiss at all for her brother.

"Old Chucky, old Chucky!" she cried,
Running across the world upon the grass   10
To Chucky's house, and listening. But alas,
Her Chucky had died.

It was a transmogrifying bee
Came droning down on Chucky's old bald head
And sat and put the poison. It scarcely bled,   15
But how exceedingly

And purply did the knot
Swell with the venom and communicate
Its rigor! Now the poor comb stood up straight
But Chucky did not.   20

So there was Janet
Kneeling on the wet grass, crying her brown hen
(Translated far beyond the daughters of men)
To rise and walk upon it.

And weeping fast as she had breath   25
Janet implored us, "Wake her from her sleep!"
And would not be instructed in how deep
Was the forgetful kingdom of death.

LITTLE BOY BLUE

He rubbed his eyes and wound the silver horn.
Then the continuum was cracked and torn
With tumbling imps of music being born.

The blowzy sheep lethargic on the ground
Suddenly burned where no fire could be found   5
And straight up stood their fleeces every pound.

The old bellwether rose and rang his bell,
The seven-days' lambs went skipping and skipped well,
And Baa Baa Baa, the flock careered pellmell.

The yellow cows that milked the savoury cud   10
Propped on the green grass or the yellow mud
Felt such a tingle in their lady blood,

They ran and tossed their hooves and horns of blue
And jumped the fence and gambelled kangaroo,
Divinely singing as they wandered Moo.   15

A plague on such a shepherd of the sheep
That careless boy with pretty cows to keep!
With such a burden I should never sleep.

But when his notes had run around the sky,
When they proceeded to grow faint and die,   20
He stuffed his horn with straw and put it by.

And when the legs were tired beneath the sheep
And there were spent and sleepy cows to keep,
He rubbed his eyes again and went to sleep.

TWO IN AUGUST

Two that could not have lived their single lives
As can some husbands and wives
Did something strange: they tensed their vocal cords

And attacked each other with silences and words
Like catapulted stones and arrowed knives.   5

Dawn was not yet; night is for loving or sleeping,
Sweet dreams or safekeeping;
Yet he of the wide brows that were used to laurel
And she, the famed for gentleness, must quarrel.
Furious both of them, and scared, and weeping.   10

How sleepers groan, twitch, wake to such a mood
Is not well understood,
Nor why two entities grown almost one
Should rend and murder trying to get undone,
With individual tigers in their blood.   15

She in terror fled from the marriage chamber
Circuiting the dark rooms like a string of amber
Round and round and back,
And would not light one lamp against the black,
And heard the clock that clanged: Remember, Remember.   20

And he must tread barefooted the dim lawn,
Soon he was up and gone;
High in the trees the night-mastered birds were crying
With fear upon their tongues, no singing nor flying
Which are their lovely attitudes by dawn.   25

Whether those bird-cries were of heaven or hell
There is no way to tell;
In the long ditch of darkness the man walked
Under the hackberry trees where the birds talked
With words too sad and strange to syllable.   30

SURVEY OF LITERATURE

In all the good Greek of Plato
I lack my roastbeef and potato.

A better man was Aristotle,
Pulling steady on the bottle.

I dip my hat to Chaucer,   5
Swilling soup from his saucer,

And to Master Shakespeare
Who wrote big on small beer.

The abstemious Wordsworth
Subsisted on a curd's-worth,   10

But a slick one was Tennyson,
Putting gravy on his venison.

What these men had to eat and drink
Is what we say and what we think.

The influence of Milton   15
Came wry out of Stilton.

Sing a song for Percy Shelley,
Drowned in pale lemon jelly,

And for precious John Keats,
Dripping blood of pickled beets.   20

Then there was poor Willie Blake,
He foundered on sweet cake.

God have mercy on the sinner
Who must write with no dinner,

No gravy and no grub,   25
No pewter and no pub,

No belly and no bowels,
Only consonants and vowels.

THE EQUILIBRISTS

Full of her long white arms and milky skin
He had a thousand times remembered sin.
Alone in the press of people traveled he,
Minding her jacinth, and myrrh, and ivory.

Mouth he remembered: the quaint orifice   5
From which came heat that flamed upon the kiss,
Till cold words came down spiral from the head.
Grey doves from the officious tower illsped.

Body: it was a white field ready for love,
On her body's field, with the gaunt tower above,   10
The lilies grew, beseeching him to take,
If he would pluck and wear them, bruise and break.

Eyes talking: Never mind the cruel words,
Embrace my flowers, but not embrace the swords.
But what they said, the doves came straightway flying   15
And unsaid: Honor, Honor, they came crying.

Importunate her doves. Too pure, too wise,
Clambering on his shoulder, saying, Arise,
Leave me now, and never let us meet,
Eternal distance now command thy feet.   20

Predicament indeed, which thus discovers
Honor among thieves, Honor between lovers.
O such a little word is Honor, they feel!
But the grey word is between them cold as steel.

At length I saw these lovers fully were come   25
Into their torture of equilibrium;
Dreadfully had forsworn each other, and yet
They were bound each to each, and they did not forget.

And rigid as two painful stars, and twirled
About the clustered night their prison world,   30
They burned with fierce love always to come near,
But honor beat them back and kept them clear.

Ah, the strict lovers, they are ruined now!
I cried in anger. But with puddled brow
Devising for those gibbeted and brave   35
Came I descanting: Man, what would you have?

For spin your period out, and draw your breath,
A kinder saeculum begins with Death.

38 *saeculum:* age.

Would you ascend to Heaven and bodiless dwell?
Or take your bodies honorless to Hell?   40

In Heaven you have heard no marriage is,
No white flesh tinder to your lecheries,
Your male and female tissue sweetly shaped
Sublimed away, and furious blood escaped.

Great lovers lie in Hell, the stubborn ones   45
Infatuate of the flesh upon the bones;
Stuprate, they rend each other when they kiss,
The pieces kiss again, no end to this.

But still I watched them spinning, orbited nice.
Their flames were not more radiant than their ice.   50
I dug in the quiet earth and wrought the tomb
And made these lines to memorize their doom:—

EPITAPH

Equilibrists lie here; stranger, tread light;
Close, but untouching in each other's sight;
Mouldered the lips and ashy the tall skull.   55
Let them lie perilous and beautiful.

47 *stuprate:* ravished.

ARCHIBALD MACLEISH

[*1892-*]

Archibald MacLeish was born in Glencoe, Illinois, on May 7, 1892. His father, Andrew MacLeish, was a Scottish immigrant who became a partner in the Carson, Pirie, and Scott Company of Chicago. After attending the Glencoe public schools and the Hotchkiss School in Connecticut, MacLeish matriculated at Yale University, where he was editor of the literary magazine. There he composed his first book of verse, TOWER OF IVORY, which was published in 1917. He was elected to Phi Beta Kappa and received his B.A. in 1915. Four years later, he graduated from Harvard Law School at the head of his class, having interrupted his studies to serve in World War I.

Following a year of teaching at Harvard, MacLeish practiced law in Boston. But the aspiring poet found that a law career interfered with his writing, and in the winter of 1923, he left for France with his wife and family in order to devote himself entirely to his poetry. In 1928 he returned to America and, after an extended stay in Mexico, he published his poem CONQUISTADOR (1932). The book won him a Pulitzer Prize and wide recognition as a poet. Throughout the 1930s he supported his family by working for FORTUNE magazine. During this period MacLeish became increasingly distressed over economic and political developments. His PANIC; A PLAY IN VERSE (1936) dealt with the Depression. His appointment in 1939 as Librarian of Congress provoked a controversy concerning his lack of professional experience as a librarian, but he retained the post until 1944. Meanwhile, he acted as Director of the Office of Facts and Figures (1941–1942) and Assistant Director of the Office of War Information (1942–1943). From 1944 until the end of the war he served as an assistant Secretary of State. Following the war, MacLeish played an important part in the founding of UNESCO.

In 1949 MacLeish was appointed Boylston Professor of Rhetoric and Oratory at Harvard, the position which he presently holds. For his COLLECTED POEMS, 1917–1952 *(1952) MacLeish was awarded the Bollingen Prize, the National Book Award, and a second Pulitzer Prize. His* J.B.: A PLAY IN VERSE *(1958) was given the Antoinette Perry Award and the Pulitzer Prize. MacLeish has published over thirty books, including poetry, prose, verse plays, and a verse ballet.*

Extensive critical assessments have been made by Cleanth Brooks, MODERN POETRY AND THE TRADITION *(1939), Oscar Cargill,* INTELLECTUAL AMERICAN: IDEAS ON THE MARCH *(1941), and by S. L. Falk,* ARCHIBALD MACLEISH, *in the Twayne Series (1966).*

THE SILENT SLAIN

We too, we too, descending once again
The hills of our own land, we too have heard
Far off—Ah, que ce cor a longue haleine—
The horn of Roland in the passages of Spain,
The first, the second blast, the failing third,   5
And with the third turned back and climbed once more
The steep road southward, and heard, faint, the sound
Of swords, of horses, the disastrous war,
And crossed the dark defile at last, and found
At Roncevaux upon the darkening plain   10
The dead against the dead and on the silent ground
The silent slain—

The Silent Slain: when first published (1926), this poem was entitled "The Too-Late Born."   3 *Ah, que ce cor a longue haleine:* Ah, the long blasts of the horn   4 *Roland:* legendary hero who warned Charlemagne's army of the Saracen advance by blowing his horn, and died defending the pass of Roncevalles.

MOTHER GOOSE'S GARLAND

Around, around the sun we go:
The moon goes round the earth.
We do not die of death:
We die of vertigo.

THE END OF THE WORLD

Quite unexpectedly as Vasserot
The armless ambidextrian was lighting
A match between his great and second toe
And Ralph the lion was engaged in biting
The neck of Madame Sossman while the drum   5
Pointed, and Teeny was about to cough
In waltz-time swinging Jocko by the thumb—
Quite unexpectedly the top blew off:

And there, there overhead, there, there, hung over
Those thousands of white faces, those dazed eyes,   10
There in the starless dark the poise, the hover,
There with vast wings across the canceled skies,
There in the sudden blackness the black pall
Of nothing, nothing, nothing—nothing at all.

1 *Vasserot:* a freak and a circus performer, as are those mentioned below.

MEMORIAL RAIN

for Kenneth MacLeish, 1894–1918

Ambassador Puser the ambassador
Reminds himself in French, felicitous tongue,
What these (young men no longer) lie here for
In rows that once, and somewhere else, were young . . .

All night in Brussels the wind had tugged at my door: 5
I had heard the wind at my door and the trees strung
Taut, and to me who had never been before
In that country it was a strange wind, blowing
Steadily, stiffening the walls, the floor,
The roof of my room. I had not slept for knowing   10
He too, dead, was a stranger in that land
And felt beneath the earth in the wind's flowing
A tightening of roots and would not understand,

Remembering lake winds in Illinois,
That strange wind. I had felt his bones in the sand   15
Listening.

>   *... Reflects that these enjoy*
> *Their country's gratitude, that deep repose,*
> *That peace no pain can break, no hurt destroy,*
> *That rest, that sleep ...*   20

                At Ghent the wind rose.
There was a smell of rain and a heavy drag
Of wind in the hedges but not as the wind blows
Over fresh water when the waves lag
Foaming and the willows huddle and it will rain: 25
I felt him waiting.

>   *... Indicates the flag*
> *Which (may he say) enisles in Flanders plain*
> *This little field these happy, happy dead*
> *Have made America ...*   30

                In the ripe grain
The wind coiled glistening, darted, fled,
Dragging its heavy body: at Waereghem
The wind coiled in the grass above his head:
Waiting—listening ...   35

>   *... Dedicates to them*
> *This earth their bones have hallowed, this last gift*
> *A grateful country ...*

             Under the dry grass stem
The words are blurred, are thickened, the words sift   40
Confused by the rasp of the wind, by the thin grating
Of ants under the grass, the minute shift
And tumble of dusty sand separating
From dusty sand. The roots of the grass strain,
Tighten, the earth is rigid, waits—he is waiting—   45

And suddenly, and all at once, the rain!

28 *enisles:* i.e., isolates.   33 *Waereghem:* site of Flanders Field, American Cemetery.

The living scatter, they run into houses, the wind
Is trampled under the rain, shakes free, is again
Trampled. The rain gathers, running in thinned
Spurts of water that ravel in the dry sand,   50
Seeping in the sand under the grass roots, seeping
Between cracked boards to the bones of a clenched hand:
The earth relaxes, loosens, he is sleeping,
He rests, he is quiet, he sleeps in a strange land.

ARS POETICA

A poem should be palpable and mute
As a globed fruit,

Dumb
As old medallions to the thumb,

Silent as the sleeve-worn stone   5
Of casement ledges where the moss has grown—

A poem should be wordless
As the flight of birds.

A poem should be motionless in time
As the moon climbs,   10

Leaving, as the moon releases
Twig by twig the night-entangled trees,

Leaving, as the moon behind the winter leaves,
Memory by memory the mind—

A poem should be motionless in time   15
As the moon climbs.

A poem should be equal to:
Not true.

For all the history of grief
An empty doorway and a maple leaf.   20

For love
The leaning grasses and two lights above the sea—

A poem should not mean
But be.

"NOT MARBLE NOR THE GILDED MONUMENTS"

The praisers of women in their proud and beautiful poems,
Naming the grave mouth and the hair and the eyes,
Boasted those they loved should be forever remembered:
These were lies.

The words sound but the face in the Istrian sun is forgotten.   5
The poet speaks but to her dead ears no more.
The sleek throat is gone—and the breast that was troubled to
        listen:
Shadow from door.

Therefore I will not praise your knees nor your fine walking
Telling you men shall remember your name as long   10
As lips move or breath is spent or the iron of English
Rings from a tongue.

I shall say you were young and your arms straight and your
        mouth scarlet:
I shall say you will die and none will remember you:
Your arms change and none remember the swish of your
        garments,   15
Nor the click of your shoe.

Not with my hand's strength, not with difficult labor
Springing the obstinate words to the bones of your breast
And the stubborn line to your young stride and the breath
        to your breathing
And the beat to your haste   20
Shall I prevail on the hearts of unborn men to remember.

"Not Marble nor the Gilded Monuments": the first line of Shakespeare's
Sonnet 55.   5 *Istrian:* a Yugoslav peninsula.

(What is a dead girl but a shadowy ghost
Or a dead man's voice but a distant and vain affirmation
Like dream words most)

Therefore I will not speak of the undying glory of women. 25
I will say you were young and straight and your skin fair
And you stood in the door and the sun was a shadow of leaves
     on your shoulders
And a leaf on your hair—

I will not speak of the famous beauty of dead women:
I will say the shape of a leaf lay once on your hair. 30
Till the world ends and the eyes are out and the mouths
     broken
Look! It is there!

YOU, ANDREW MARVELL

And here face down beneath the sun
And here upon earth's noonward height
To feel the always coming on
The always rising of the night:

To feel creep up the curving east 5
The earthy chill of dusk and slow
Upon those under lands the vast
And ever climbing shadow grow

And strange at Ecbatan the trees
Take leaf by leaf the evening strange 10
The flooding dark about their knees
The mountains over Persia change

And now at Kermanshah the gate
Dark empty and the withered grass
And through the twilight now the late 15
Few travelers in the westward pass

And Baghdad darken and the bridge
Across the silent river gone

You, Andrew Marvell: see pp. 86–101.   9 *Ecbatan:* a city in Persia.

And through Arabia the edge
Of evening widen and steal on   20

And deepen on Palmyra's street
The wheel rut in the ruined stone
And Lebanon fade out and Crete
High through the clouds and overblown

And over Sicily the air   25
Still flashing with the landward gulls
And loom and slowly disappear
The sails above the shadowy hulls

And Spain go under and the shore
Of Africa the gilded sand   30
And evening vanish and no more
The low pale light across that land

Nor now the long light on the sea:

And here face downward in the sun
To feel how swift how secretly   35
The shadow of the night comes on . . .

IMMORTAL AUTUMN

I speak this poem now with grave and level voice
In praise of autumn, of the far-horn-winding fall.
I praise the flower-barren fields, the clouds, the tall
Unanswering branches where the wind makes sullen noise.

I praise the fall: it is the human season.   5
                    Now

No more the foreign sun does meddle at our earth,
Enforce the green and bring the fallow land to birth,
Nor winter yet weigh all with silence the pine bough,

But now in autumn with the black and outcast crows
Share we the spacious world: the whispering year is gone: 10
There is more room to live now: the once secret dawn
Comes late by daylight and the dark unguarded goes.

Between the mutinous brave burning of the leaves
And winter's covering of our hearts with his deep snow
We are alone: there are no evening birds: we know   15
The naked moon: the tame stars circle at our eaves.

It is the human season. On this sterile air
Do words outcarry breath: the sound goes on and on,
I hear a dead man's cry from autumn long since gone.

I cry to you beyond upon this bitter air.   20

MEN

Our history is grave noble and tragic.
We trusted the look of the sun on the green leaves.
We built our town of stone with enduring ornaments.
We worked the hard flint for basins of water.

We believed in the feel of the earth under us.   5
We planted corn grapes apple-trees rhubarb.
Nevertheless we knew others had died.
Everything we have done has been faithful and dangerous.

We believed in the promises made by the brows of women.
We begot children at night in the warm wool.   10
We comforted those who wept in fear on our shoulders.
Those who comforted us had themselves vanished.

We fought at the dikes in the bright sun for the pride of it.
We beat drums and marched with music and laughter.
We were drunk and lay with our fine dreams in the straw. 15
We saw the stars through the hair of lewd women.

Our history is grave noble and tragic.
Many of us have died and are not remembered.
Many cities are gone and their channels broken.
We have lived a long time in this land and with honor.   20

LINES FOR AN INTERMENT

Now it is fifteen years you have lain in the meadow:
The boards at your face have gone through: the earth is
Packed down and the sound of the rain is fainter:
The roots of the first grass are dead.

It's a long time to lie in the earth with your honor: 5
The world, Soldier, the world has been moving on.

The girls wouldn't look at you twice in the cloth cap:
Six years old they were when it happened.

It bores them even in books: "Soissons beseiged!"
As for the gents they have joined the American Legion.   10

Belts and a brass band and the ladies' auxiliaries:
The Californians march in the OD silk.

We are all acting again like civilized beings:
People mention it at tea . . .

The Facts of Life we have learned are Economic: 15
You were deceived by the detonations of bombs.

You thought of courage and death when you thought of
        warfare.
Hadn't they taught you the fine words were unfortunate?

Now that we understand we judge without bias:
We feel of course for those who had to die.   20

Women have written us novels of great passion
Proving the useless death of the dead was a tragedy.

Nevertheless it is foolish to chew gall:
The foremost writers on both sides have apologized.

The Germans are back in the Midi with cropped hair: 25
The English are drinking the better beer in Bavaria.

You can rest now in the rain in the Belgian meadow—
Now that it's all explained away and forgotten:
Now that the earth is hard and the wood rots:

Now you are dead . . .   30

POLE STAR

Where the wheel of light is turned,
Where the axle of the night is
Turned, is motionless, where holds
And has held ancient sureness always:

Where of faring men the eyes   5
At oar bench at the rising bow
Have seen—torn shrouds between—the Wain
And that star's changelessness, not changing:

There upon that intent star,
Trust of wandering men, of truth   10
The most reminding witness, we
Fix our eyes also, waylost, the wanderers:

We too turn now to that star:
We too in whose trustless hearts
All truth alters and the lights   15
Of earth are out now turn to that star:

Liberty of man and mind
That once was mind's necessity
And made the West blaze up has burned
To bloody embers and the lamp's out: 20

Hope that was a noble flame
Has fanned to violence and feeds
On cities and the flesh of men
And chokes where unclean smoke defiles it:

Even the small spark of pride   25
That taught the tyrant once is dark

7 *wain:* the Big Dipper.

246

Where gunfire rules the starving street
And justice cheats the dead of honor:

Liberty and pride and hope—
Every guide-mark of the mind   30
That led our blindness once has vanished.
This star will not. Love's star will not.

Love that has beheld the face
A man has with a man's eyes in it
Bloody from the slugger's blows   35
Or heard the cold child cry for hunger—

Love that listens where the good,
The virtuous, the men of faith,
Proclaim the paradise on earth
And murder starve and burn to make it—   40

Love that cannot either sleep
Or keep rich music in the ear
Or lose itself for the wild beat
The anger in the blood makes raging—

Love that hardens into hate,   45
Love like hatred and as bright,
Love is that one waking light
That leads now when all others darken.

SPEECH TO THE DETRACTORS

What should a man do but love excellence
Whether of earth or art,
Whether the hare's leap or the heart's recklessness?

What honor has any man but with eagerness,
Valuing wasteless things,
To praise the great and speak the unpraise meagerly?

Because the heroes with the swords have vanished
Leaving us nearer by
Actual life and the more human manhood—

Because the common face, the anonymous figure,   10
The nameless and mortal man,
Is our time's birth to bear and to be big with—

Because the captains and the kings are dust—
Need we deny our hearts
Their natural duty and the thing they must do?   15

Not to the wearers of wreaths but those who bring them,
Coming with heaped-up arms,
Is fame the noble and ennobling thing.

Bequeathers of praise, the unnamed numberless peoples
Leave on the lasting earth   20
Not fame but their hearts' love of fame for keeping.

They raise not alone memorial monuments:
Outlasting these
They raise their need to render greatness honor.

The ignorant and rabble rain erases   25
Dates and the dead man's kind.
It leaves the blindness of the stones that praised him.

Why then must this time of ours be envious?
Why must the great man now—
Sealed from the mouths of worms—be sucked by men's mouths? 30

Refusing ribbons that the rest have clowned for—
Dying and wishing peace—
The best are eaten by the envy round them.

When Lawrence died the hate was at his bier.
Fearing there might have lived   35
A man really noble, really superior—

Fearing that worth had lived and had been modest—
Men of envious minds
Ate with venom his new buried body.

We cheat ourselves in cheating worth of wonder.   40
Not the unwitting dead
But we who leave the praise unsaid are plundered.

"DOVER BEACH"—A NOTE TO THAT POEM

The wave withdrawing
Withers with seaward rustle of flimsy water
Sucking the sand down, dragging at empty shells,
The roil after it settling, too smooth, smothered . . .
After forty a man's fool to wait in the   5
Sea's face for the full force and the roaring of
Surf to come over him: droves of careening water.
After forty the tug's out and the salt and the
Sea follow it: less sound and violence.
Nevertheless the ebb has its own beauty—   10
Shells sand and all and the whispering rustle.
There's earth in it then and the bubbles of foam gone.

Moreover—and this too has its lovely uses—
It's the outward wave that spills the inward forward
Tripping the proud piled mute virginal   15
Mountain of water in wallowing welter of light and
Sound enough—thunder for miles back. It's a fine and a
Wild smother to vanish in: pulling down—
Tripping with outward ebb the urgent inward.

Speaking alone for myself it's the steep hill and the   20
Toppling lift of the young men I am toward now—
Waiting for that as the wave for the next wave.
Let them go over us all I say with the thunder of
What's to be next in the world. It's we will be under it!

"Dover Beach": a poem by Matthew Arnold, Victorian poet and critic
(1822–1888).

THE SUNSET PIECE

For Phelps Putnam upon the completion of our
fortieth year in this place

Christ but this earth goes over to the squall of time!
Hi but she heels to it—rail down, ribs down, rolling
Dakotas under her hull! And the night climbing
Sucking the green from the ferns by these Berkshire boulders!

She'll roll the two of us clean of her one day lifting—   5
Draining the dark from her gutters with slick slide,
The night running off from her—you and me like driftwood:
Men we've known like litter on a tide.

She'll roll us clear of her, drowned in a dragging wake,
Time going over us, touching us like a sea—   10
You and me that bragged our berths were taken
For death's eventual wharves and foreign quay:
You and me that bragged of an end to the journey—
The bow brought fast, the stern warped in, the screw
Dead in a dirty wash and the sea gulls turning: 15
Earnest faces and no face we knew.

You and me!
                And watch her! She's God's planet!
She luffs in the wind and she logs in the seaway rolling
The earth's no ship to board for any land—   20
Even for death's.
                    The night among the boulders . . . .

THE QUARREL

I never said that you were changed.
I said—and if I looked at you
With fear it was my natural heart—
I said dear love that you were true.

I said your body was still yours   5
And bore no bruise where he had been:
Your mouth was still the mouth I knew,
The hair was yours, the throat, the skin.

I said I could not see his eyes
In your eyes doubled: could not hear   10
The whisper of his actual breath
Beneath your hair, against your ear.

I never said that you were changed:
I said—in dread as though you came
Unaltered from the earth of death—   15
I said your eyes were still the same!

FROM *"The Woman on the Stair"*

THE RECONCILIATION

Time like the repetitions of a child's piano
Brings me the room again the shallow lamp the love
The night the silence the slow bell the echoed answer.

By no thing here or lacking can the eyes discover
The hundred winter evenings that have gone between   5
Nor know for sure the night is this and not that other.

The room is here, the lamp is here, the mirror's leaning
Searches the same deep shadow where her knees are caught:
All these are here within the room as I have seen them.

Time has restored them all as in that rainy autumn: 10
Even the echoes of that night return to this—
All as they were when first the earthy evening brought them.

Between this night and that there is no human distance:
There is no space an arm could not out-reach by much—
And yet the stars most far apart are not more distant.   15

Between my hand that touched and her soft breast that
    touches
The irremediable past, as steep as stone,
Wider than water, like all land and ocean stretches:

We touch and by that touching farness are alone.

FROM *"The Woman on the Stair"*

THE ROOM BY THE RIVER

They think in each other's arms of the sound of the surf:
(The sound in that street is of barges:
The wake v's out, curves,
Breaks on the bulkhead blurring the water stars.)

They think how the sound of the surf is the sound of forever 5
Turning upon the returning of time—
Bringing the wave back that has left them—
Taking their knees again with the sea's climbing.

(The sound in that street is the sound of the barges:
The one wave breaks along the brackish shore: 10
Nothing returns . . . .)

                  He rises from her arms to
Dress in silence and go out the door.

FROM *"The Woman on the Stair"*

THE REMEMBRANCE

I have forgotten you. There is grey light on my
Hands and I have forgotten you. There is light enough.
There is light enough left to forget your face by—
Voice by, to forget you. As long as the
Light lasts on my hands I forget you.   5
There needs be some light: a little.
A man remembers by night—even the

Windows barely a sure shape and the
Shadows anything—standing for anything.
Night is never alone: it remembers.   10
At night the hair mouth eyes—
The eyes—at night they return to us.

Between the night and me this light,
Little enough, a thin cover,
Fragile defense against the meaning dark   15
Where eyes are always but not seen till night comes.
Now for a little there is light between.

FROM *"The Woman on the Stair"*

TRICKED BY ETERNITY THE HEART

Corruptible if all things are,
Corruption yet has eyes to see.
Dead for a hundred years, the star
Still burns for us above the tree.

Between the cause and the effect,   5
Time, like the custom of the street,
Teaches our eyes till they expect
What is no longer theirs to meet:

Teaches our eyes until the face
That smiles in mirrors when we smile—   10
Still young, still fair, still full of grace—
Stands for our aging hearts awhile.

CALYPSO'S ISLAND

I know very well, goddess, she is not beautiful
As you are: could not be. She is a woman,
Mortal, subject to the chances: duty of

Childbed, sorrow that changes cheeks, the tomb—
For unlike you she will grow grey, grow older,   5
Grey and older, sleep in that small room.

She is not beautiful as you, O golden!
You are immortal and will never change
And can make me immortal also, fold

Your garment round me, make me whole and strange   10
As those who live forever, not the while
That we live; keep me from those dogging dangers—

Ships and the wars—in this green, far-off island,
Silent of all but sea's eternal sound
Or sea-pine's when the lull of surf is silent.   15

Goddess, I know how excellent this ground,
What charmed contentment of the removed heart
The bees make in the lavender where pounding

Surf sounds far off and the bird that darts
Darts through its own eternity of light,   20
Motionless in motion, and the startled

Hare is startled into stone, the fly
Forever golden in the flickering glance
Of leafy sunlight that still holds it. I

Know you, goddess, and your caves that answer   25
Ocean's confused voices with a voice:
Your poplars where the storms are turned to danccs;

Arms where the heart is turned. You give the choice
To hold forever what forever passes,
To hide from what will pass, forever. Moist,   30

Moist are your well-stones, goddess, cool your grasses!
And she—she is a woman with that fault
Of change that will be death in her at last!

Nevertheless I long for the cold, salt,
Restless, contending sea and for the island   35
Where the grass dies and the seasons alter:

Where that one wears the sunlight for a while.

CROSSING

At five precisely in the afternoon
The dining car cook on the Boston and Albany
Through train to somewhere leaned and waved
At the little girl on the crossing at Ghent, New York—
The one with the doll carriage.   5

                               Who understood it best?
She, going home to her supper, telling her Pa?
The Negro cook, shutting the vestibule window,
Thinking: She waved right back she did? Or I,
Writing it down and wondering as I write it   10
Why a forgotten touch of human grace
Is more alive forgotten than its memory
Pressed between two pages in this place?

THEODORE ROETHKE

[*1908–1963*]

Theodore Roethke was born in Saginaw, Michigan. His father and uncle owned extensive greenhouses and a game preserve and he grew up with a love and understanding of animals and growing things. He was educated at the University of Michigan and at Harvard where, while working for his M.A., he was encouraged in his early attempts at poetry by Robert Hillyer.

In 1941 his first book of poems, OPEN HOUSE, *received favorable comment from W. H. Auden, Louise Bogan, and Yvor Winters. With the publication of* THE LOST SON AND OTHER POEMS *in 1948 he was firmly established as a major American poet.* PRAISE TO THE END! *was published in 1951; in 1954 Roethke won the Pulitzer Prize for* THE WAKING. THE FAR FIELD *was published posthumously in 1964.*

Roethke taught at Bennington, Lafayette, Penn State, and, in 1947, he accepted a position at the University of Washington where he remained until his death. An exceptionally fine teacher, Roethke exerted great influence on young poets, attracting a number of them as students, visitors, or teachers to the Pacific northwest.

Besides the Pulitzer Prize, Roethke was honored with two National Book Awards and, in 1959, the Bollingen Prize.

A useful short piece on the poet is Ralph Mills' THEODORE ROETHKE *(in the University of Minnesota Pamphlets on American Writers series) and* ON THE POET AND HIS CRAFT: SELECTED PROSE OF THEODORE ROETHKE, *edited by Ralph J. Mills, offers much insight into Roethke's work. Arnold Stein has edited* THEODORE ROETHKE: ESSAYS ON THE POETRY.

OPEN HOUSE

My secrets cry aloud.
I have no need for tongue.
My heart keeps open house,
My doors are widely swung.
An epic of the eyes   5
My love, with no disguise.

My truths are all foreknown,
This anguish self-revealed.
I'm naked to the bone,
With nakedness my shield.   10
Myself is what I wear:
I keep the spirit spare.

The anger will endure,
The deed will speak the truth
In language strict and pure.   15
I stop the lying mouth:
Rage warps my clearest cry
To witless agony.

DEATH PIECE

Invention sleeps within a skull
No longer quick with light,
The hive that hummed in every cell
Is now sealed honey-tight.

His thought is tied, the curving prow   5
Of motion moored to rock;
And minutes burst upon a brow
Insentient to shock.

257

TO MY SISTER

O my sister remember the stars the tears the trains
The woods in spring the leaves the scented lanes
Recall the gradual dark the snow's unmeasured fall
The naked fields the cloud's immaculate folds
Recount each childhood pleasure: the skies of azure   5
The pageantry of wings the eye's bright treasure.

Keep faith with present joys refuse to choose
Defer the vice of flesh the irrevocable choice
Cherish the eyes the proud incredible poise
Walk boldly my sister but do not deign to give   10
Remain secure from pain preserve thy hate thy heart.

INTERLUDE

The element of air was out of hand.
The rush of wind ripped off the tender leaves
And flung them in confusion on the land.
We waited for the first rain in the eaves.

The chaos grew as hour by hour the light   5
Decreased beneath an undivided sky.
Our pupils widened with unnatural night,
But still the road and dusty field kept dry.

The rain stayed in its cloud; full dark came near;
The wind lay motionless in the long grass.   10
The veins within our hands betrayed our fear.
What we had hoped for had not come to pass.

PRAYER

If I must of my Senses lose,
I pray Thee, Lord, that I may choose
Which of the Five I shall retain
Before oblivion clouds the brain.
My Tongue is generations dead,   5
My Nose defiles a comely head;
For hearkening to carnal evils
My Ears have been the very devil's.
And some have held the Eye to be
The instrument of lechery,   10
More furtive than the Hand in low
And vicious venery—Not so!
Its rape is gentle, never more
Violent than a metaphor.
In truth, the Eye's the abettor of   15
The holiest platonic love:
Lip, Breast and Thigh cannot possess
So singular a blessedness.
Therefore, O Lord, let me preserve
The Sense that does so fitly serve,   20
Take Tongue and Ear—all else I have—
Let Light attend me to the grave!

MID-COUNTRY BLOW

All night and all day the wind roared in the trees,
Until I could think there were waves rolling high as my
      bedroom floor;
When I stood at the window, an elm bough swept to my knees;
The blue spruce lashed like a surf at the door.

The second dawn I would not have believed: 5
The oak stood with each leaf stiff as a bell.
When I looked at the altered scene, my eye was undeceived,
But my ear still kept the sound of the sea like a shell.

THE BAT

By day the bat is cousin to the mouse.
He likes the attic of an aging house.

His fingers make a hat about his head.
His pulse beat is so slow we think him dead.

He loops in crazy figures half the night   5
Among the trees that face the corner light.

But when he brushes up against a screen,
We are afraid of what our eyes have seen:

For something is amiss or out of place
When mice with wings can wear a human face.   10

NO BIRD

Now here is peace for one who knew
The secret heart of sound.
The ear so delicate and true
Is pressed to noiseless ground.

Slow swings the breeze above her head,   5
The grasses whitely stir;
But in this forest of the dead
No bird awakens her.

ON THE ROAD TO WOODLAWN

I miss the polished brass, the powerful black horses,
The drivers creaking the seats of the baroque hearses,
The high-piled floral offerings with sentimental verses,
The carriages reeking with varnish and stale perfume.

I miss the pallbearers momentously taking their places,   5
The undertaker's obsequious grimaces,
The craned necks, the mourners' anonymous faces,
—And the eyes, still vivid, looking up from a sunken room.

ACADEMIC

The stethoscope tells what everyone fears:
You're likely to go on living for years,
With a nurse-maid waddle and a shop-girl simper,
And the style of your prose growing limper and limper.

WEED PULLER

Under the concrete benches,
Hacking at black hairy roots,—
Those lewd monkey-tails hanging from drainholes,—
Digging into the soft rubble underneath,
Webs and weeds,   5
Grubs and snails and sharp sticks,
Or yanking tough fern-shapes,
Coiled green and thick, like dripping smilax,
Tugging all day at perverse life:
The indignity of it!—   10
With everything blooming above me,
Lilies, pale-pink cyclamen, roses,
Whole fields lovely and inviolate,—
Me down in that fetor of weeds,
Crawling on all fours,   15
Alive, in a slippery grave.

CHILD ON TOP OF A GREENHOUSE

The wind billowing out the seat of my britches,
My feet crackling splinters of glass and dried putty,
The half-grown chrysanthemums staring up like accusers,

Up through the streaked glass, flashing with sunlight,
A few white clouds all rushing eastward,   5
A line of elms plunging and tossing like horses,
And everyone, everyone pointing up and shouting!

MY PAPA'S WALTZ

The whiskey on your breath
Could make a small boy dizzy;
But I hung on like death:
Such waltzing was not easy.

We romped until the pans   5
Slid from the kitchen shelf;
My mother's countenance
Could not unfrown itself.

The hand that held my wrist
Was battered on one knuckle;   10
At every step you missed
My right ear scraped a buckle.

You beat time on my head
With a palm caked hard by dirt,
Then waltzed me off to bed   15
Still clinging to your shirt.

PICKLE BELT

The fruit rolled by all day.
They prayed the cogs would creep;
They thought about Saturday pay,
And Sunday sleep.

Whatever he smelled was good: 5
The fruit and flesh smells mixed.
There beside him she stood,—
And he, perplexed;

He, in his shrunken britches,
Eyes rimmed with pickle dust,   10
Prickling with all the itches
Of sixteen-year-old lust.

THE RETURN

I circled on leather paws
In the darkening corridor,
Crouched closer to the floor,
Then bristled like a dog.

As I turned for a backward look,   5
The muscles in one thigh
Sagged like a frightened lip.

A cold key let me in
That self-infected lair;
And I lay down with my life,   10
With the rags and rotting clothes,
With a stump of scraggy fang
Bared for a hunter's boot.

NIGHT CROW

When I saw that clumsy crow
Flap from a wasted tree,
A shape in the mind rose up:
Over the gulfs of dream
Flew a tremendous bird   5
Further and further away
Into a moonless black,
Deep in the brain, far back.

THE CYCLE

Dark water, underground,
Beneath the rock and clay,
Beneath the roots of trees,
Moved into common day,
Rose from a mossy mound   5
In mist that sun could seize.

The fine rain coiled in a cloud
Turned by revolving air
Far from that colder source
Where elements cohere   10
Dense in the central stone.
The air grew loose and loud.

Then, with diminished force,
The full rain fell straight down,
Tunneled with lapsing sound   15
Under even the rock-shut ground,
Under a river's source,
Under primeval stone.

ELEGY FOR JANE

My Student, Thrown by a Horse

I remember the neckcurls, limp and damp as tendrils;
And her quick look, a sidelong pickerel smile;
And how, once startled into talk, the light syllables leaped for
    her,
And she balanced in the delight of her thought,
A wren, happy, tail into the wind,   5
Her song trembling the twigs and small branches.
The shade sang with her;
The leaves, their whispers turned to kissing;
And the mold sang in the bleached valleys under the rose.

Oh, when she was sad, she cast herself down into such a pure
    depth,   10
Even a father could not find her:
Scraping her cheek against straw;
Stirring the clearest water.

My sparrow, you are not here,
Waiting like a fern, making a spiny shadow.   15
The sides of wet stones cannot console me,
Nor the moss, wound with the last light.

If only I could nudge you from this sleep,
My maimed darling, my skittery pigeon.
Over this damp grave I speak the words of my love: 20
I, with no rights in this matter,
Neither father nor lover.

TWO POEMS FROM:
FOUR FOR SIR JOHN DAVIES

I THE DANCE

Is that dance slowing in the mind of man
That made him think the universe could hum?
The great wheel turns its axle when it can;
I need a place to sing, and dancing-room,
And I have made a promise to my ears   5
I'll sing and whistle romping with the bears.

For they are all my friends: I saw one slide
Down a steep hillside on a cake of ice,—
Or was that in a book? I think with pride:
A caged bear rarely does the same thing twice   10
In the same way: O watch his body sway!—
This animal remembering to be gay.

I tried to fling my shadow at the moon,
The while my blood leaped with a wordless song.

Four for Sir John Davies: Sir John Davies: Attorney-general for Ireland
and poet (1569–1626).

Though dancing needs a master, I had none   15
To teach my toes to listen to my tongue.
But what I learned there, dancing all alone,
Was not the joyless motion of a stone.

I take this cadence from a man named Yeats;
I take it, and I give it back again: 20
For other tunes and other wanton beats
Have tossed my heart and fiddled through my brain.
Yes, I was dancing-mad, and how
That came to be the bears and Yeats would know.

4 THE VIGIL

Dante attained the purgatorial hill,
Trembled at hidden virtue without flaw,
Shook with a mighty power beyond his will,—
Did Beatrice deny what Dante saw?
All lovers live by longing, and endure: 5
Summon a vision and declare it pure.

Though everything's astonishment at last,
Who leaps to heaven at a single bound?
The links were soft between us; stil'. we kissed;
We undid chaos to a curious sound: 10
The waves broke easy, cried to me in white;
Her look was morning in the dying light.

The visible obscures. But who knows when?
Things have their thought: they are the shards of me;
I thought that once, and thought comes round again;   15
Rapt, we leaned forth with what we could not see.
We danced to shining; mocked before the black
And shapeless night that made no answer back.

The world is for the living. Who are they?
We dared the dark to reach the white and warm.   20
She was the wind when wind was in my way;
Alive at noon, I perished in her form.
Who rise from flesh to spirit know the fall:
The word outleaps the world, and light is all.

THE WAKING

I wake to sleep, and take my waking slow.
I feel my fate in what I cannot fear.
I learn by going where I have to go.

We think by feeling. What is there to know?
I hear my being dance from ear to ear.   5
I wake to sleep, and take my waking slow.

Of those so close beside me, which are you?
God bless the Ground! I shall walk softly there,
And learn by going where I have to go.

Light takes the Tree; but who can tell us how?   10
The lowly worm climbs up a winding stair;
I wake to sleep, and take my waking slow.

Great Nature has another thing to do
To you and me; so take the lively air,
And, lovely, learn by going where to go.   15

This shaking keeps me steady. I should know.
What falls away is always. And is near.
I wake to sleep, and take my waking slow.
I learn by going where I have to go.

THE DREAM

I

I met her as a blossom on a stem
Before she ever breathed, and in that dream
The mind remembers from a deeper sleep:
Eye learned from eye, cold lip from sensual lip.
My dream divided on a point of fire;   5
Light hardened on the water where we were;

A bird sang low; the moonlight sifted in;
The water rippled, and she rippled on.

2

She came toward me in the flowing air,
A shape of change, encircled by its fire.   10
I watched her there, between me and the moon;
The bushes and the stones danced on and on;
I touched her shadow when the light delayed;
I turned my face away, and yet she stayed.
A bird sang from the center of a tree;   15
She loved the wind because the wind loved me.

3

Love is not love until love's vulnerable.
She slowed to sigh, in that long interval.
A small bird flew in circles where we stood;
The deer came down, out of the dappled wood.   20
All who remember, doubt. Who calls that strange?
I tossed a stone, and listened to its plunge.
She knew the grammar of least motion, she
Lent me one virtue, and I live thereby.

4

She held her body steady in the wind;   25
Our shadows met, and slowly swung around;
She turned the field into a glittering sea;
I played in flame and water like a boy
And I swayed out beyond the white seafoam;
Like a wet log, I sang within a flame.   30
In that last while, eternity's confine,
I came to love, I came into my own.

ALL THE EARTH, ALL THE AIR

1

I stand with standing stones.
The stones stay where they are.
The twiny winders wind;

The little fishes move.
A ripple wakes the pond.   5

2

This joy's my fall. I am!—
A man rich as a cat,
A cat in the fork of a tree,
When she shakes out her hair.
I think of that, and laugh.   10

3

All innocence and wit,
She keeps my wishes warm;
When, easy as a beast,
She steps along the street,
I start to leave myself.   15

4

The truly beautiful,
Their bodies cannot lie:
The blossom stings the bee.
The ground needs the abyss,
Say the stones, say the fish.   20

5

A field recedes in sleep.
Where are the dead? Before me
Floats a single star.
A tree glides with the moon.
The field is mine! Is mine!   25

6

In a lurking-place I lurk,
One with the sullen dark.
What's hell but a cold heart?
But who, faced with her face,
Would not rejoice?   30

WORDS FOR THE WIND

I

Love, love, a lily's my care,
She's sweeter than a tree.
Loving, I use the air
Most lovingly: I breathe;
Mad in the wind I wear   5
Myself as I should be,
All's even with the odd,
My brother the vine is glad.

Are flower and seed the same?
What do the great dead say?   10
Sweet Phoebe, she's my theme:
She sways whenever I sway.
"O love me while I am,
You green thing in my way!"
I cried, and the birds came down   15
And made my song their own.

Motion can keep me still:
She kissed me out of thought
As a lovely substance will;
She wandered; I did not: 20
I stayed, and light fell
Across her pulsing throat;
I stared, and a garden stone
Slowly became the moon.

The shallow stream runs slack;   25
The wind creaks slowly by;
Out of a nestling's beak
Comes a tremulous cry
I cannot answer back;
A shape from deep in the eye—   30
That woman I saw in a stone—
Keeps pace when I walk alone.

2

The sun declares the earth;
The stones leap in the stream;
On a wide plain, beyond 35
The far stretch of a dream,
A field breaks like the sea;
The wind's white with her name,
And I walk with the wind.

The dove's my will today. 40
She sways, half in the sun:
Rose, easy on a stem,
One with the sighing vine,
One to be merry with,
And pleased to meet the moon. 45
She likes wherever I am.

Passion's enough to give
Shape to a random joy:
I cry delight: I know
The root, the core of a cry. 50
Swan-heart, arbutus-calm,
She moves when time is shy:
Love has a thing to do.

A fair thing grows more fair;
The green, the springing green 55
Makes an intenser day
Under the rising moon;
I smile, no mineral man;
I bear, but not alone,
The burden of this joy. 60

3

Under a southern wind,
The birds and fishes move
North, in a single stream;
The sharp stars swing around;
I get a step beyond 65
The wind, and there I am,
I'm odd and full of love.

Wisdom, where is it found?—
Those who embrace, believe.
Whatever was, still is,   70
Says a song tied to a tree.
Below, on the ferny ground,
In rivery air, at ease,
I walk with my true love.

What time's my heart? I care.   75
I cherish what I have
Had of the temporal:
I am no longer young
But the winds and waters are;
What falls away will fall;   80
All things bring me to love.

4

The breath of a long root,
The shy perimeter
Of the unfolding rose,
The green, the altered leaf,   85
The oyster's weeping foot,
And the incipient star—
Are part of what she is.
She wakes the ends of life.

Being myself, I sing   90
The soul's immediate joy.
Light, light, where's my repose?
A wind wreathes round a tree.
A thing is done: a thing
Body and spirit know   95
When I do what she does:
Creaturely creature, she!—

I kiss her moving mouth,
Her swart hilarious skin;
She breaks my breath in half;   100
She frolicks like a beast;
And I dance round and round,
A fond and foolish man,

And see and suffer myself
In another being, at last.   105

SHE

I think the dead are tender. Shall we kiss?—
My lady laughs, delighting in what is.
If she but sighs, a bird puts out its tongue.
She makes space lonely with a lovely song.
She lilts a low soft language, and I hear   5
Down long sea-chambers of the inner ear.

We sing together; we sing mouth to mouth.
The garden is a river flowing south.
She cries out loud the soul's own secret joy;
She dances, and the ground bears her away.   10
She knows the speech of light, and makes it plain
A lively thing can come to life again.

I feel her presence in the common day,
In that slow dark that widens every eye.
She moves as water moves, and comes to me,   15
Stayed by what was, and pulled by what would be.

THE SURLY ONE

1
When true love broke my heart in half,
I took the whiskey from the shelf,
And told my neighbors when to laugh.
I keep a dog, and bark myself.

2
Ghost cries out to ghost—   5
But who's afraid of that?
I fear those shadows most
That start from my own feet.

PLAINT

Day after somber day,
I think my neighbors strange;
In hell there is no change.
Where's my eternity
Of inward blessedness?   5
I lack plain tenderness.

Where is the knowledge that
Could bring me to my God?
Not on this dusty road
Or afternoon of light   10
Diminished by the haze
Of late November days.

I lived with deep roots once:
Have I forgotten their ways—
The gradual embrace   15
Of lichen around stones?
Death is a deeper sleep,
And I delight in sleep.

"THE SHIMMER OF EVIL" *Louise Bogan*

The weather wept, and all the trees bent down;
Bent down their birds: the light waves took the waves;
Each single substance gliddered to the stare;
Each vision purely, purely was its own:
—There was no light; there was no light at all: 5

Far from the mirrors all the bushes rang
With their hard snow; leaned on the lonely eye;
Cold evil twinkled tighter than a string; a fire
Hung down: And I was only I.
—There was no light; there was no light at all: 10

Each cushion found itself a field of pins,
Prickling pure wishes with confusion's ire;
Hope's holy wrists: the little burning boys
Cried out their lives an instant and were free.
—There was no light; there was no light at all.   15

SNAKE

I saw a young snake glide
Out of the mottled shade
And hang, limp on a stone:
A thin mouth, and a tongue
Stayed, in the still air.   5

It turned; it drew away;
Its shadow bent in half;
It quickened, and was gone.

I felt my slow blood warm.
I longed to be that thing,   10
The pure, sensuous form.

And I may be, some time.

INDEX OF FIRST LINES